THE WORLD TURNED UPSIDE DOWN

The Complex Partnership between China and Latin America

Series on Contemporary China (ISSN: 1793-0847)

*Published**

Vol. 22 China and The Global Economic Crisis
edited by Zheng Yongnian & Sarah Y. Tong

Vol. 23 Social Cohesion in Greater China: Challenges for Social Policy and Governance
edited by Ka Ho Mok & Yeun-Wen Ku

Vol. 24 China's Reform in Global Perspective
edited by John Wong & Zhiyue Bo

Vol. 25 The Transition Study of Postsocialist China: An Ethnographic Study of a Model Community
by Wing-Chung Ho

Vol. 26 Looking North, Looking South: China, Taiwan, and the South Pacific
edited by Anne-Marie Brady

Vol. 27 China's Industrial Development in the 21st Century
edited by Mu Yang & Hong Yu

Vol. 28 Cross-Taiwan Straits Relations Since 1979: Policy Adjustment and Institutional Change Across the Straits
edited by Kevin G. Cai

Vol. 29 The Transformation of Political Communication in China: From Propaganda to Hegemony
by Xiaoling Zhang

Vol. 30 The Great Urbanization of China
edited by Ding Lu

Vol. 31 Social Structure of Contemporary China
edited by Xueyi Lu

Vol. 32 East Asia: Developments and Challenges
edited by Yongnian Zheng & Liang Fook Lye

Vol. 33 China and East Asia: After the Wall Street Crisis
edited by Peng Er Lam, Yaqing Qin & Mu Yang

Vol. 34 The World Turned Upside Down:
The Complex Partnership between China and Latin America
by Alfredo Toro Hardy

*To view the complete list of the published volumes in the series, please visit:
http://www.worldscientific.com/series/scc

Series on Contemporary China – Vol. 34

THE WORLD TURNED UPSIDE DOWN

The Complex Partnership between China and Latin America

Alfredo Toro Hardy

NEW JERSEY • LONDON • SINGAPORE • BEIJING • SHANGHAI • HONG KONG • TAIPEI • CHENNAI

Published by

World Scientific Publishing Co. Pte. Ltd.
5 Toh Tuck Link, Singapore 596224
USA office: 27 Warren Street, Suite 401-402, Hackensack, NJ 07601
UK office: 57 Shelton Street, Covent Garden, London WC2H 9HE

British Library Cataloguing-in-Publication Data
A catalogue record for this book is available from the British Library.

Series on Contemporary China — Vol. 34
THE WORLD TURNED UPSIDE DOWN
The Complex Partnership between China and Latin America

ISBN 978-981-4452-56-4

In-house Editor: DONG Lixi

Typeset by Stallion Press
Email: enquiries@stallionpress.com

Printed in Singapore.

To the pillars of my life:
Gabriela, my wife,
and my children Daniela, Alfredo and Bernardo.

Contents

Foreword by Geoffrey Hawthorn

I was teaching at Harvard in the autumn of 1989 where the joke was that the Cold War was over and Japan had won. That was not quite right; Japan was just then entering what proved to be long a deflationary spiral. But the decision of the United States to finance Japan's recovery against the communist victory in China had led also to the growth of Taiwan, South Korea, Hong Kong and Singapore. And the United States was for a moment able to strengthen its influence. Indebtedness in Latin America in the later 1980s and in the smaller countries of East Asia in the later 1990s had allowed a new 'Washington Consensus', the impetus in which was to allow governments in East Asia to continue to buy American bonds and those in Latin America to reduce their spending and allow more private investments from the North. But that is now past.

The Cold War is over and it is now clear that China has won. The United States is by most economic measures declining, and the European Union is in difficulty also. It is they who are now facing the problems of debt. They are still strong markets for imports, but exporting and growth have moved elsewhere. China will soon be the largest economy and already has a far wider range of economic options than any other country. What one might now describe as the Old North is naturally refusing to accede to the shift in power, but in time, one imagines, will have to do so.

Alfredo Toro Hardy offers a wonderfully lucid and well-informed account of the genesis and nature of this new 'upside-down world', all the more refreshing for being free of ideological assumptions. His central question, however, is what place there might be in the new world for the countries of Latin America. He explains that these are not in an ideal position. They cannot compete in many high value-added manufactures or with the cheap labour of Asia and Africa also in the future. Their sovereign wealth funds are not large. And they have understandably been tempted to move back to supplying commodities for manufacturing elsewhere. But they have advantages for more profitable growth, he explains, that others may not have noticed and which they themselves may not quite appreciate. His grasp of these is informed. His sense of the differences in the region as well as what the countries have in common is acute. And, he offers a convincing account of how the prospects of the region as a whole do and do not match those of East Asia.

My personal regret is that Toro Hardy was not able to accept election to the Simon Bolívar Professorship at Cambridge. This book reveals what that the university has missed. But that now is available to all. I know of no account of the present international economic order which is at once so comprehensive, balanced, persuasive, accessible and free of tedious polemic; none which takes a more imaginative view of the prospects for Latin America. Unlike most writing of its kind, it is also exciting. I cannot think of anyone at any level of expertise who would not enjoy reading it and benefit greatly from doing.

Geoffrey Hawthorn

Emeritus Professor on International Politics and Political Theory and former Director of the Political Sciences Department at the University of Cambridge.

Foreword by Xulio Ríos

This book by Alfredo Toro Hardy contains an excellent, updated and profound analysis of a momentous historical change: the rebalancing between East and West and the specific development of the China–Latin America relationship within that process.

The awakening of China within the frontlines of politics and world economy is the most important event of the international system of the century that has just begun. The dynamic economic growth of China and its emergence as a world power have been accompanied by an increasing interaction with Latin America. The current is a decisive moment within a period of historical change that started with the end of the bipolar world and where, despite some unequivocal trends, nothing remains more certain than uncertainty. Both regions are facing enormous geostrategic challenges amidst a context marked by what many consider to be the inevitable economic decline of the United States and that of the European Union, but where emerging countries are also submitted to eventful transformations. Changes suggested by these challenges involve alterations in traditional trade flows and predict the creation of new actors with increasing influence within the global institutional architecture, especially around the BRICS.

The emergence of China and Asia in general, as engines of growth, has been crucial for the return of Latin America to a path of growth that remained elusive for decades. However, behind the uniformity of this general trend, complexity emerges. On the one hand, not all countries of the region are rich in natural resources. In Central America, for example, where many countries are net importers of raw materials, the 'China effect' only generates gloomy prospects. Even in South

America, commodities' producing economies have to be differentiated. Those oriented to the production of metals are in a different category from those that are more agricultural in nature, while the two of them have to be distinguished from fuel producing economies where volatility is greater. We face therefore a heterogeneous scenario, as clearly suggested in this prescient work by Alfredo Toro Hardy.

The first decade of the 21st century has been especially fruitful in bilateral trade relations. In just 10 years, China went from capturing 1% of Latin American exports to 8% in 2010. During that period, Latin American exports rose from 2% to 14%. In 2011, trade totalled US$241,500 million, which meant a 31.5% increase over the previous year. China is the third largest trading partner in the region, but it is the first one for Brazil, Peru and Chile and the second one for Argentina, Cuba, Uruguay and Venezuela. In 2015, Latin America may become China's fourth trading partner. Additional elements show the same kind of overwhelming impulse. In 2010, China invested US$15.548 in Latin America, which represented 9% of the total investments received by the region. That placed China as the third largest investor in Latin America amidst the perception of a rapid increasing trend in this area.

As the industrialised countries are suffering a serious economic crisis, the moment is well suited to rethink alliances and strategies. Opportunities for South–South cooperation in trade, investment, but also in other matters are emerging. As bilateral ties are developing it is both necessary and desirable to shape a strategic understanding based on mutual benefits and that looks beyond the diversity of regional integration strategies.

In parallel, it should be recognised that not everything are opportunities. There are also challenges, especially when it comes to avoiding reproduction of a centre–periphery pattern in which the region becomes over dependant in primary products, something ephemeral in the long run. It is fundamental to avoid the consolidation of a primary-export model, which comes accompanied by a concentration of income, wealth and power in the hands of few, precisely in a moment when progress in democracy and in a more equitable distribution of income is being made.

In the context of a crisis where industrialised economies are not offering suitable answers, the interaction between China and Latin America can create a different and alternative path, able to redefine the role of the latter in the ongoing distribution of global power. This requires of a long-term strategic vision and an efficient management of opportunities. The economies of many Latin American countries depend less and less on the United States and Europe. South–South trade is growing at more than twice the speed of that of developed economies, which by extension means that growth in developing countries depends more on their partnership with China than on their relation with the G-7 economies. This forces to revise development strategies and alliances policies.

China, which is increasingly giving more importance to its relations with Latin America, can help to improve regional integration while, at the same time, becoming instrumental in developing the region's integration to the international economy. Indeed, the Asian giant is being seen as an economic counterweight in times of crisis, but it can be a lot more than that if both parties are able to start a new stage in their relations with emphasis on political dialogue. Prime Minister Wen Jiabao confirmed, during his tour around the region in June 2012, the global nature of its strategic alliance with Brazil and proposed, among other ambitious initiatives, a free trade area with Mercosur. Above all, however, he announced a policy change towards Latin America with the formalisation of a Cooperation Forum China–Latin America and the Caribbean, the institutionalisation of a foreign ministers' dialogue and other measures that would enable new frameworks to expand common interests and to arrange a regional agenda of priorities.

The emergence of China is changing the distribution of world power. China wants a deeper and long-term relationship with Latin America. Herein lays a historic opportunity for Latin America. This work by Alfredo Toro Hardy provides us with a clear and convincing reflection on this subject in a well structured and easy to read manner. This book could have not been published at a better time.

Xulio Ríos

Coordinator of the Iberian–American Network of Sinologists, he has authored 10 books and numerous academic articles on China.

Foreword by L. Enrique García

The World Upside Down' is a defying metaphor that captures the transformations of an international scenario that was almost impossible to imagine just 20 years ago. Asia — particularly China — and Latin America have become the most dynamic regions in the global economy, in a world that sees its central axis shifting from the Atlantic Basin to the Pacific Rim parallel to the emergence of a new global South.

As Alfredo Toro Hardy points out in this scholarly account of recent economic history, sustained growth in both regions over the last decade has not only produced significant results in terms of poverty reduction and the appearance of a burgeoning middle-class, but it has also modified the structure of world trade.

Moreover, these changes occur precisely as a consequence of increased interaction between both the regions, triggered by Chinese demand for raw materials. This has been one of the main factors behind the exponential increase in Latin American exports, which is the engine of this region's growth. Similarly, the increase in imports from China has also had positive effects, including widespread access to material welfare for the low-income sectors in Latin America.

All this could augur a favourable scenario for Latin America, as an ever more intense interaction unleashes the region's full potential for growth, under the condition that it overcomes the formidable challenges it faces in making the most of its *'complex partnership'* with China.

This book makes a compelling case for Latin America to seize this opportunity by forging a stronger and more balanced relationship with China. Its call to prioritise investment in physical infrastructure, to attract quality foreign investment in strategic areas for productive transformation and to design an intelligent strategy of international integration must be taken seriously.

This is unavoidable reading for decision-makers, businessmen and scholars who are confronted to the key question of how Latin America should prepare to cope with the new global powers of the 21st century.

L. Enrique García
President
CAF — Development Bank of Latin America

Acknowledgements

I would like to express my deep gratitude to the following persons and institutions whose support was fundamental in bringing this book to the readers.

The Rockefeller Foundation Bellagio Center hosted me as a Resident Scholar at Villa Serbelloni in Bellagio, Italy, during September 2011. It was a marvelous experience that allowed me to conceptualise this book while writing its first general draft. The combination of a contemplative atmosphere within the most beautiful surrounding imaginable and the interaction with a group of co-residents coming from the most diverse backgrounds, each working in their own projects, was a magical formula for creativeness. With Pilar Palacia, Director of the Villa, taking perfect care of our needs, it was easy to concentrate on the daily intellectual work while mingling and interchanging ideas at meals and social time with fellow residents. Among the latter were Mary Robinson, former President of Ireland and former United Nations High Commissioner for Human Rights; Roger Cohen, columnist of the *New York Times* and the *International Herald Tribune* and Gabor Lovey, Senior Scientist at the Flakkebjerg Research Centre at Aarhus University in Denmark. Their insightfulness helped me to see from different perspectives some of the ideas upon which I was working.

Xulio Rios is Coordinator of the Iberian–American Network of Sinologists, Director of two well-known Spanish think-tanks — IGADI and El Observatorio de la Política China — and Editor of the academic review *Tiempo Exterior*, besides probably being the main expert on China in the Spanish-speaking world. Enrique García is a former Minister of Finance from Bolivia and since 1990 the President of CAF, Development Bank of Latin America. Both he and the institution that he chairs have been instrumental in numerous projects of regional development. Few people are as knowledgeable of Latin American economic realities as he is. Geoffrey Hawthorn is an Emeritus Professor on International Affairs and Political Theory at the University of Cambridge where he was Director of its Political Sciences Department. He is a well known author as well as a member of the editorial board of the Cambridge Review of International Affairs. The three of them have honoured me by writing the forewords of this book.

Kishore Mahbubani is the Dean of the Lee Kuan Yew School of Public Policy at the National University of Singapore. A former President of the United Nations Security Council and a well-known author, he has been listed by *Foreign Policy* as one of the top 100 most influential public intellectuals of the world. Ambassador Jorge Alberto Lozoya is a former Secretary General of the Iberian–American Cooperation Secretariat, former Chief of Advisers on Foreign Policy to the President of Mexico and a well-known scholar and author. Both read the book and endorsed it with their generous comments. Gloria Carnevali, former Director of the Bolivar Hall in London, gave me her assessment on the book and corrected some of my English language deficiencies.

Gabriela, my wife, provided me with the necessary atmosphere for writing this work and helped me with its footnotes while Alfredo my son supported me in the process of finding an editor.

Geomar Cattafi and Sonely Arocha were also of invaluable help.

Last, but I would like to mention them in a very particular way, the East Asian Institute of the National University of Singapore and World Scientific Publishing kindly decided to shelter this book under the prestige of the Series on Contemporary China. Professor Zheng Yongnian, Director of the former and Dr. Phua Kok Khoo, Chairman of the latter were instrumental in such an endeavour. Ms. Dong Lixi and Ms. Lu Shan desk editors of this book from World Scientific, were in charge of the edition in a highly professional manner.

Introduction

Within little more than 20 years, the correlation of economic powers in the world has experienced an upturn of immense dimensions. At the beginning of the 90s, the Northern Hemisphere presented itself as all-powerful, while developing economies found themselves down on their knees. Nowadays, these countries are emerging with an unstoppable force, while developed ones are immersed in a clear process of decline.

The 80s of the previous century marked their end with a quite particular convergence of phenomena: the collapse of communism, the crisis of third world countries' external debt, the strengthening of financial markets, the fall in the price of commodities, the re-emergence of the General Agreement on Trade and Tariffs (GATT), the International Monetary Fund (IMF) and the World Bank. In short, the West stood unbeatable while developing nations appeared impoverished, indebted to the bone, and forced to align with the emerging economic paradigm: the market economy.

On the one hand, the Washington Consensus made its appearance, imposing its Decalogue of market oriented rules. On the other hand, the negotiations between developed and developing economies within the frame of the GATT Uruguay Round were confined to a process of multiple concessions by the latter. The Washington Consensus and the Uruguay Round presented themselves as two huge pincers squeezing the body of the Third World and dictating the acceptance of the dominant economic order. As if that were not enough, the largest financial and multimedia centres of the West converged around that economic order, imposing credibility or ostracism parameters among developing economies, according to their acceptance or rejection of such rules.

Since the end of 1999, however, the pendulum started to move in the opposite direction on a progressive but unstoppable way. At the World Trade Organization (WTO) summit at Seattle, developing nations became much more assertive, after being confronted with new sacrifices and because of the frustration created by the lack of reciprocity obtained in relation to their previous concessions. China's entry into the WTO in 2001 and the combined power of this nation with the two other big emerging economies — India and Brazil — gave way to a new platform of Southern Hemisphere's power that would be felt at subsequent negotiations within that organisation. At the same time, a succession of economic and political crises in several latitudes resulting from the implementation of the Washington Consensus policies, led to its progressive discredit and abandonment. In turn, the spectacular economic growth obtained by China transformed its economic model into an alternative paradigm for developing nations. The Chinese economic growth generated a new boom in commodities that pulled up most of the economies of the Southern Hemisphere, kick-starting an era of prosperity for them.

Moreover, market economy was creating the conditions for the developed economies decline. By promoting the inclusion into the labour global equation of 1.3 billion Chinese, 1.2 billion Indians or 250 million Indonesians, within the context of a race to the bottom of production costs, Western nations began transforming themselves into embattled fortresses. The combination of a shareholder-value-driven capitalism and official passivity was indeed a good prescription for trouble. That implied quarterly oriented corporations lacking perspective as well as any sense of stakeholder mentality in relation to their own societies and governments that eluded long-term structural considerations amidst a "*laissez faire*" attitude.

Even if inevitable the sliding process of developed economies was evolving in a gradual way. Nonetheless, events dramatically hastened since 2008, when developed countries were hit by the worst economic crisis in 78 years. The excesses of deregulation and of the so-called shadow banking system in the United States, resulting again from market economy "*laissez faire*", were responsible for that. They not only unleashed an international recession but created a spiral of mistrust that later evolved from private institutions into governments.

The concatenation of high indebtedness, sluggish growth and lack of confidence made evident the systemic crisis of the developed economies. More economic stimulus means debt increase and hence loss of confidence by the private sector and the financial markets. Austerity, on the other hand, means more economic contraction. Even worst, austerity and lack of confidence are appearing at the same time. While Europe is in the worst position, the United States is in very difficult one as well. Surrounded by deflation and debt, Japan is not better off. Not only American hegemony is at its sunset but decay has been accelerated in the former mighty triad of the Northern economies.

While the above happens, developing economies are being lifted up by the strength of China. Moreover, emerging economies are becoming increasingly interconnected boosting each other in the process. This has given rise to a new phenomenon: a growing decoupling between developed and developing countries, to the extent that the latter have continued to grow despite the crisis of the former. Global demand indeed has markedly shifted in favour of emerging markets, which currently account for 75% of its growth.[1] Within this context, China and Latin America are two of the fastest growing areas of the planet and their strong but complex economic partnership epitomises well the shift taken place in the global economy.

China's trade with the latter attained US$178.6 billion in 2010 and it was projected that it would displace the European Union as second largest Latin American export market in 2014 and as second largest import market in 2015. Nonetheless, in 2011, trade between Latin America and China reached US$233.7 billion with the latter already surpassing the European Union as that region's No. 2 largest import market.[2] Such trade is having a game changing effect for Latin American economies and its implications are not only felt directly but indirectly as well, as the price of their commodities have risen substantially in the global markets thanks to the Chinese consumption and development policies. Even if the effects are more modest for China, they are still relevant as Latin America has become China's most dynamic export market with an annual growth of 31% between 2005 and 2010, versus 16% for the rest of the world.[3]

This new trade wave has been also accompanied by a spate of investments and financing. In 2010, China became the third largest investor in Latin America, after the United States and the European Union. Conversely, investments in the opposite direction are also on the table. At the same time, China has transformed itself into a very important financial source for the region, having made loans of around US$75 billion since 2005 which is more than what the World Bank, the US Export Bank and the Inter-American Development Bank combined lent during the same period.[4]

But, even if this emerging economic partnership has produced impressive results, it does not flow easily from a Latin American perspective. Costs as well as benefits are involved in the process even for the winners as they are consolidating a primary-export model as the prevailing pattern of its international trade. But together with the winners, which represent the majority, there are losers as well. The latter are those Latin American countries for which the Chinese juggernaut has meant the loss of export markets for their manufactures as well as foreign direct investments that had been redirected to China. It is thus a complex relation that entails winners and losers as well as costs and benefits. This is a normal occurrence within an economic relationship still in the making.

This increased Latin American dependence on commodities has generated conflicting points of views by two important multilateral bodies. While the World Bank presents a fairly positive interpretation of such phenomenon, the United Nations Commission for Latin America and the Caribbean is mainly pessimistic. According to the former, if it had not been for the commodities' export boom, Latin America would not be showing its current economic strength and resilience. The latter believes to the contrary that Latin America is establishing a 21st century pattern of relation with China that mirrors the export structure that it had during the 19th century.

Commodities' producers such as Norway, Canada, Australia and New Zealand, though, have been able to sustain high economic growth rates while creating productive crosslinks of higher value added. That being the case, the only constructive thing for Latin Americans to do is to define a route map that allows obtaining the best possible advantages from the current set of conditions while avoiding risks and minimising vulnerabilities.

Such a route map should consider the obvious fact that commodities are at the mercy of economic cycles. And, clearly enough, the current expansive cycle is highly dependent of China's urbanisation and infrastructural development process, which will reach its ceiling in a not such a distant future. It could be argued, of course, that India with its 1.2 billion people and its current growth rates would take China's place when that moment arrives. Nonetheless, this is far from certain as India's development model did not follow the classic Asian strategy of labour intensive-export oriented economy, emphasising on the contrary services over industry and high technology over low-skilled manufacturing.

But even if China's role as a big magnet for commodities was to be taken by India or by a combination of smaller emerging economies in Asia or by both of them, it is always possible that technology curtails the commodities expansive cycle in dramatic ways. Biotechnology and steam cells technology are two cases in point. The former threatens with creating agricultural foodstuff in closed laboratories while the latter already allows growing beef in laboratories in small scale for human consumption.

The current expansive cycle for Latin American commodities will reach an end sooner or later. China's impressive emergence, and the subsequent bonanza that many Latin American countries enjoy today, have to be seen as a window of opportunity to prepare for what might lay ahead. It is the fat cows–lean cows logic. But where should Latin America aim to? There seems to be certainty in at least one thing: Latin Americans cannot look forward, as they once did, to industrialisation as a panacea. Indeed, this road seems to be blocked both at the top and the bottom. Latin America will never be able to compete in the high-tech manufacturing sector and it is finding extremely difficult to do so in the labour-intensive one as well. It is a classic middle income trap situation, as its economies are unable to compete with advance ones in high-skilled innovations or with low income, low wage economies, in manufacture exports.

A first line of defense would involve protecting their commodities against the uncertainties of volatility by diversifying their offer while creating crosslinks of higher value added for them. A second and more important line would imply transcending commodities by allocating resources and efforts to the development of human capital, international tradable services that are the new exports frontier, infrastructure and sovereign wealth funds. The aim of such a process would be to widen the scope of their available economic options. The latter strategy applies as well to those Latin American countries that have specialised in labour-intensive industries and that are, as a result, suffering the direct impact of China's competition. This is a difficult and demanding endeavour but an inescapable one if Latin America is to have an economic future.

Endnotes

1 Alejandro Izquierdo and Ernesto Talvi, coord., *One Region, Two Speeds?* (Washington D.C.: Inter-American Development Bank, March 2011).

2 Juan Miguel González Peña, "Una aproximación a las relaciones económico-comerciales entre China y América Latina y el Caribe", *Observatorio de la Política China*, 13 de septiembre 2011; CEPAL, *La República popular China y América Latina y el Caribe: Diálogo y Cooperación ante los Nuevos Desafíos de la Economía Mundial* (Santiago de Chile: Junio de 2012).

3 "Exports from Latin America and the Caribbean will increase in 27% in 2011", Economic Commission for Latin America and the Caribbean, ECLAC, Press Release, 31 August 2011, <http://www.caribbeanpress-release.com/articles/8630/1/ECLAC-Exports-from-Latin-America-and-the-Caribbean-Will-Increase-by-27-in 2011/Page1.html>.

4 Chris Arsenault, "The dragon goes shopping in South America", *Aljazeera.net*, 21 December 2011, <http://www.aljazeera.com/category/person/chris-arsenault>.

Chapter 1

Emerging China

Shareholder capitalism versus Stakeholder capitalism

The Soviet system collapsed not because it was military defeated but because of the shortcomings of its economic system and its incapacity to sustain the economic challenge posed by the West. The winner thus was the capitalist model. A model that presented different variants: all of which could claim the right to be its best expression. Among these versions were the Anglo-Saxon and the East Asian as well as the varieties of capitalism prevailing in continental Europe.[1]

Germany and East Asia highlighted the search for consensus and work stability within a stakeholder mentality, while in France and East Asia free market and State planning complemented each other. In all of them, companies were guided by a long-term approach to business. The Anglo-Saxon version excluded the State and had a much more flexible attitude towards employment and social benefits, while it

[1] Michel Albert, *Capitalisme contre Capitalisme* (París: Editions du Seuil, 1991); Will Hutton and Anthony Giddens, edit., *Global Capitalism* (New York: New York Press, 2000).

combined an economics shareholder mentality with a short-term vision for profits. In sum, the market-oriented capitalism imposed during the Reagan–Thatcher years, plus the subordination of manufacture to finance that focuses the attention of companies in profit maximisation and immediate returns at the expense of its long-term strengths.

Within an international economic environment that was becoming highly competitive the United States possessed a fundamental advantage: no one could match its profit maximisation. Despite the German productivity increase of 1.8% a year between 1979 and 1993, twice the United States productivity, the return of capital in Germany was only 7% compared with 9% in the United States.[2] In an economic context where profit margins were turning out to be the fundamental consideration, there was no room for disparities in the return on capital and in that area the Americans had no rivals.

But in addition to purely economic reasons, there was also the fact that the United States not only remained as the sole superpower after the collapse of its Soviet rival, but represented the pinnacle of a network of multilateral organisations and alliance systems that Washington had created at the end of World War II or in subsequent years. The convergence and feedback of all of those strengths projected an overwhelming sense of leadership and direction that no one dared to contradict.

The United States version of capitalism was thus to be transformed into the dominant economic paradigm destined to lead the globalisation process. "Globalisation favours shareholder-value-driven capitalism, and is being driven by it, so it is hardly surprising that other variants of capitalism that try to balance the other interests in the enterprise, like those of the workers, and to behave more ethically — stakeholder capitalisms — are under pressure."[3]

This emerging economic paradigm would be felt across the developing world basically through two means: the Washington Consensus

---

[2] Alfredo Toro Hardy, *Tiene Futuro América Latina?* (Bogotá: Villegas Editores, 2004).

[3] Will Hutton and Anthony Giddens in Will Hutton and Anthony Giddens, edit. *op. cit.*, p. 31.

and the GATT Uruguay Round. Consensus and Round presented themselves as two huge pincers, forcing the acceptance of the dominant economic order within such economies.

The Washington Consensus

The term "Washington Consensus" was coined in 1989 by economist John Williamson to comprise the 10 directives set out by the US Treasury Department, the International Monetary Fund, the World Bank and a group of think tanks based at that capital, as a panacea for economic reform. In Moises Naim words: "Its appeal was helped by its self-assured tone, its prescriptive orientation and sense of direction and its origin in Washington, the capital of the victorious empire."[4]

In other words, the Washington Consensus became the most visible symbol of the new economic order. Within its 10 prescriptions were the following: trade liberalisation, privatisation, deregulation, fiscal discipline, reduction of public expending, etc. As Joseph Stiglitz explains: "These market fundamentalist ideas were reflected in the basic strategy for development ... advocated, beginning of the 1980s, by the IMF, the World Bank, and the US Treasury, a strategy various referred to as 'neo-liberalism' or, because the major players planning it were all in Washington, the 'Washington Consensus'."[5]

The debt crisis represented the perfect opportunity for spreading the new creed around the world. Developing countries whose debts had become unmanageable as a result of the combination of the high interest rates that surged at the end of the 70's and the decline in the price of their commodities after the beginning of the 80's (as well as embattled former communist countries transitioning to capitalism) were in need of economic relief.

The International Monetary Fund was officially entrusted with managing that relief: "As part of the rescue packages, the International

---

[4] "Washington Consensus or Washington Confusion". *Foreign Policy* (Spring 2000), p. 90.

[5] Joseph Stiglitz, *Globalization and its Discontents* (London: W.W. Norton & Company, 2002), p. 229.

Monetary Fund became ... a sort of international bankruptcy receiver."[6] The IMF became, indeed, the custodian of the gate that gave access to the creditors' cartel. Without its blessing, debtor countries were not able to accede to the loans of the World Bank, other multilateral financial bodies, the G-7 countries or the private banks. In other words, compliance with the Washington Consensus rules, as implemented by the IMF, became the only way through which indebted economies could borrow fresh money.

The International Monetary Fund assumed this function with an inflexibility that became proverbial. Two factors were responsible for that. Firstly, the collapse of the Bretton Woods system in the early 70's seemed to have deprived the Found from a sense of institutional purpose, which reappeared — thanks to the debt crisis. The latter gave the IMF the possibility to intervene in the management of world economies, providing an institutional resurrection that was experienced with the intensity of those coming back to life after having lost it.

Secondly, because of a similar comeback to life of a set of ideas on the virtues of the market that had been consigned to oblivion during a good part of the 20th century and that, thanks to the Reagan–Thatcher synergy, were now in the pinnacle. Economists and thinkers such as von Hayek, von Mises, Friedman, Stigler, Becker, Lucas or Joseph, economic faculties such as Chicago and think tanks such as the Mont Pelerin Society or London's Institute of Economic Affairs, became icons of the emerging economy after a long ostracism.[7] Once victorious, the followers of these lonely preachers of the "truth" brought about the fundamentalist style that had allowed them to maintain their faith alive all along their long walk in the desert. The technocrats of the International Monetary Fund transformed themselves into the best expression of this fundamentalism. Keynes could have told them what he once wrote to Hayek: "You greatly underestimate the practicability of the middle course."

---

[6] Daniel Yergin and Joseph Stanislaw, *The Commanding Heights* (New York: Simon & Schuster, 1998), p. 132.

[7] *Ibid.*

But in addition to institutional and ideological zeal, double standards and abuse of dominant position were also involved. In Joseph Stiglitz words:

> "The critics of globalisation accuse Western countries of hypocrisy, and the critics are right. The Western countries have pushed poor countries to eliminate trade barriers, but kept up their own barriers, preventing developing countries from exporting their agricultural products and so depriving them of desperately needed exports income. The United States was, of course, one of the prime culprits and this was an issue about which I felt intensely. When I was chairman of the Council of Economic Advisers, I fought hard against this hypocrisy. ... But even when not guilty of hypocrisy, the West has driven the globalisation agenda, ensuring that it garners a disproportionate share of the benefits, at the expense of the developing world."[8]

Thanks to the International Monetary Fund, Western economies and in particular the United States, were able to open the developing markets to their products, their investments and their services in an indirect way. It was indeed a subtle but incontrovertible mechanism to instrument collective power to their benefit. For developing economies, though, it implied submitting to institutional and ideological zeal and the abuse of dominant position.

In parallel with the Washington Consensus and the implementation of its policies by the International Monetary Fund, the negotiations of the GATT Uruguay Round were taking place. Albeit they had started in 1986, three years before the definition of the fundamentals of the Consensus, the collapse of communism and the emergence of the new economic paradigm deeply affected such negotiations that were to conclude in 1993.

The GATT Uruguay Round

Between 1974 and the first years of the 80's, the developing world had showed both ambition and cohesion in its quest for a more equitable

---

[8] *op. cit.*, pp. 6, 7.

economic order. During that period, its fight for what was called the New International Economic Order (NIEO) was channelled through the United Nations Conference for Trade and Development (UNCTAD). A North–South dialogue was institutionalised covering a wide range of trade, financial, commodity and debt related issues.

Within such negotiations, the developing countries managed to present a common position via the so-called G-77. Such common position aimed at restructuring the world's economy so as to give them greater participation and access to benefits. It was meant to be a revision of the prevailing economic order that implied, by extension, replacing the collapsing Bretton Woods system, which in their opinion had benefited the richer countries at their expense, by a more fair system.[9]

The conjunction of the external debt and the collapse in the price of commodities, including the loss of negotiating power by the Organization of Petroleum Exporting Countries, seriously shattered the strength and the cohesion of the G-77 and led these countries into a much more flexible attitude. According to Joan E. Spero and Jeffrey A. Hart: "The new realities of the 1980s altered the trade strategy of the developing countries. The South's demand for a new international economic order was undermined by the collapse of commodity power, including the OPEC threat ... and by the weakened economic position of the South, especially the debt crisis."[10] The weakened position of developing economies became evident after the so-called UNCTAD VI conference held in Belgrade in the year 1983. Indeed: "The rapid build-up of debt reached its peak at a bad time — just the moment when, owing to recession in industrial countries, demand was weakening for the primary products that made up the livelihood of most developing countries. That meant lower prices for their goods and

---

[9] Jahangir Amuzegar, "The North-South Dialogue: From Conflict to Compromise", *Foreign Affairs*, Vol. 54, (March/April 1976), pp. 56–65; Robert L. Rohthstein, *Global Bargaining: UNCTAD and the Quest for a New International Economic Order* (Princeton: Princeton University Press, 1979); Robert Looney, *Routledge Encyclopedia of International Political Economy* (London: Routledge, 1999).

[10] *The Politics of International Economic Relations* (Belmont, Ca.: Thompson/ Wadsworth, 2003), p. 249.

thus lower incomes. At the same time, the high interest rates of the early 1980s, aimed at counteracting the inflation in the industrial countries, raised the cost of developing countries' floating debt, increasing the repayment burden."[11]

As reported by the Spanish newspaper *El País* at the conclusion of the UNCTAD VI negotiations: "Mexico, Argentina and Brazil, a trio that owes more than 200,000 million dollars, induced restrain in the table of debtor countries...The three main indebted nations of the world recommended not to irritate the international financial markets in order to avoid been included in black lists."[12]

As a result of the impaired position of Third World countries, negotiations with the industrialised economies returned to the General Agreement on Trade and Tariffs. In Joan E. Spero and Jeffrey A. Hart words: "The new forces of the 1980s also called into question the effectiveness of the South's preferred forums for governance, especially the UNCTAD ... As the strategy of confrontation and the NIEO collapsed, developing countries shifted their focus to the GATT."[13] The GATT went back in time to 1947 and was among the group of organisms and agreements that came to light under the auspices of the United States, on the years that followed World War II, with the aim of regulating the world economy. In this sense, the GATT, the International Monetary Fund and the World Bank had a common background. The Bretton Woods spirit was back in place as developed nations wanted to open a new round of trade negotiations within a friendlier and familiar framework.

According to Ngaire Woods: "Until 1993, international trade was regulated globally under the auspices of the GATT, a very loose institution whose rules and procedures were developed in an *ad hoc* way. Within this arrangement, there was a clear inequality of power with the 'Quad' (the US, the European Union, Japan, and Canada) being able to work behind the scenes to shape most decisions."[14]

---

[11] Daniel Yergin and Joseph Stanislaw, *op. cit.*, p. 132.

[12] 29 September 1983.

[13] *op. cit.*, p. 249.

[14] "Order, Globalization and Inequality" in David Held and Anthony McGrew, edit.

For Joseph Stiglitz, the hypocrisy and the abuse of dominant position were parts of this game as well:

> The US and Europe have perfected the art of arguing for free trade while simultaneously working for trade agreements that protect themselves against imports from developing countries. Much of the success of the advanced industrial countries has to do with shaping the agenda — they set the agenda so that markets were opened up for the goods and services that represented their comparative advantage. Western negotiators almost take for granted that they can control what gets discussed, and determine the outcome.[15]

In Ngaire Woods words: "The results were trading rules, which had a very uneven impact on countries. ... Importantly, these results reflected a process, which magnified inequalities among members. The GATT operated as a club with a core membership empowered to decide who to admit and on what conditions."[16]

Such negotiations within the GATT, known as the Uruguay Round, were called to cover the "new trade areas". That is to say, services, intellectual property and investments. Agriculture would also be included. In contrast with the confrontational attitude experienced within the framework of the North–South Dialogue, the developing countries would enter here into a process of multiple concessions. These concessions materialised in areas such as foreign investment liberalisation, reduction of tariffs and export subsidies, extension of international trade law to the service sector, reduction of limits to imports of foreign goods, acceptance of the intellectual property guidelines from the North, etc. The decisive reason for this complacent attitude before the demands of the developed world responded to what may be called the "credibility syndrome".

This weakened position of developing economies resulting from the conjunction of the debt crisis and the collapse in commodity prices, together with the emergence of a new economic paradigm, left

---

The Global Transformations Reader (Cambridge: Polity Press, 2000), p. 392.

[15] *Making Globalization Work* (London: Allen Lane, 2006), pp. 78, 79.

[16] *op. cit.*, p. 392.

them with no other option but to give in to the prevailing order. According to Joan E. Spero and Jeffrey A. Hart: "Although many developing countries were reluctant to mar the appearance of Southern unity in international forums, these countries frequently chose to pursue a more pragmatic strategy ... believing that only those who played the game had any chance of winning concessions."[17] The burden of proof regarding reliability as an international interlocutor fell on these countries. That is to say, in order to be taken seriously it was necessary to accept the new rules of the game. This way, developing economies started to liberalise their trade and economic regimes as a mean to earn the required credibility before the powerful coalition that sustained the emerging ideas.

Such dominant coalition was composed by the multilateral financial organisms as well as by the governments, the financial markets and the multimedia conglomerates of the North or, should we better say, the West. Special mention has to be made to the mighty financial and media centres. The former had exponentially grown since the "Big Bang" of the London Stock Exchange in 1986, while the latter had managed to consolidate in a few corporations by way of several gigantic fusions.

On the one side of the street was the oligopoly represented by the financial centres where a small group of investment banks, financial conglomerates, insurance companies and credit rating assessment companies ruled supreme. With 90% of the assessment sector controlled by Standard & Poor, Moody and Fitch, their ratings could by themselves determine the way in which the financial market portrayed any economy. On the other side of the street was the multimedia oligopoly that could define the terms in which the potential investors and the general public perceived them. Within the multimedia sector, where news and entertainment had conglomerated, two large categories could be found: one with a world coverage made up of nine big groups and another of regional or specialised dimensions.

In the first tier were Time-Warner, Sony, News Corporation, Disney (mainly in the entertainment business), Viacom, Seagram, Bertelsmann and, to a lesser extent, General Electric and AT&T,

[17] *op. cit.*, p. 253.

which achieved that rank through the acquisitions of NBC and Liberty Media. In the second tier were media such as Dow Jones, *New York Times*, Gannet, Hearst or Advance Publications in North America; BBC, Pearson, Kirch, Havas, Mediaset, Hachette, Prisa and Canal Plus groups in Europe. According to Benjamin Barber: "The concept that drives the new media merger frenzy carries the fashionable name 'synergy', which describes what is supposed to be the cultural creativity and economic productivity that arises out of conglomerating the disparate industries that once, quite separately, controlled all segments ... Synergy is a polite way of saying monopoly and in the domain of information, monopoly is a polite way of saying uniformity, which is a polite word for virtual censorship."[18]

Financial and multimedia centres converged around the new economic order and imposed credibility or ostracism parameters among nations, according to their acceptance or rejection of such order. But in addition to the credibility syndrome derived from such situation there was something more. Developing economies were also led to believe that compliance to the new set of rules would be met by future concessions on the other side. In Joseph Stiglitz words: "The Uruguay Round had been based on what become known as the 'Grand Bargain', in which the developed countries promised to liberalise trade in agriculture and textiles (that is, labour-intensive goods of interest to exporters in developing countries) and, in return, developing countries agreed to reduce tariffs and accept a range of new rules and obligations on intellectual property rights, investments and services. Afterward, many developing countries felt that they had been misled into agreeing to the Great Bargain: the developed countries did not keep their side of the deal."[19]

The pendulum starts swinging back

The decade of the 90's represented the climax of this era, marked by the predominance of the West. The turning point began at the World

[18] *Jihad vs. McWorld* (New York: Ballantine Books, 1966), p. 137.
[19] *Making Globalization Work*, p. 77.

Trade Organization (WTO) summit in Seattle during November–December 1999, when the pendulum started to swing back on a progressive but unstoppable way. The WTO had been created in 1995 as the natural heir to the GATT, and it was there where subsequent international negotiations in trade and investments were to take place.

In Seattle, developing economies, faced with the fact that the costly sacrifices that they had made in the areas of services, intellectual property and trade liberalisation, had not been met with due reciprocity, began to assume a much more assertive position. The credibility syndrome and the implicit acceptance of the developed economies based on good faith, were reaching its end. "Significant differences existed between the North and the South. The developed countries pressed for the inclusion of new issues such as labour and environmental standards while the developing countries demanded a focus on dismantling existing barriers to trade in agricultural goods and apparel and on tempering antidumping measures in developed economies."[20]

At the time of this summit, the United States not only did continue passing stricter trade regulations and raising its non-tariff barriers, but most of the industrialised countries had not reduced agricultural subsidies as offered during the Uruguay Round, that is to say, 20% reduction by 2000. According to Joseph Stiglitz, it was clearly a one-way highway: "Western countries pushed trade liberalisation for the products that they exported, but at the same time continued to protect those sectors in which competition from developing countries might have threatened their economies. This was one of the bases of the opposition to the new round of trade negotiations that was supposed to be launched in Seattle."[21]

The new attitude of the Southern Hemisphere would be consolidated during the three subsequent WTO summits at Doha, Cancun and Hong Kong (the Doha Round) as a natural counterpart to the arrogance showed by developed economies. In Joan E. Spero and Jeffrey A. Hart words: "In Seattle in 1999 and Doha in 2001, the

---

[20] Joan E. Spero and Jeffrey A. Hart, *op. cit.*, p. 106.

[21] *Globalization and its Discontents*, pp. 60, 61.

developing countries argued that they have achieved little in the Uruguay Round and had made important and costly concessions to the developed countries in services and intellectual property ... The South was strongly opposed to including new issues in the next round until old issues were satisfactorily resolved."[22]

But while the United States was inflexible regarding the subsidy to its cotton producers and Japan insisted on its committed support to its rice producers, the European Union remained as the most protracted provider of agricultural subsidies. In Kishore Mahbubani's words: "The Doha Round is not making progress ostensibly because both the EU and the US refuse to adhere to their previous commitment and end the massive subsidies to their agricultural sectors. Each year, the EU spends an average of 49 billion Euros (US$67.5) and the US more than US$20 billion on agricultural subsidies."[23] Nonetheless, they kept putting pressure on developing countries to negotiate new rules on areas such as investments, competition, easing of trade and government acquisitions.

China's entry into the WTO in 2001 and the combined leverage of this nation with the other two big emerging economies, India and Brazil, provided the developing world with a new platform. The weakness and prostration that had prevailed among these countries during the Uruguay Round was definitively left behind. A new feeling of empowerment was in the air. This entailed a raising awareness to the fact that the unity of the weak was tantamount to the weakness of the powerful.

The Doha Round of negotiations showcased the confrontation between developed and developing economies. Within such Round, developing economies forged common positions around matters such as elimination of agricultural subsidies, access to industrialised markets for non-agricultural goods, special and differential treatment, the special case of cotton, and the so-called "Singapore issues" (investments, competition, public markets transparency and trade easing).

---

[22] *op. cit.*, p. 258.

[23] *The New Asian Hemisphere: The Irresistible Shift of Global Power to the East* (New York: Public Affairs, 2008), p. 38.

This eye-to-eye relation with the developed world was the sign of a new time.

The empowerment of the South at multilateral trade negotiations came together with the progressive discredit of the Washington Consensus, whose devastating effects were been felt all around the world. According to Joseph Sitglitz: "Fiscal austerity, privatisation and market liberalisation were the three pillars of the Washington Consensus ... The problem was that many of these policies became ends in themselves, rather than means to more equitable and sustainable growth. In doing so, these policies were pushed too far, too fast and to the exclusion of other policies that were needed."[24] Moreover referring to the mistakes made, he adds:

> Perhaps of all the IMF blunders, it is the mistakes in sequencing and pacing, and the failure to be sensitive to the broader social context that have received more attention — forcing liberalisation before safety nets were put in place; before there was an adequate regulatory framework; before countries could withstand the adverse consequences of sudden changes ... forcing policies that led to job destruction before the essentials for job creation were in place; forcing privatisation before there where adequate competition and regulatory frameworks. Many of the sequencing mistakes reflected fundamental misunderstandings of both economic and political processes. Misunderstandings particularly associated with those who believed in market fundamentalism.[25]

As a result of those mistakes, a series of economic crisis that frequently entailed social revolts of high political impact eroded the support for the consensus. Again in Joseph Stiglitz words: "The Asian financial crisis of 1997, the global financial crisis that followed the year after, with crises in Russia and Brazil, made it clear that *something* was wrong. It was, or should have been, clear that there were systemic problems. When there is a bend in the road and a single car has an accident, one can blame the driver. But when, day after day, crashes

[24] *Globalization and its Discontents*, pp. 53, 54.
[25] *ibid.*, p. 73.

occur at the same spot, one suspect there is something wrong with the road."[26]

There were known costs associated with the Washington Consensus. Among them were the high unemployment and the dramatic social costs resulting from the reduction or disappearance of the social safety nets provided by the State, there was also the loss of important parcels of the national wealth, through the privatisation of state industries and public utilities and the abandonment of endogenous research and development efforts. The Latin American experience in these areas is extensively analysed in Chapter 3.

There were unpredictable costs as well. The expansive waves of each tsunami, with known epicentre, could in turn threaten other emerging economies that had not only reasonably complied with the set rules, but which were located at distant places. With surprising ease, indeed, countries or entire regions lost overnight the trust of investors and were left entirely vulnerable. Countries that had reduced the income-expenditure gap, deregulated their financial sectors, massively privatised industries and state services and liberalised their trade — and which in the process had incurred in immense social tensions — fell out of favour of the markets in sudden ways. Despite the immense sacrifices made by compliant nations, the disfavour of investors could become immediate and implacable as soon as fissures were detected and the risk of potential contagion was feared. And the nature of the reforms made those fissures a common event. Nobody was safe independently of the efforts and sacrifices incurred.

To put oneself in the hands of the market meant to surrender the defence mechanisms of society to an impatient and heartless master. Between the Mexican crisis in 1994 and the Argentinean one in 2001–2002, there were many economic crises in between caused by the implementation of the IMF policies. But the social destitution, the loss of national wealth and the economic ravage experienced by Russia when confronted with the shock therapy prescribed by the IMF, were probably the more extreme. Moreover, when the contagion effect of

---

[26] Stiglitz, *The Roaring Nineties*, pp. 221, 222.

the 1997 Asian crisis hit the Russian economy in 1998, all the fissures within the system detonated a huge financial crisis.

The shock therapy put in place in Russia after the fall of communism implied rapid privatisation and liberalisation. Sudden price liberalisation brought with it a first sickness: hyperinflation. This in turn was treated with two medicines, tight monetary policy and fiscal austerity. Such medicines produced new sicknesses: deep recession and depression. Meanwhile, rapid privatisations were giving away, at laughable prices, the country's most valuable assets to insiders who had neither the incentives nor the capital to perform the necessary deep restructuring of the enterprises. This created a new class of oligarchs who took money out of the country much faster than the inflow of money that the IMF was pouring in as assistance. At the same time, capital markets were liberalised under the assumption that money will be induced to come in, attaining precisely the opposite result: a massive capital flight. Capital market liberalisation pushed by the IMF made it easier for the oligarchs, who had stripped assets from the corporations they controlled, to take all the money they could outside the country. Huge amounts of capital left Russia and were spent on luxury goods or real estate or placed in safe havens, instead of being put to productive use in the country. In 1996, and after seven years of continuous decline, the country's GDP had dropped more than 40% in relation to 1989.[27]

The impact resulting from the contraction on social spending was even more dramatic. The high-quality education of the country, one of communism legacies deteriorated profoundly. About 20 million people were dropped under the poverty line. Life expectancy fell to unimaginable levels, in par with India: 59 years. The mortality rate increased substantially, multiplying by 10-fold just between 1993 and 1994, as people began to die from minor illnesses amid the crumbling of healthcare services. Infrastructure, on its side, fell in rapid decay amid the lack of investment and maintenance.[28]

---

[27] Joseph Stiglitz, *Making Globalization Work*; UNCTAD/UNECE, "The Russian Crisis of 1988", October 1998, <http://www.twnside.org.sg/title/1998-cn.htm>.
[28] Joseph Stiglitz, *ibid.*; *The Economist: The World in 2005.*

Then the Asian financial crisis, that had begun the year before, impacted Russia in 1998. Given Russia's fragile economy, the rapid decline in the prices of crude oil and other export commodities derived from the weakening of global demand, caused economic turmoil. Such natural resources represented 80% of merchandise exports, and the fall in their prices in the aftermath of the Asian crisis, had a major impact on Russia's external and fiscal balances. The cracks within the system did the rest. According to a joint report by UNCTAD and the United Nations Economic Commission for Europe (UNECE): "Whilst the crisis must be seen in the context of policy failures and abortive reforms during the 1990's, its unfolding reflected mismanagement of the opening of the country's financial markets to foreign lenders and investors, which left the country vulnerable to the risk that domestic financial difficulties could be transformed into a full-blown currency crisis."[29]

On 13 August of that year he Russian stock, bond and currency markets collapsed, as a result of fears from investors that the government would devalue the ruble or default on its domestic debt or both. From January to August, the market had already lost more than 75% of its value. Then, on 17 August, the Russian government fulfilled the worst fears by devaluing the ruble and defaulting on its debt.

What about the crisis where the Russian contagion came from? Some have argued that the Asian crisis of 1997 could not be attributed to market economy faults and that it was different in nature to other economic crises of that period. Was it so?

The Asian crisis

The East Asian economic model had been a tremendously successful one, so much that according to the World Bank it was able to reduce the number of poor people from 716 million to 435 million during 1975–1995.[30] "The combination of high savings rates, government

---

[29] *op. cit.*, p. 1.

[30] Lee T.Y., "Crecimiento de las Economías Asiáticas", PECC XII, Papel de Trabajo, Santiago de Chile (30 septiembre–2 octubre 1997).

investment in education, and state-directed industrial policy all served to make the region an economic powerhouse. Growth rates were phenomenal for decades and the standard of living rose enormously for tens of millions of people."[31] So impressive had been the performance that it was widely described as the "East Asia miracle". Nonetheless, in 1997 East Asian economies entered into a deep crisis.

Both the East Asian and the Anglo-Saxon market economy models found themselves in the dock as a result of that crisis. For Asian economies where the crisis originated, the blame was on the other side. From their perspective, had they not liberated and deregulated their markets according to the neoliberal model, the crisis would have never occurred.

For those in favour of market economy, the responsibility was laid on the Asian side. According to their judgement, the irrational use of lent funds ignited the recessive spiral. Joseph Stiglitz explains the situation:

> When the crisis broke out, I was surprised at how strongly the IMF and the US Treasury seemed to criticise the countries — according to the IMF, the Asian nation's institutions were rotten, their government corrupt, and wholesale reform was needed. These outspoken critics were hardly expert on the region, but what they said contradicted so much of what I knew about it.[32]

Both sides intended to keep distances with the alleged offender. Malaysia, Hong Kong, Taiwan, Singapore, South Korea and the rest started to take measures to protect themselves from the Western influx. Not in vain, some people even spoke of an Asian run versus the Anglo-Saxon market model. Those in favour of the market economy, for their part, were willing to dissociate themselves as much as possible from the East Asian economies. In fact, the damage caused to those countries with the stampede of capitals, was out of proportion to their mistakes.

---

[31] *Globalization and its Discontents*, p. 92.

[32] *ibid.*, p. 90.

The fact is that the massive availability and accessibility to foreign capital resulting from an international market inundated with liquidity, together with the liberation of their domestic financial systems, led to excessive indebtedness. The abundant offer of cheap foreign funds exacerbated asset prices, which in turn increased the pledge value of these, promoting new and bigger loans. This contributed to raise even more assets' prices. On this base huge speculative bubbles were created, particularly at real estate and the stock exchange.

In 1995, the US dollar started to re-evaluate against the other currencies. Given the fact that the economies of the region, with the exception of Japan, had their currencies pegged to the dollar, their products began to become more expensive in relation to their competitors. This situation affected their exports and increased its current account deficits.

The two previous elements together with the unstoppable increase in stock and in real estate prices rang the alarm bells for big speculators. When George Soros and his pairs decided to step out of the region, they triggered panic in the markets. Unavoidably, all the big speculative bubbles exploded one by one and in a few months hundreds of billions of dollars went bust and a hundred million people went back to poverty. During the depths of the crisis in 1998, the aggregate output in the ASEAN-5 countries (Indonesia, Malaysia, the Philippines, Thailand and Singapore) plunged by 8.3% while the real GDP in South Korea contracted by 5.7%.[33]

No doubt, there were important responsibilities at both sides. Nevertheless, it is evident that none of this would have happened without a market inundated with liquidity where an international caste of professional borrowers reacted with paranoia when faced by bad news. By liberalising their economies and putting themselves on that caste hands the successful Asian model opened its doors to uncertainty. According to Joseph Stiglitz: "The countries in East Asia had no need for additional capital, given their high savings rate, but still capital account liberalisation was pushed on these countries in the late 80s and early 90s. I believe that capital account liberalisation was *the single most*

[33] Stephen Roach, "Asia's take on austerity", *Project Syndicate*, 28 February 2012.

important factor leading to the crisis."[34] As it was common in these situations, the massive stampede of capitals, out of rational proportions, led the countries involved down on their knees: "Probably no country could have withstood the sudden change in investor sentiment, a sentiment that reversed this huge inflow to a huge outflow ..."[35]

What about the medicine proposed to face the crisis? "The International Monetary Fund — executor of the *laissez faire* Washington Consensus — prescribed drastic medicine for countries like Thailand, the Philippines, Singapore and South Korea. They were told to cut government spending, even in the teeth of recession; to raise interest rates; to severe links between banks and the state; and to deregulate."[36]

It happened though that those that did not follow the IMF prescription were the ones that overcome the crisis faster:

> Indeed, many of the countries that did the best during and after the Asian crisis were those that did not follow the standard IMF/Treasury prescriptions. China avoided a downturn by pursuing expansionary monetary and fiscal policies — precisely the opposite of what the Treasury and IMF had imposed elsewhere in the region. Malaysia, the country with the shortest and shallowest downturn, not only had no IMF program but imposed capital controls, for which it was sharply criticised by the US Treasury, the IMF, and others. By following its own course, Malaysia was left with a legacy of debt far smaller than those who had listened to the treasury/IMF advice ... Thailand, the country that followed IMF/Treasury advice most closely, is only just now returning to the levels of GDP that it had half a decade before the crisis.[37]

Notwithstanding the above, to the rest of the world, the East Asian model became discredited while market economy emerged on

[34] *Globalization and its Discontents*, p. 99.
[35] *ibid.*, p. 99.
[36] David Pilling, "Capitalism in crisis: Perilous route to prosperity", *Financial Times*, 16 January 2012.
[37] Joseph Stiglitz, *The Roaring Nineties* (London: Allan Lane, 2003), pp. 217, 218.

a stronger footing. However, after East Asians got the taste of approaching too much to the American model, they drew their own conclusions. As the Russians and the Latin Americans, they would know in the future the risks involved by this. That implied, among other things, relying on their own international reserves. As Gordon Brown explains: " ... because the penalties imposed by the IMF were simply too high to be paid by their people again."[38] "Never more" was indeed the battle cry of East Asian economies. The reaction against the IMF and its market economy policies was growing. Region after region were simply getting fed up.

While this process was in course, an alternative economic paradigm based on the outstanding economic emergence of China was shaping up. To understand what happened, it is necessary to go back to 1979. During that year, Deng Xiaoping initiated a process of economic change based on a new lecture of the international order. The central pillars of his proposal were to leave behind the period of "war and revolution" to step into a new era of "economic openness without political change'": "It was one of those great strategic intuitions by a historical leader, a *coup d'oeil* that defined the basis of all that was to come afterwards."[39]

The Beijing Consensus

However, Deng Xiaoping not only assumed, as a priority, the need for economic development but the fact of doing it in an endogenous way. He called it "socialism with Chinese characteristics" while others talked of "capitalist measures with Chinese characteristics".[40] It was, though, a fusion of the Chinese mentality with the knowledge derived from the failure of globalisation in other parts of the world.[41]

---

[38] *Beyond the Crash* (London: Simon & Schuster UK Ltd, 2010), p. 81.

[39] Joshua Cooper Ramo, *Brand China* (London: The Foreign Policy Centre, February 2007), p. 28.

[40] Dorothy J. Solinger, *Chinese Business under Socialism* (Berkeley: University of California Press, 1984).

[41] Joshua Cooper Ramo, *The Beijing Consensus* (London: The Foreign Policy Centre, May 2004).

It could not have been otherwise given the strength of its culture: “The Chinese, in constantly making reference to what they describe as their 5,000-year history, are aware that what defines them is not a sense of nationhood but of civilisation. In this context, China should not primarily be seen as a nation-state but rather as a civilisation-state.”[42]

This implied a highly pragmatic model; away from the Washington Consensus characteristic shock therapies that provoked so much damage everywhere. Instead of the inflexible directions of the Washington Consensus, China chose a path that allowed trial and error. While clearly defining a goal to aim at through strategic planning, the country allowed itself an ample tactical room of manoeuvring, leaving space to react to undesirable effects or changing circumstances. According to a Deng’s aphorism this was tantamount to “crossing the river by feeling the stones”.

Such a process took a pathway of progressive stages and periodic adjustments in which transitory policies acted as bridges from one stage into the next one: “The reform process has been gradual and pragmatically introduced in progressive stages that build on, and adjust to, experience in the development of greater market forces in the economy. This incrementalism involves the interaction of initial conditions with transitional policies.”[43]

The gradualness of the model was shown through the management of its export and domestic production industries. The former was channelled through special areas that subsequently expanded while the latter saw a progressive reduction of the levels of protection assigned to them.

The establishment of the Special Economic Zones in 1979 initiated the opening up of the Chinese economy to foreign investments and globalisation. They began in South-East China having as its initial centres the newly created cities of Shenzhen, Zhulai and Shantou in

---

[42] Martin Jacques, *When China Rules the World* (London: Allen Lane, 2009), p. 13.

[43] Inter-American Development Bank, *The Emergence of China: Opportunities and Challenges for Latin America and the Caribbean* (Washington D.C.: March 2005), p. 32.

the province of Guangdong and Xiamen in the province of Fujian. In 1983, eight additional zones for priority investments were established in the Beijing-Bohai Bay area, the Shanghai Zone, the Wuhan Zone and the Pearl River Delta Zone. In 1984, 14 additional coastal cities were opened up for foreign investment (Tianjin, Shanghai, Dalian, Qinhuangdao, Lianyungang, Nantong, Ningbo, Wenzhou, Fuzhou, Guangzhou, Zhanjiang and Beihai). In 1985, 52 Pearl River Delta and Yangtze River Delta cities were incorporated to the opening process. In 1988, the East coast open belt, also called gold coast, covering a total area of 320 square kilometres and comprising 160 million people was also opened. These open regions were formed by special economic zones, coastal open cities and the larger coastal open economic areas. In 1994, the Chinese authorities permitted the Singapore government to open an industrial park in Souzhou, followed by another in Wixi in 1995.[44] The next step was to take China into the global economy as a full participant. That took shape by joining the WTO in 2001. Economic openness ceased thus to be confined to "islands" and spread out in waves to the rest of the country.

The opening process was not only gradual but also strategically planned to promote specific sectors and activities through selective policies. A first step in industrial policy was taken with the Town and Villages Enterprises, which received access to low-interest credit, tax holidays and special allocations in budget. In early 1990s, priority was given to investments in energy, basic materials and related infrastructure. In the mid 1990s, the policy was focused on "pillar industries" that were capital intensive and with scale economies such as machines, autos, electronics and petrochemicals. In the late 1990s, industrial policy shifted again in order to provide support to technologically advanced enterprises. In the mid 2000s, software, integrated circuits and autos were the priority industries.[45] Currently,

---

[44] Leslie Skalair, *Globalization, Capitalism & its Alternatives* (Oxford: Oxford University Press, 2002); Xulio Ríos, *China: de la A a la Z* (Madrid: Editorial Popular, 2008); Xulio Ríos, *Mercado y Control Político en China* (Madrid: Los Libros de la Catarata, 2007).

[45] Inter-American Development Bank, *op. cit.*

Hong Kong is being seen by analysts as the laboratory for Beijing's experiment in opening up China's financial system with the intention of developing deeper financial sophistication to power its own growth. Moreover, effective 30 January 2012, China is encouraging domestic and foreign private investments into energy saving and environmentally-friendly technologies, new generation information technology, biotechnology, high-end equipment manufacturing, alternative energy, advance materials and alternative fuel cars.[46]

Domestic tariffs successively fell down in direct relation with the capacity of Chinese companies to face foreign competition: 55% in 1982, 24% in 1996 and 12% in 2003. In 2006, due to China's entry in the WTO in 2001 and the need to comply with its rules, its tariffs went down to 6%.[47]

The gradualness of this process, though, should not make us lose sight of its velocity. The extraordinary magnitude of changes occurred in such a little time is the best proof of its speed, whose result has been the fastest growth in a major economy in the documented history of humanity: an average 9% during 30 years. Between 1980 and 1990, the country's GDP doubled; and between 1990 and 2000, it was doubled again. According to the IMF, China's GDP rose from US$309 billion in 1980 to US$1.2 trillion in 2000.[48] At the beginning of this reform process, China's GDP only reached 9% of that of the US, while its GDP per capita represented 2% of the American one. Projections by the IMF estimate that in 2017 China's GDP will be surpassing by 3% that of the US, while its GDP per capita will have become a quarter of that of the US.[49] Such amazing growth has made possible for China to take out of poverty 600 million human beings while quadrupling the average income of every citizen.

---

[46] David Yeo and Philip Ng, "China's Twin Paradigm Shift: Beacons in a Sea of Change", *IE Insights*, International Enterprise Singapore (Vol. 1/July 2012).

[47] Inter-American Development Bank, *op. cit.*

[48] John and Doris Naisbitt, *China's Megatrends* (New York: Harper Business, 2010).

[49] CEPAL, *La República popular China y América Latina y el Caribe: Diálogo y Cooperación ante los Nuevos Desafíos de la Economía Mundial* (Santiago de Chile: Junio de 2012).

Since 2010, China has been the second largest economy in the world. That year, the United States GDP measured at purchasing power parity was US$14,802,081 whereas China's was US$9,711,244 and, according to Euromonitor International estimations, in 2020 China's GDP should be US$23,124,870 whereas the United States should be US$22,644,910.[50]

That would imply passing from being an "iron rice bowl" economy to become the largest economy of the world in less than four decades. Shenzhen exemplifies well the dimension of such change: from a small city of 20,000 inhabitants in 1979, it has become a metropolis of more than 10 million people and one of the most modern cities in the world. China produces today two-thirds of the world's photocopiers, shoes, toys and microwave ovens; half of its DVD players, digital cameras and textiles; one-third of its DDVD-ROM drives and desktop computers and a quarter of its mobiles, television sets, PDAs and car stereos.[51] Meanwhile, it is rushing up the technological ladder and beginning to pose a challenge to the American leadership in the high-tech sector.

Moreover, during the period 2000–2008, the Chinese economy grew at 9.9% per year while the total productivity of factories was 4.2% a year. In other words, 42% of the GDP growth can be attributed to a more efficient use of both work and capital. This applies as well to the period 1990–2000.[52] Not surprisingly a so-called Beijing Consensus attracted the imagination of developing economies:

> China has something more to offer than a simple inspiring story. It also provides an alternative theory of development and international relations. Joshua Cooper Ramo coined the term "Beijing Consensus" in 2004 to refer to it. According to his reasoning, developing countries already saturated their tolerance regarding the ideological content of the "Washington Consensus" and are increasingly

---

[50] <http://blog.euromonitor.com/2010/07/special-report-to-10-largest-economies-in2020.html>

[51] Martin Jacques, *op. cit.*

[52] CEPAL, *op. cit.*

impressed by the Chinese model that emphasises pragmatism, innovation, social cohesion and self determination.[53]

If in the past China had followed a "communism with Chinese characteristics" now it was immersed in a "globalisation with Chinese characteristics".[54] As Joseph Stiglitz puts it:

> A decade of unparalleled American influence over the global economy was also a decade in which one economic crisis seemed to follow another- every year there was another crisis ... Meanwhile, China, following its own course, showed there was an alternative path of transition which could succeed both in bringing the growth that market promised and in markedly reducing poverty.[55]

The Singapore model

But if Deng was the father of this "alternative path", Lee Kuan Yew could be seen as an inspirer of the model. Indeed, Singapore's success both preceded and inspired the Chinese model. As part of his response to the Vietnamese invasion to Cambodia, Deng visited Bangkok, Kuala Lumpur and Singapore in November 1978. His trip to Singapore was an eye opener as to the possibilities of an "open door" policy. Following this visit, he called on the Chinese people to learn from this country: "Singapore enjoys good social order and is well managed ... We should tap their experience and learn how to make things better than they do."[56]

And indeed, they tapped from Singapore, as numerous Chinese delegations visited the city-State to study and learn about its experience and Dr. Goh Keng Swee, Singapore's co-founding father, was invited to serve as economic advisor to the State Council of China on coastal development from 1985 to 1990. At the beginning of the 90s,

---

[53] Gideon Rachman, "The hard evidence that China's soft power is working", *Financial Times*, 20 February 2007.
[54] Cooper Ramo, *The Beijing Consensus.*
[55] *The Roaring Nineties*, p. 21.
[56] Quoted by Mahbubani Kishore, *op. cit.*, p. 76.

the China–Singapore Suzhou Industrial Park was established in China with the aim of developing a modern industrial township that followed Singapore's management methods and that could transmit its know-how. This Industrial Park was followed by a new one in Wixi in 1995. Moreover, a "special relationship" developed between Deng Xiaoping and Lee Kuan Yew, two "straightforward realists'" with strategic minds, who met again in 1980, 1985 and 1988 with the former admiring the latter's capacity to grasp long-term trends and dealing in extraordinarily successful terms with practical issues.[57] Not surprisingly Deng's dream was to "plant thousand Singapores in China".[58]

What was the secret of Singapore that Deng wanted to follow? In Henri Ghesqiere words: "In Singapore, the State and not the local private sector, has been the driver for development. The invisible hand that serves the common good through self-interest is guided by the strong visible arm of the government."[59] The State not only assumes a direct entrepreneurial role through public enterprise, but also acts as agenda-setter to the private sector.

While being highly open to foreign investments, a meritocratic led State directs these investments according to strategic and carefully planned industrial policies. Foreign capital not only serves to finance and develop strategic objectives, but also provides an invaluable spill over of knowledge to local firms and Singaporean citizens. The State plans sets of quantitative targets to be reached at future time points, carefully monitoring its results in order to evaluate if public policies are in track.

Moreover, a continuous process of reinvention takes place though the periodical renewal of its strategic aims: from the oil refining and petrochemical sectors to the electronic and pharmaceutical industries; from port services to financial services; from off-shore drilling

[57] Ezra F Vogel, *Deng Xiaoping and the Transformation of China* (Cambridge: Harvard University Press, 2011).

[58] Quoted by Henri Ghesquiere, *Singapore's Success* (Singapore: Thompson, 2007), p. 1.

[59] *ibid.*, p. 92.

equipment manufacture to biotechnology; from R&D to high end services. As a result, higher value-added activities are densely concentrated and clustered in a network of world class hubs that make the country one of the most globalised on earth.

Following always the long view and having as creed a pragmatic problem-solving approach, Singapore had reached the third largest GDP per capita in the world on purchasing power parity basis in 2012 — US$59,711.[60]

At the same time, it was ranked as the third most competitive city in the world by The Economist Intelligence Unit's 2012 Global City Competitiveness Index.[61] Singapore's success story bears indeed few comparisons. It has been argued that in a global economy that forces nations to move with speed in order to remain competitive, small size is a blessing as it brings flexibility of manoeuvre and incentives to look for outside markets. That is why of the 10 richest countries of the world in GDP per capita terms, only two have a population that surpasses 5 million inhabitants: the US and Switzerland. In a globalised economy, small is undoubtedly beautiful.[62]

According to such reasoning, it may be understandable how an island with an area of less than 40 Km by 20 Km and a population of around 5 million has been so successful. But then, what about China? With its 1.3 billion citizens and a contour size reasonable comparable to that of the US, China has been able to move with incredible speed and shown a flexibility of manoeuvre that would have seem impossible for a country of such dimensions. Perhaps the answer lies in a combination of the model and the cultural traits of the Chinese people that both countries share: Confucianism, pragmatism, work ethic, etc. In any case, China has been able to fulfil Deng's dream to "plant a

---

[60] International Monetary Fund, *World Economic Outlook Database* (Washington D.C., April 2012).

[61] "The World's richest countries", *Forbes*, 22 February 2012; "Singapore, the most competitive city in Asia", *Today*, 14 March 2012.

[62] Alberto Alesina and Enrico Spolaore, *The Size of Nations* (Cambridge: MIT Press, 2003).

thousand Singapores" in its soil and, not surprisingly, China has been called a "giant Singapore".[63]

Nonetheless, the consequences of China's emergence have not been linear for the developing world. Its economic take-off has resulted in both negative and positive elements for them. The more obvious of the first has been the impact of its low-cost manpower that has left many emerging economies with no capacity to compete. That has resulted not only in these countries losing export markets, but also losing direct foreign investments that have been redirected to China. However, there are several areas in which China's emergence is positive for the developing world. Let us talk about them.

China and the developing world

After the decline of China and India, from the beginning of the 19th century onwards, the world became Eurocentric. From free trade to Marxism, any paradigm with universal aspirations had to come, by definition, from the West, only valid source of legitimacy. The Washington Consensus became the last of these totalising paradigms. China's revival, based on the strength of its civilisation, came over to put an end to this universalism in singular and gave way to a universalism in plural where there is no room for "unique thoughts". Thanks to China, multiculturalism has emerged and it has become impossible for hegemonic visions to take hold.

Notwithstanding, the strength of its culture and history, or precisely as a result of it, China has an inward looking vision at odds with the search for global hegemony. According to Kishore Mahbubani: "The Chinese mind has always focused on developing Chinese civilisation, not developing global civilisation. China today is willing to be a responsible stakeholder in the global order, but it shows little interest in leading the creation of a new global order."[64] Consequently, "China's unwillingness to intervene is consistent with its overall policy of live and let live ... Where the United States often attempted to

[63] Niall Ferguson, *Civilization: the West and the Rest* (London: Allen Lane, 2011).
[64] *op. cit.*, p. 239.

dictate to its allies and adversaries, China approached relations with other countries in terms of mutual interests."[65] China's economic dealings with rest of the developing world come, thus, with no strings attached.

For a long time, economic pre-eminence and development were synonyms. However, despite being the second economic power of the planet, China remains a developing country and still will be at the time it reaches the first place. This surprising duality makes of China an invaluable standard-bearer of the developing world, as it has been proved in numerous multilateral negotiations. Indeed, as Goh Sui Noi explains: "China has rejected the idea of a G-2, which would have meant playing second fiddle to the US. It is also reluctant to break with the developing world. Being part of a collective that represents the developing world would be just right for it."[66]

The Chinese economic expansion and the huge investments made in infrastructure and urbanisation developments, have determined a boom period in relation to commodity prices. A few examples: China accounts for more than 30% of global growth in oil demand, while it surpassed 40% of the world's consumption of aluminium, copper, nickel, coal and iron ore.[67] Thanks to that, Latin America, Africa, the Middle East and many countries in Asia have been economically pulled up, enjoying of a sustained economic growth that will probably continue for several decades ahead. The downturn of this boom for many developing countries, though, has been the increase of international food and energy prices.

China has become an important investor in developing economies. This reached a new momentum on 9 March 2007, when its government announced the creation of the China Investment Corporation, with the aim to invest abroad an important part of its international reserves. In 2010, those reserves amounted up to

---

[65] Zachary Karabell, *Superfusion* (New York: Simon & Schuster, 2009), p. 243.

[66] "BRICS need to build stronger unity", *The Straits Times*, 2 June 2011.

[67] David Zweig and Bi Jianhai, "China's Global Hunt for Energy", *Foreign Affairs*, Vol. 84, (September/October 2005), pp. 25–38; CEPAL, *op. cit.*

US$2.4 trillion while in 2012 they have reached US$3.2 trillion.[68] An important part of these resources is being directed to investments and loans in countries owning raw materials of strategic value for China.

China's low-cost products are accessible by disenfranchised populations from all over the world. Consumers from around the globe benefit from products that were previously out of their reach. Moreover, thanks to their lower prices, inflation has been kept under control in many developing economies. The huge caveat though is depriving other emerging economies from competitiveness.

The balance of the Chinese economic growth seems to lean, thus, on the positive side for developing countries. And albeit the Chinese expansion has deprived many emerging economies of competitiveness, others have been able to imbricate their economies with China through supply chains of production. Such chains have become feasible thanks to information technology and cheaper global transportation costs. The former allows managing the puzzle represented by goods moving on different steps through different countries within the same production process. The latter allows those goods coming together for final assembly through a system of virtual spanning arteries composed by trucks, trains, ships and planes. While information technology solves the logistical problems involved in following up scattered manufacture parts in different places, lower transportation cost makes possible the joining together of those parts. China will frequently be the final destination of such production process as, since 2005, it became the centre of the Asian productive chain.[69]

There are, nonetheless, emerging economies whose manufacturing processes are not interconnected with China and that have clearly been affected by its lower production costs. If climbing through the technological ladder is not an option for them, these economies

---

[68] Yu Yongding, "China can stay the course- for now", *Today*, 7 August 2012.
[69] Robyn Meredith, *The Elephant and the Dragon* (New York, W.W. Norton & Company, 2007); Zachary Karabell, *op. cit.*; CEPAL, *op. cit.*

should try to lean towards the commodities and service sectors so as to avoid direct competition with China.

The international tradable services sector would offer them an important possibility to integrate their economies with global value chains steam-driven by China. Through these chains, manufacturing and services join together as the two sides of the same coin. Thanks to the revolutions in telecommunication and informations technologies, white-collar and blue-collar jobs can interact within the same production processes.[70] For countries whose economies have been overwhelmed by Chinese cheaper products, that would allow interconnecting their economies to China though global production chains. Hence, its designers, accountants, marketing analysts, legal researchers, software engineers, financial consultants or managers could be part of global manufacturing processes whose final assembly point takes place in China.

Other downturns for developing economies have also been mentioned. One would be the hike in international food or energy prices. But, of course, there are many additional responsible factors for that hike in addition to China's increased consumption. Not least, among them, the improvement in feeding and living standards in most developing countries whose uplift has been precisely dependent on Chinese demand.

Accusations of neocolonialism have also been directed against China, especially in relation to its deals with Africa. Nonetheless according to Martin Jacques:

> "China, with its own experience of colonisation, its anti-colonial record and its status as a developing country, has more legitimacy and enjoys a greater affinity with the African nations than does the West. That is reflected in the fact that in the 2007 Pew Global Attitudes Survey, for example, respondents in 10 African countries expressed far more favourable attitudes towards China than they did to the United States."[71]

---

[70] Andrés López, Daniela Ramos e Iván Torres, *Las Exportaciones de Servicio y su Integración a las Cadenas Globales de Valor* (Santiago de Chile: Comisión Económica para América Latina y el Caribe, marzo 2009).

[71] *op. cit.*, p. 332.

The answer to those accusations may rather be found in the Chinese harshness as a negotiator or in its redoubtable and cold-blooded pragmatism. But if that is the case, major international corporations and Western governments have had also to deal with it. China may not be an easy partner but as many have concluded it is an unavoidable and profitable one. On the other hand, having such a kind of negotiator making common cause with developing economies is not a bad thing.

However, some analysts consider that the days of high economic growth rates are numbered for China. And with it the position of No. 1 global exporter that, according to the WTO, the country holds since 2009. The conjunction of much talked about strikes and the pay raise in iconic companies has rung the alarms of Western media regarding China. Much is said about the country reaching what economists call the "Lewis turning point". Such "point" is named after Arthur Lewis, a Nobel laureate in economics, and describes the stage in the development of an emerging economy when labour shortages bring on inflation and slowing economic growth. Some analysts argue that as China will inevitably be forced to rush up in the technological ladder, jobs and companies will migrate to Vietnam and other centres of cheaper manpower.

The Lewis turning point

It is correct to point out that manpower costs are raising and that the country is rushing in up the technological ladder, but this is happening at the coastal provinces where the industrial production has been concentrated until now. While in inland China, there is still an immense human mass that may absorb the non-specialised jobs to be abandoned at coastal provinces.

According to *The Economist*: "In fact, there is good reason to doubt that the turning-point is here ... China's economic hinterland remains vast. About 40% of the country's labour force remains in agriculture, where their productivity is about one-sixth of its level in the rest of the economy."[72] Not surprisingly, the Taiwan giant

---

[72] "Is China's labour market at a turning point?", 12 June 2010.

Foxconn reaction was to move inland after intense scrutiny due to several suicides at its factories in coastal Shenzhen that coincided with a spate of strikes and wage protests at other nearby factories. According to Wesley J. Smith: "The planned relocation, aimed at containing rising costs, also indicates a move by labour-intensive manufactures out of coastal regions, reported *Global Times. The Financial Times*, citing unnamed executives, said yesterday that Foxconn will move some production from its long-time manufacturing hub in Shenzhen to northern Tianjin and central Henan province ... China has been pushing Taiwan, Hong Kong and other foreign investors to focus more on building manufacturing plants in inland regions closer to where most migrant workers come from."[73]

It is indeed a bit premature, to say the least, to talk about the Lewis turning point when China has at its disposal a working-age population of 977 million people that in 2015 will rise to 993 million. Although the one-child policy will subsequently reduce the number of new entrants into the work market and the fact that they will be 30% less in 10 years time, the sheer magnitude of the numbers involved makes exaggerate to talk about manpower scarcity.[74] Moreover, the one-child policy is not written with indelible ink.

According to Keith Bradsher, three elements would prevent the movement of foreign factories, currently located in China, to other Asian economies. Firstly, because those economies — Vietnam, Indonesia, Bangladesh, etc. — are also raising the cost of their manpower: "But wages are rising as quickly or more so in many of these countries, following China's example ... Bangladesh raised its minimum wage by 87% last year, yet apparel factories there are still struggling to find enough workers to complete ever rising numbers of orders." Secondly, because corporations prefer to have their plants where their sales are growing faster, "if the market is in China, which in many cases it now is, there is much less incentive to move". Thirdly, because of the sales currency: "Manufacturing in China

[73] "Near slave labour sweat shops in China lead to worker suicides", *The Straits Time,* 30 June 2010.

[74] *The Economist, op. cit.*

allows companies to incur costs in Renminbi, the same currency as a growing part of their sales."[75]

As for technological specialisation, the immense Chinese financial resources devoted to research and development, its capacity to accede to technology by acquiring it abroad or through transfer by transnational corporations producing or researching in China, the capacity of its universities to produce hundreds of thousands of engineers per year or the large pool of Chinese Scientist trained in the US, are tools of great importance to reconvert its coastal provinces. In fact, this is a process in high-speed motion: "But almost unnoticed by the outside world, over the past four years China has been moving toward a new stage of development. It is quietly and deliberately shifting from a successful low- and middle-tech manufacturing economy to a sophisticated high-tech one."[76]

According to a 2008 study on technological competitiveness by the Georgia Institute of Technology, it will not be long before China surpasses the United States in critical capability to develop science and technology and to transform these developments in products and services available in the market.[77] Already in 2005, a report from the National Academy of Sciences of the United States alerted that this country might lose, in not such a distant future, its status as world's technological leader. The report pointed out among other things that in the previous year, China had graduated 600,000 engineers while the US had only produced 70,000. This showed that for every qualified US engineer, China had 11.[78] On the other hand, China has rocketed into second place in the number of articles published in internationally recognised science magazines and according to a

[75] "World pays more as China's wages rise", *International Herald Tribune*, 2 June 2011.

[76] Thomas M Hout and Ghemawat Pankaj, "China vs. the world", *Harvard Business Review* (December 2010), pp. 95–103.

[77] "China is passing the USA in technology development", *Next Big Future*, 24 January 2008, <http://nextbigfuture.com/2008/01/china-is-passing-usa-in-technology.html>.

[78] Fareed Zakaria, *The Post-American World and the Rise of the Rest* (London: Penguin Books, 2009).

report by the Royal Society of London it may surpass the United States in 2013.[79]

Numerous examples are proof of China's impressive technological advancements. In 2010, it inaugurated the fastest train on earth, capable of running at 350 kilometres per hour, while in the final days of 2011 it unveiled the test version of an even faster train capable of hitting 500 kilometres per hour. So far, the government has built almost 10,000 kilometres of high speed rail tracks. But there is also the stealth J-20 that competes with the American F-22 Raptor in fifth generation war airplanes or the Dong Feng 21-D anti naval missile with an action radio of 1.500 kilometres. Moreover, the country's lunar probe projects have launched two successful lunar probes (the Change's-1 in 2007 and the Chang'e-2 in 2010), while in 2011 it launched the Tiangong-1 unmanned space module with the aim of establishing a space laboratory in 2016 and a manned space station in 2020. In 2012, China successfully launched its most ambitious space mission to date, putting three astronauts (taikonauts), including the country first woman, into orbit. The Shenzhou IX spacecraft realised manual docking manoeuvres with the orbiting Tiangong-1 space module.[80]

As for clean technology, Frances Beinecke President of the United States Council of Natural Resources stated in October 2009 that China was on the brink of surpassing his country in this sector. Barely a player in the solar industry a few years ago, China is currently producing more than half of the solar panels in the world. Moreover, according to a report commissioned by the World Wide Fund for Nature (WWF), China's production of green technology has been growing at a remarkable 77% a year, being the world's largest producer of such technology in money terms, even though it is surpassed by Denmark in terms of percentage of its GDP.[81]

---

[79] Agence France-Press, "China set to overtake the US in science research", *The Straits Time*, 30 March 2011.

[80] *International Herald Tribune*, 23 June 2011; *International Herald Tribune*, 6 January 2011; *Straits Times*, 30 September 2011; *Financial Times*, 28 December 2011; *Daily Shanghai*, 30 December 2011; *Straits Times*, 17 June 2012.

[81] Kevin Bullis, "Is China beating the U.S. in clean tech?", *Technology Review*,

In Information Technology, China's advances are surprising. In 2010, it put into work the Tianhe-1A that was for a while the world's fastest supercomputer with capacity to process 2.507 trillion calculi per second.[82] In 2011, another Chinese supercomputer, the Sunway BlueLight MPP broke the so-called "petaflop barrier" representing a quadrillion calculations per second. In David Barboza and John Markoff words:

> "That machine proved even more surprising in the West. Not only was it based on a Chinese-made microprocessor, it achieved a significant advance in low-power operation. That might indicate that the Chinese now have a significant lead in performance per watt — a measure of energy-efficient computing that will prove crucial to reaching the next generation of so-called exascale supercomputers, which are computers that will be a thousand times faster than the world's fastest today ... What scares competitors is that China has begun producing waves of amazing hardware engineers and software programmers, winning international competitions and beginning to dominate the best engineering programs in the US ... Now innovation is accelerating, and in the future, patents on smartphones and tablets will be originated by the Chinese people."[83]

Chinese high-technology manufacturing exports tell, on its part, a very impressive story. In fact, they grew more than 100,000% between 1985 and 2006, capturing the largest share of this market's growth. In Kevin P. Gallager and Roberto Porzecanski words:

> "According to our calculations, the EU15 captured the greatest share of growth of high-tech exports with almost 30% (of which 11.29% growth was captured by Germany). China comes in second and

Massachusetts Institute of Technology, 9 October 2009, <http:/www.technologyreview.com/business/23653.html>; Associated Press, "China leads push to go green", *International Herald Tribune* , 9 May 2010; Keith Bradsher, "Subsidies propel China in clean energy", *International Herald Tribune*, 10 September 2010.

[82] *International Herald Tribune*, 29 October 2010.

[83] "China reaches for high-tech dominance", *International Herald Tribune*, 6 December 2011.

> captured 27.44% between 2000 and 2006. It was the largest growth captured by a single country and represented more than all the growth captured by East Asia and the Pacific (including Japan), which captured 20.62% ... In 1990, China's high-tech exports were a mere 10% of total manufacturing exports. By 2006, China's high-tech share was approaching 40% of its total manufactures exports ... In 1985, China was in 29th place among high-technology exporters. By 2006, China ranked first with 13.7% of the global high-tech market."[84]

Of course, high-technology exports statistics and classification may be deceptive due to the fact that global production has become increasingly fragmented. Hence, a product whose parts have been imported can be assemble in a labour intensive production facility, and then exported as "high-tech". Nonetheless, China's increasing sophistication in this area is evident not only as a result of the important degree of research and development taking place in the country but also due to the high level of foreign transferred technology. Indeed, "China is now beginning to export final products under its own brands such as Lenovo and is domestically manufacturing high volumes of parts rather than importing them".[85] Moreover China is currently producing 300,000 inventory patents and about an equal number of "utility-model patents" annually and aims to reach two million patents a year by 2015.[86]

But the fact that China is advancing towards technological leadership does not have to affect its high economic growth rates. If anything, being able to excel both in intensive manpower and in technology gives China an exceptional economic room to manoeuvre. To that we have to add two additional elements. The first is the huge process of urbanisation and infrastructure development that is currently taking place in China and, that according to its 11th five-year plan, aims to move 300 million people from the country side to urban

---

[84] *The Dragon in the Room* (Stanford: Stanford University Press, 2010), p. 64.

[85] *ibid.*, p. 74.

[86] President's Council of Advisors on Science and Technology, "Report to the President on Ensuring American Leadership in Advanced Manufacturing", Washington D.C., June 2011, <http://www.whitehouse.gov/sites/default/files/microsites/ostp/pcast-advanced-manufacturing-june2011>.

areas.[87] The second corresponds to the emphasis given to domestic consumption by the 12th five-year plan.

China's ruder

In relation to the former, let us just mention the urban and infrastructural expansion involved in the reconfiguration of the axis of development of the Pearl and Yangtze rivers deltas. A super region that will penetrate 1,000 miles inland is being developed within the Pearl River while a gigantic corridor is following the Yangtze River until remote inland territories.[88] Hundreds of new cities are planned to emerge within this process. According to Michael Schuman: "Much of the new infrastructure links the already rich coastal areas to fast-growing second-third and fourth-tier cities in the west."[89] The dimension of the process in course is, as all things in China, immense. According to Peh Shing Huei:

> "More and more Chinese cities are aiming to upsize in the next decade ... Such observations appeal to some a half dozen Chinese cities that plan to balloon to megacity size, a status which in China usually means a population of more than 10 million and a built-up area of more than 500 sq km. These aspirants to mega status are mostly inland ... If successful, they will join the current club of six giants, which have largely concentrated near the coast. These megacities are suitable for China, said foreign and Chinese urban planning experts, since more than a billion people are expected to live in cities by 2030, up from today's 660 million."[90]

As for the rise in domestic consumption, the 12th five-year plan aims at taking the economically and socially "balanced" model of high-income Western societies as a benchmark.[91] Searching to correct

[87] Alfredo Toro Hardy, *Hegemonía e Imperio* (Bogotá: Villegas Editores, 2007).
[88] "China's new axes of development", *Oxford Analytica*, 15 December 2005.
[89] "Trading Up", *Time*, 7 November 2011.
[90] "More megacities for China", *The Straits Times*, 1 October 2011.
[91] Yongsheng Zhang, "The impact of China's 12th five year plan", *East Asia Forum*, 24 April 2011, <http://www.eastasiaforum.org/2011/04/24/the-impact-of-china-s-12th-five-year-plan/>.

the excesses and vulnerabilities deriving from its export oriented economic model, especially after the 2008 world crisis, China looks inwards in order to create a more self sustainable economic growth process. Professor Kay Shimizu of the Wheterhead East Asian Institute of Columbia University noted that the newly released 12th Five-year Plan (2011–2015) signified that "China is ready to go on the next phase in economic growth by staring wealth among its people and allowing the public share the fruits of reform and development".[92]

Indeed, nothing less than a "structural break" has been considered in relation to domestic consumption stimulus. In Gordon Brown's words: "We are about to see the implementation of a new medium-term plan targeted on stimulating consumption. Chinese officials stated to the IMF that they are taking other measures that amount to a 'structural break' with the past. If they succeed, it could reduce the current-account surplus about 4% of GDP and make consumer spending the fastest growing on any country by rising, on average, by more than 8% or even more per year. The Chinese government does not usually publish figures that it does not plan to reach."[93]

According to China's President Hu Jintao, total retail sales in the country are expected to grow at an annual rate of more that 15% between 2012 and 2017.[94] Bearing in mind that between 2001 and 2007 Chinese savings rose above 40% of its GDP and that on average Chinese households save more than a fifth of the money they make, while corporations retain even more in the form of retained earnings, China seems to be quite prepared to shift into a consumer society.[95] Current China's consumption level is too low. At 40% is well behind the United States with 70% and even India with 56%. In 2012, China's authorities were particularly promoting domestic tourism,

---

[92] "China's 12th Five-Year Plan signifies a new phase in growth", *Chinadaily*, 27 October 2011, <http://www.chinadaily.com.cn/bizchina/2010-10/27/content_11463985.htm>.

[93] Brown, *op. cit.*, p. 157.

[94] Agence-France Presse, 12 December 2011.

[95] Ferguson, *op. cit.*, 2011.

online shopping and spending on energy saving products.[96] Moreover, with social safety nets improving, the motivation for precautionary saving has weakened given a new boost to consumption while, at the same time, the consumption rate of luxury goods is rising.[97]

The country enjoys thus of an extraordinary room of manoeuvre resulting not only from its strengths in the areas of intensive labour and medium and high technology, but also by its capacity to play simultaneously in three different scenarios: exports, domestic consumption and urban and infrastructure development. China, of course, is not free of problems. The uncertainty of their European and American markets, inflation, bad debt left behind by past excesses, overpriced property markets, pollution, the "hukou" or urban housing registration system, among other considerations, are generating a great deal of anxiety. Nonetheless, no other country in the world can exhibit such an array of economic options and tools at its disposal.

But together with the spacious economic room of manoeuvre, China enjoys a political one as well. While in Europe and the United States every step in any given direction is constrained by huge contending forces, China's leadership faces little opposition when moving the economic ruder in any chosen way. Legitimacy, according to the country's political tradition, is measured by tangible results, able to generate satisfaction within its population. That guarantees that little opposition will emerge as results keep coming and, according to Martin Jacques, general satisfaction with the Chinese Central Government currently exceeds 90%.[98] While that keeps being the case, its leaders will have little problem in manoeuvring with relative ease.

The country's capacity to implement and reverse policies according to their economic needs have indeed proven to be extraordinary. The stimulus package of US$500 billion unveiled by Beijing only six weeks after the Lehman Brothers collapse and the subsequent

---

[96] David Yeo and Philip Ng, *op. cit.*

[97] Yu Yongding, "Dip bodes well for China's rebalancing act", *Today*, 4 October 2012.

[98] "How China will Change the World", Lee Kuan Yew School of Public Policy Lecture, Singapore, 24 September 2012.

monetary balancing act (initially pulling back on the levers to contain inflation and latter on relaxing its lending policy), are good examples of this. The capacity to obtain results is also quite amazing. While the stimulus package kept the economy growing at high percentages amid an international recession, the policies subsequently implemented to contain inflation on the one hand while easing lending on the other, were equally successful. In September 2012, China's consumer price inflation, at 1.9%, was under control while producer prices have dropped by 3.6% from a year earlier. At the same time in September and October 2012 evidence showed that lending was perking up and the pro-growth measures were gaining traction.[99]

The simple fact that China is targeting a slower growth rate in order to rebalance its economy speaks by itself. Indeed, the country's authorities are aiming at an annual growth of 7.5% in 2012 and 7% in the current five year plan period in order to encourage stronger domestic demand and higher value-added industries, while keeping consumer price rises under control (although 2012 projections by multilateral bodies estimated that economic growth during the period 2013–2017 will oscillate between 8.5% and 8.8%).[100] When compared to the US or the European Union economic blind alleys and decision-making deadlocks, China's availability of options and capacity to move the ruder of the economic ship in any given direction, looks simply amazing.

[99] Reuters, "China inflation eases to 1.9%", *The Straits Times*, 16 October 2012; Reuters, Agence France-Presse, "China showing signs of recovery", *The Straits Times*, 25 October 2012.

[100] CEPAL, *op. cit.*

Chapter

2

A Declining West

Mighty Chiindia

There is another nation that is normally associated with China: India. The relevance of these two emerging economies has led to the coining of a term frequently used these days: Chiindia. The same makes reference to the combined force of two countries that until 1820 represented almost 50% of the world GDP and which are on their way to reclaim their former pre-eminence. In Kishore Mahbubani's words:

> ...the kind of incredible domination of the world that America and the West enjoyed for the last 200 years was a hugely artificial moment of history. For 1,800 of the last 2,000 years, the two largest economies in the world were consistently China and India. So by 2050, or earlier, the No. 1 economy will be China, No 2 India, No 3 the United States of America that is the normal scheme of things.[1]

[1] "The seesaw of power: a conversation with Joseph Ny, Dambisa Moyo and Kisshore Mahbubani", *International Herald Tribune Magazine*, 24 June 2011.

A bit of historical economic data is required to bring perspective into this matter. Between 1600 and the beginning of the 19th century, China accounted for between a quarter and a third of the global GDP.[2] In 1750, the combined manufacturing production of China and India represented 57.3% of the global output while Europe just accounted for 23.2%.[3] At that point in time, these two countries constituted the main "central" regions of the world.[4] In 1700, India was responsible for 24% of the world manufacturing output while Great Britain just represented 3%.[5] According to Adam Smith, in 1776 China was richer than all of Europe put together.[6] In 1900, nonetheless, China and India together just represented 7% of the world manufacturing output.[7] About 50 years later, their combined GDP share of the world economy was only 8.8%.[8]

After much humiliation and pillage by Western powers (including the deindustrialisation imposed on them through coercion and unfair trade treaties) and after many big mistakes of their own making, China and India are back. And all seems to point out that Western predominance may end up being a brief 200 year interlude within Asia's multi-millenary economic supremacy. Indeed, China and India represent approximately 37% of the world's population and about 10% of global GDP. Moreover, in 2030, China's share in world GDP is expected to reach 23.1% and India's 10.4%, whereas in 2040, China should attain 40% and India 12%. In other words, with an expected combined percentage of 52% of the world's GDP in 2040,

---

[2] Angus Maddison, *The World Economy: Historical Statistics* (Paris: OECD, 2003).
[3] Philip S. Golub, "Quand la Chine et L'Inde dominaent le monde", *Maniere de Voir*, París, Janvier-March 2006.
[4] Andre Gunder Frank, "The World Economic System in Asia before European Hegemony", *The Historian*, Vol. 56, Issue 2 (December 1994), pp. 259–276.
[5] Ferguson Niall, *Empire: How Britain Made the Modern World* (London: Penguin Books, 2004).
[6] Golub, *op. cit.*
[7] *ibid.*
[8] T.N. Srinivasan, *Growth, Sustainability, and India's Economic Reforms* (Oxford: Oxford University Press, 2011).

they will be surpassing its combined GDP global share of 1820, which reached 48.9%.[9]

Starkly put,

> China and India are changing the rules of the global game. They are two of the world's 10 largest and the two fastest growing economies. Thus, they account for the two biggest growth opportunities for almost any product or service. They are two of the world's poorest economies in terms of per capita income. Thus, they offer some of the lowest wage rates for blue- and white-collar work that can have a transformational effect on competitive advantage. They are the world's two largest producers of science and engineering graduates. Thus, they represent an opportunity to radically expand a company's intellectual capabilities without a proportionate increase in cost structure. And finally, they are the breeding ground for a new cohort of ambitious, aggressive, and fast-moving global champions.[10]

At the same time, the combination of rapid growth and big population that characterises both these nations, offers them a spectacular advantage. Despite its fast growth in the previous decades, Japan could have never expected to surpass the United States for the simple reason that its population is hardly 40% of America. On the contrary, China would only require that its per capita income becomes a quarter of that of the United States in order to surpass in size the American GDP. Hereafter, its population dimension would allow China to guarantee itself several additional decades of sustained economic growth at high rates. Something similar could be said about India.

In GDP per capita terms, China is today where Japan was in 1965 and India is where Japan was in 1950, which means that there is still a lot of tissue to cut upon. Not surprisingly, it has been estimated that during the decade of 2040, both countries will represent 40% of the

---

[9] Srinivasan, *op. cit.*; Edward M. Kerschener and Naeema Huq, "Asian Affluence: The Emerging 21st Century Middle Class", Morgan Stanley Smith Barney, New York, June 2011.

[10] Anil K. Gupta and Haiyan Wang, *Getting China and India Right* (San Francisco: Jossey-Bass, 2009), pp. 1, 2.

total world market. Indeed, according to the Organisation for Economic Co-operation and Development (OECD), China's middle class spending will surpass that of the United States in 2020 and surpass the 27 European Union countries in 2027, whereas India will move ahead of the United States in 2021 and the European Union in 2026.[11]

Let us just mention that according to a Euromonitor International study, China's middle class will reach 700 million people in 2020, representing 48% of the total population of the country, whereas McKinsey estimates that by 2025 India's middle class will reach 583 million people representing 41% of its total population.[12] In other words, a combined middle class consumer market of 1,283 million people.

The Indian model

According to Kishore Mahbubani: "The Indian economy began to open up in 1991, mostly because of the balance of payments crisis, but partially also because of the lessons from China as well as the fear of being left behind."[13] That year, Prime Minister P.V. Narasimha Rao and Finance Minister Manmohan Singh, being forced to tackle the debt crisis but also impressed with China's impressive economic growth rates, began dismantling India's byzantine web of regulations and permits known as the "License Raj".[14] Under this system, it was impossible to open a factory, launch a product line or import technology without an overbearing bureaucratic peregrination that required

[11] *ibid.*; Jacques Attali, "Regional Outlook Forum", Institute of Southeast Asian Studies lecture, Singapore, 12 January 2011; Edward M. Kerschener and Naeema Huq, *op. cit.*

[12] *People's Daily Online*, 20 July 2010, <http://english.people.com.cn/90001/90778/90862/7072426.html>; "The 'Bird of Gold': The Rise of India's Consumer Market", McKinsey Global Institute, May 2007, <http://www.mackinsey.com/Insights/MGI/Research/Asia/The_bird_of_gold.html>.

[13] *The New Asian Hemisphere: The Irresistible Shift of Global Power to the East* (New York: Public Affairs, 2008), p. 78.

[14] Michael Schuman, "Think big. Act bold", *Time*, 29 October 2012.

countless permits. The reforms yielded spectacular results with a GDP growing average of 6.5% a year ever since.

Nonetheless, instead of adopting the classic Asian strategy of labour intensive-export oriented economy, India has relied more on its domestic market. It has also emphasised services over industry and high technology over low-skilled manufacturing. As a result, it has been successful in high-end services and capital and knowledge intensive manufacturing, but has not been able to create a broad industrial base. And even though it is now the fourth largest economy of the world and is expected to surpass Japan in 2035 to become No. 3, it has been argued that it would have to create more manufacturing jobs in order to overcome the huge inequality gap and expand the domestic demand.[15]

India's insufficient physical infrastructure has been closely related to the limitations of its industrial base and to the possibilities of an export-oriented economy.[16] Nevertheless, the strength of its service sector, which now accounts for 54% of India's GDP has made some analysts wonder if India can skip the industrial revolution altogether and jump directly from an agricultural economy to a service economy. According to *The Economist*, this would be highly unlikely as none of the Asian economies, including high-end services centres like Hong Kong and Singapore, were able to overcome poverty or even low-end incomes without a manufacturing boom.[17] A World Bank paper argues, though, that the "Indian experience has led researchers to challenge the conventional notion that industrialisation is the only plausible route to rapid economic development".[18]

According to this perspective, services have to be seen under a different light as they have ceased to be simple inputs for trade in goods, in order to become tradable elements in themselves. That is,

---

[15] Gurcharan Das, "The India Model", *Foreign Affairs*, Vol. 85 (July/August, 2006), pp. 2–16.

[16] Robyn Meredith, *The Elephant and the Dragon* (New York, W.W. Norton & Company, 2007); Anil K. Gupta and Haiyan Wang, *op. cit.*

[17] "Now for the hard part: A survey of business in India", 3 June 2006.

[18] Saurabh Mishra, Susanna Lundstrom and Rahul Anand, "Service Sophistication and Economic Growth", The World Bank, South Asia Region Policy Research, Working Paper 5606 (March 2011), p. 2.

"final exports" for direct consumption. Thanks to revolutionary advances in the information and the telecommunication technologies, brought about with the advent of the Internet age, services that can be provided at distance such as banking, insurance, business-related services, call centres or education, to mention just a few, have proliferated. That has resulted in a profound shift on the nature, productivity, and tradability of services.[19]

India's distinctive comparative advantages in tertiary education, native fluency in the English language, telecommunication, soft infrastructure, etc., have indeed positioned the country at the forefront of international tradable services. According to Anil K. Gupta and Haiyan Wang:

> India is far ahead of China in software services as well as most other types of services that can be delivered remotely by information technology. Examples of the latter range from low-end commodity services (such as call centres) to high-end knowledge-intensive services (such as software development, chip design, market research, marketing analytics, legal research, securities analysis, drug discovery services and so forth).[20]

Moreover, in their words:

> India's IT services sector is more than five times as large as that of China. Also, paralleling China's comparative advantage in manufacturing, India's lead in IT services rests on multiple factors: a very strong export orientation, extensive experience at remote delivery of IT services to global clients, highly developed process rigor, in-depth knowledge of specific industries, and fluency in the English language.[21]

Nonetheless, the World Bank paper suggestion that high-end services can challenge the conventional notion that industrialisation is the

---

[19] *ibid.*

[20] *op. cit.*, p. 42.

[21] *ibid.*, p. 53.

only plausible route to rapid economic development is not accepted by T.N. Srinivasan, one of India's top economist: "The suggestion that India could leap-frog the manufacturing activity altogether and shift labour from low skill primary activities to the high skill-technology component of services is *prima facie* a pipe dream".[22]

Indeed, even if services that can be delivered remotely by information technology are able to provide important economic growth rates while generating middle class jobs, it does not follow that this is a reasonable option to overcome poverty or even low-end incomes. What about other types of services?

Services in india can be classified into three groups: traditional, traditional/modern and modern. The first is made of retail and wholesale trade, transport and storage, public administration and defence. The second is a combination of traditional and modern services mainly consumed by households: education, health and social works, hotels and restaurants and other community, social and personal services, whose shares rise linearly with the per capita income. The third relates to business services, computer services, communications, banking, financial intermediation, legal and technical services, etc. This group is directly linked to the international tradable services and move on towards the direction of high-end knowledge-intensive services.

Evidence suggests that the first group of services stagnated following a period of rapid growth, but this is not linear: public administration and defence as well as miscellaneous personal services seem to have levelled off, whereas the transport sector has grown rapidly. The second group has continued growing steadily with particular reference to hotels, restaurants, education and health. Finally, the third has been the fastest growing group, having accelerated since 1990. More broadly, though, communication, business services, financial services, education, health, hotels and restaurants and transport have in fact risen to the point where they roughly transport for half of total growth in services during the period 2000–2006.[23]

---

[22] *op. cit.*, p. 77.

[23] Barry Eichengree and Poonam Gupta, *The Service Sector as India's Road to*

It appears then that services job creation is transversal to the three aforementioned groups with emphasis in certain sectors. But would this be sufficient to skip labour-intensive manufacturing in a country plagued by poverty? It seems highly unlikely. What about the agricultural sector that represents 22% of the GDP versus 27% in industry? Luckily for India, agriculture is an important option on the table, which certainly is not the case for China given its mountainous topography. According to Gurcharan Das:

> In the short term, the best way for India to improve the lot of the rural poor might be to promote a second green revolution. Unlike in manufacturing, India has a competitive advantage in agriculture, with plenty of arable land, sunshine and water. To achieve such a change, however, India would need to shift its focus from peasant farming to agribusiness and encourage private capital to move from urban to rural areas. It would need to lift onerous controls, allow large retailers to contract with farmers, invest in irrigation, and permit the consolidation of fragmented holdings.[24]

The caveat though is that agricultural industry's productivity and job creation do not follow the same direction. Agribusiness could certainly overcome the current low productivity associated to the peasant farming system, but it would do so at the expense of making redundant an important part of the population that works in the land. For a country with high poverty rates, it may not be a wise decision to emphasise economic growth at the cost of a dramatic increase on unemployment and urban misery. The debate that has surrounded the opening of the retail sector to foreign wholesale companies is a good example of the dilemma that exists between modernisation of backward economic sectors and the job losses implicit in such a process.

If the most dynamic industries of the Indian's economy do not provide sufficient new jobs and the low productive sectors are the job intensive ones, logic would advise the necessity of a trade off

---

Economic Growth?, Indian Council on International Economic Relations, Working Paper No. 249 (April 2010).

[24] *op. cit.*, p. 8.

between this two conflicting trends. According to the rating company Crisil, between 2000 and 2005 net employment in India increased by 93 million people, whereas in the following five years, growth in employment slowed to the meagre number of 2 million.[25] During those last five years, though, India had an impressive economic growth. Hence, there seems to be an inverse correlation between economic growth and job creation that has to be corrected in order to preserve the social tissue of the country. Redistributive social policies could become a necessary tool in order to attack poverty reduction, a good example of which was a landmark Bill that secured Cabinet approval in December 2011, guaranteeing heavily subsidised grains to poor families.

In any case, it is up to India to define the specifics of its model, as the "one size fits all" prescription has lost its appeal. As former Prime Minister Vajpayee once said: "India has adapted itself to globalisation, but globalisation has been adapted to 'indianisation'".[26] A "Washington Consensus" would be as out of context as an "Asian model" or a "Beijing Consensus", as India has to cross its particular river "by feeling the stones". The Chinese experience could provide general lessons such as the usefulness of a well-defined long-term strategy, the convenience of emphasising pragmatism and flexibility over shock therapies and the benefits of industrial policies, but more than that India and China represent distinct cultures and different political systems. Moreover, they represent "civilisation-states".[27]

A multicultural globalisation

This takes us back to an enlightening exercise of scenarios realised by Shell in 2002. According to the same, two alternative routes existed to the year 2020. The first was represented by the so-called "Executive Class" scenario, the second by the "Prism". The former implied a

[25] Andy Mukherjee, "Work and wages versus wealth and welfare", *The Straits Times*, 17 November 2011.
[26] *India Today*, 24 March 2004.
[27] Martin Jacques, *When China Rules the World* (London: Allen Lane, 2009).

continuation of the Washington Consensus leading the globalisation process. A world characterised by a single modernity, where an all powerful and tight international elite supported market-oriented values. The latter as a "prism" dispersed different colours, symbolising a multicultural world economy in which a plural modernity prevailed. That meant different economic strategies defined in accordance to cultural, national or regional specificities.[28]

It seems rather clear that the world economy is no longer defined by Washington or Western values and standards, having set off in the route of the "prism", which means a multicultural globalisation process. This requires some additional explanation. Globalisation is both fact and content. The fact derives from the information, telecommunication and transport revolutions, which have created what has been labelled as the "death of distance".[29] The result has been a mobile economy where capital sweeps across countries at electron speed, where manufactures and services move flexibly among nations, where goods are conceived, produced and assembled in several countries and where services and manufactures are integrated within the same production processes.

But coexisting with globalisation as a fact we found the substance of globalisation, which enters into the realm of ideology. This conforms the notion of hegemony as defined by Antonio Gramsci, for whom the capacity to define the political agenda through ideological and cultural persuasion and consensual acceptance was the most stable and effective form of predominance.[30]

Globalisation as content was identified with three interacting elements: a market-oriented economic model, an ideology based on the virtues of the market and a double standard Western controlled system. As explained above, the ideological zeal and the hypocrite

---

[28] Shell Group of Companies, *Peoples and Connections: Global Scenarios for 2020* (London: 2002).

[29] Frances Cairncross, *The Death of Distance* (Boston: Harvard Business School Press, 1997).

[30] David Forgacs, *Antonio Gramsci Reader* (London: Lawrence & Wishart, 2001); Alfredo Toro Hardy, *Hegemonía e Imperio* (Bogotá: Villegas Editores, 2007).

double standards were resented by many, particularly in the developing world, and were instrumental in bringing down the Washington Consensus and in blocking the Western led multilateral trade negotiations. That meant the loss of consensual acceptance on the prevailing values by a substantial part of the international community. The emergence of two civilisation-states, China and India, as major economies also helped to convince developing economies about the existence of powerful alternatives. In other words, the idea of a single modernity ceased to be acceptable by the majority.

Globalisation as a fact has not, and could not, been affected, but globalisation as a substance has been deprived from its hegemonic content. The "prism" represents a new multicultural approach to globalisation where the "one size fits all" prescriptions are no longer admissible, and where the time in which a reduced group of countries could define the world's economic agenda in self-serving terms, has elapsed. According to Charles Kupchan: "We are heading toward no-one's world, a world of multiple modernities, interdependent and globalised without a political center or model."[31] In Martin Jacques words:

> In the future, then, instead of there being one dominant Western modernity, they will be many distinct modernities. It is clear that we have already entered this era of multiple modernities...Hitherto, we have lived in a Western-made and Western-dominated world, in which the economic, political and cultural traffic has been overwhelmingly one-directional, from the West to others.[32]

And he adds:

> The emergence of new modernities not only means that the West no longer enjoys a virtual monopoly of modernity, but that the histories, cultures and values of these societies will be affirmed in a new way and can no longer be equated with backwardness or, worse

[31] Quoted by Roger Cohen, "How bad are things, really?", *International Herald Tribune Magazine*, December 2011.
[32] *op. cit.*, p. 142.

> still, failure. On the contrary, they will experience a new sense of legitimacy ... The West has thought of itself to be universal, the unquestioned model and example for all to follow.[33]

This new plural modernity is the natural background for the impressive emergence of developing economies. Indeed, even if the leading role of China and India in shaping a new reality has been fundamental, there is a long list of countries that have to be taken in consideration. Brazil together with the two of them and Russia (the latter not a South hemisphere country and perhaps not even a developing economy), was part of the so-called BRIC. Moreover, Goldman Sachs, that in 2003 had coined the acronym BRIC, mooted in 2005 their successors, calling them the Next 11 (N11). Among their rank were Vietnam, Mexico, Turkey, Indonesia, the Philippines, Egypt and Bangladesh. Moreover, Goldman Sachs guru's Jim O'Neill, who invented the BRIC acronym, suggested the term "growth markets" in 2011, defining them as emerging economies that account for more than 1% of the global GDP.

In 2006, PricewaterhouseCoopers published a report called *The World in 2050*, where it listed its own emerging candidates under the so-called E7: China, India, Brazil, Mexico, Indonesia, Turkey and Russia. In 2010, the BRIC, already a formal group, decided to incorporate South Africa as one of them, giving birth to the BRICS. A year before, the OECD had coined the term BRIICS, including not only South Africa but also Indonesia. In 2006, the BRICs Economic Research Institute of Japan created the acronym VISTA to include their own list: Vietnam, Indonesia, South Africa, Turkey and Argentina. In 2009, Robert Ward, Global Forecasting Director of the Economist Intelligence Unit, produced the acronym CIVETS to list his favourite emerging economies: Colombia, Indonesia, Vietnam, Egypt, Turkey and South Africa. And the list goes on.

Nonetheless, Chiindia, the BRIC, the BRICS, the BRIICS, the growth markets, the CIVETS, the VISTA, the N11 or the E7 are just the tip of the Iceberg of the emerging economies. And even though emerging and developing economies are not synonymous concepts,

---

[33] *ibid.*, p. 144.

and this is something that has to be outlined, the fact remains that the great majority of the former comes from the latter. According to Brazil's Foreign Minister, Antonio Patriota, in his remarks to Reuters: "It has become clear that the engines for growth and dynamism in the world economy have been economies that share some common traits; they still have large segments that are underdeveloped or that live in poverty, but at the same time they have demonstrated a capacity to generate high levels of growth and expanding markets."[34] Emerging and developing economies are thus two notions that can be easily equated for practical purposes, even though there are developing economies that are not emerging and emerging economies that already overcame the developing phase.

The truth of the matter is that when Western economies transformed "shareholder-value-driven capitalism" in the essence of globalisation, they were promoting, at the same time, their own economic decline and the strengthening of the Global South. The short-term vision, the concomitant lack of strategic aims and the race to the bottom of production costs that characterises such a model has indeed caused tremendous damage to Western predominance. According to Jim O'Neill, during the period 2011–2020, the five BRICS countries will double the G7 in its contribution to the increase of the global GDP.[35] Such damage has materialised through several steps.

The Global South and shareholder capitalism

Western economies offshored their blue-collar jobs to developing economies, which was tantamount to transferring its industrial might to those economies. Manufacturing now accounts for less than a 10th of private sector American jobs, its lowest share since the early 20th century.[36] At the same time, around 450 of the largest

---

[34] "Brazil: No BRICS expansion wanted for now", Reuters, 16 November 2011, <http://www.reuters.com/article/2011/11/16/us-brazil-brics-idUSTRE7AFOP92111116.html>.

[35] "Puns and punditry", *The Economist*, 10 December 2011.

[36] Edward Luce, *Time to Start Thinking: America and the Spectre of Decline* (London: Little, Brown, 2012).

500 multinationals have invested in China.[37] According to the World Bank, 20 years ago developing countries provided just 14% of rich countries' manufacturing imports, but by 2006 that figure increased to 40%, and by 2030 it should rise to more than 65%.[38] In Zachary Karabell's words:

> A substantial portion of China's trade with the world since the beginning of the millennium has been generated by foreign firms sourcing products in China in order to sell them somewhere else, and not because Chinese factory owners figured out what foreigners want and decided to produce low-cost versions. ... In addition, it has been estimated that more than 50 percent of China's exports were paid for by foreign firms and were the result of foreign investment in China that led to the construction of the factories that produced those goods.[39]

Western economies have been offshoring their white-collar jobs to developing economies as well, which implies relying on the strength of foreign brains at the expense of making their own brains increasingly redundant. According to Robyn Meredith: "By 2008, the United States will have moved 2.3 million service-industry jobs overseas, and the United Kingdom will have offshore 650,000".[40] In Edward Luce words: "In the past decade, some of America's most impressive companies shifted large chunks of their corporate brains offshore. In 2003, IBM had 6,000 employees in India and 135,000 in the United States. Now it has 110,000 employees in India, which has overtaken the company's US workforce".[41] But the situation is much worse than that as it has been estimated that impersonal services — those than can be provided at distance — will tend to disappear from developed nations in order to be relocated in developing ones. A 2006 study by consulting firm Booz Allen Hamilton stated that white-collar offshoring included high-end work that had

---

[37] Xulio Ríos, *op. cit.*

[38] Robyn Meredith, *op. cit.*

[39] *Superfusion* (New York: Simon & Schuster, 2009), pp. 156, 157.

[40] Robyn Meredith, *op. cit.*, p. 79.

[41] *op. cit.*, p. 146.

traditionally been considered 'core' to the business, such as chip design, financial and legal research, clinical trial management, book editing, etc. The convergence of lower costs and the huge pool of talent available in those countries — as the case of India shows — lead in that direction. That may imply tens of millions of jobs migrating from the West. Moreover, it would seem that high-wage jobs, performed by highly educated employees in the US are, if anything, more offshorable than other service jobs.[42]

Western economies have been transferring their technologies to China in a massive way. That materialises as a mean to gain access to its huge potential market or through direct sale. General Electric is a good example of the former, as it is handing over its most sophisticated aeronautical electronic technology in order to benefit from Chinese aeronautical market, which is expected to generate 400 billion dollars in sales during the next 20 years. Technology selling by American or European companies to China frequently implies selling the companies that are producing it, which has gone from Volvo to MG, from IBM's Personal Computers Division and France's Thompson to numerous medium size Silicon Valley corporations. A study, commissioned by the Asia Society in New York forecasts that over the next decade, China could invest as much as 2 trillion dollars to acquire overseas companies, plants or property.[43] It is of course easy to imagine what type of companies China is looking for: "One of the main worries in the Western world is the nature of the companies that China is buying abroad ... They are just interested in accessing their knowhow, their technology."[44]

---

[42] Alan S. Blinder, "Offshoring: The Next Industrial Revolution", *Foreign Affairs,* Vol. 85 (March/April 2006), pp. 113–128; Alan S. Blinder and Alan B. Krueger, "Alternative Measures of Offshorability" in Working Paper 15287, National Bureau of Economic Research, August 2009, <http://www.nber.org/papers/w15287>; Arianna Huffington, *Third World America* (New York: Crown Publishers, 2010); Saurabh Mishra, Susanna Lundstrom and Rahul Anand, *op. cit.*; President's Council of Advisors on Science and Technology, *op. cit.*

[43] David Barboza, "China's Growing Overseas Portfolio", *International Herald Tribune*, 4 May 2011; "China buys up the world", *The Economist*, 11 November 2010.

[44] "El gigante chino se va de compras por el mundo", *La Razón*, 19 enero 2011.

After having promoted China's trade surplus, by offshoring to them their blue-collar jobs, Western economies and very particularly the United States let China finance their own spending binge. Trade surplus with the US grew from US$28 billion in 2001 to US$251 billion in 2007.[45] Not surprisingly, as Fareed Zakaria points out, China became such a good lender: "Through their accumulation of massive quantities of American debt, the Chinese ended up subsidising the behaviour that caused it — American consumption. They financed our spending binge and built up a vast hoard of dollars IOUs."[46] China's lending was not only responsible for the United States living beyond their means but also created the cheap money that encouraged all kind of financial excesses. To begin with, it was the underlying reason why the mortgage market in the United States was so full of cash that it became possible to obtain a 100% mortgage without income, jobs or even assets: the spark that unleashed the American financial fire.

The creative destruction associated with shareholder capitalism has unforeseeably brought, indeed, a lot of creation to developing economies and substantial destruction to the developed ones. The leverage of the former has increased in a very relevant way as, in addition to their preponderance in commodities and new markets, they have gotten a substantial hold on manufacturing industries, brainwork, technology, and cash. Conversely, Western economies have cornered themselves. Thanks to this process, among many other things, some American cities are experiencing what demographers say is the greatest urban population decline since the Black Death in 13th century Europe.[47] In Kishore Mahbubani's words: "The rest of the world, paradoxically, is more ready than Americans for a globalisation that Americans themselves are creating."[48]

---

[45] Brahma Chellaney, *Asian Juggernaut* (New York: Harper, 2010).

[46] *The Post-American World and the Rise of the Rest* (London: Penguin Books, 2009), p. xx.

[47] Edward Luce, *op. cit.*

[48] "The seesaw of power: a conversation with Joseph Nye, Dambisa Moyo and Kisshore Mahbubani", *International Herald Tribune Magazine*, 24 June 2011.

The West: An embattled fortress

A June 2008 Harvard Business School study reported that up to 42% of American jobs, which represents more than 50 million of them, are vulnerable to being sent offshore.[49] By promoting the inclusion into the labour global equation of 1.3 billion Chinese, 1.2 billion Indians or 250 million Indonesians, within the context of a race to the bottom of production costs, Western nations created huge economic and social problems for themselves while becoming embattled fortresses.

As Georgetown Professor of International Affairs Charles Kupchan, clearly explains:

> A crisis of governability has beset the Western world. It is no accident that the United States, Europe and Japan are simultaneously experiencing political breakdown; globalisation is producing a widening gap between what electorates are asking of their governments and what those governments can deliver ... Globalisation was supposed to have played to the advantage of liberal societies, which were presumably best suited to capitalise on the fast and fluid global marketplace. But instead, for the better part of two decades, middle-class wages in the world's leading democracies have been stagnant and economic inequality is rising sharply. The plight of the West middle class is the consequence primarily of the integration into global markets of billions of low-wage workers from developing economies.[50]

But while the social fabric of Western nations risks a fracture — the "Occupy" movement, the hate rhetoric of the Tea party, the Spanish "indignados" or the London rioters are but feeble signs of it — Western corporations have been obtaining disproportionate profit margins. According to the Ohio based hedge fund manager John Hussman, profit margins for private sector investors are today 50% higher than historical levels.[51]

---

[49] Arianna Huffington, *op. cit.*

[50] "Refounding good governance", *The New York Times*, 19 December 2011.

[51] Andy Mukherjee, "Work and wages versus wealth and welfare", *The Straits Times*, 17 November 2011.

And, of course, when faced with the competition of foreign lower wages that they promoted by offshoring jobs, Western corporations' natural response has been to multiply job-killing technologies home in order to reduce costs. "That so many of the jobs we now create are low end underscores a growing debate over technology and its role. Many of the jobs that have disappeared from the US economy have done so not only because they were outsourced but also because they are now done by computers or robots."[52] As for the jobs that still remain in the United States, a 2011 McKinsey report stated that more than half of American employers surveyed said they planned to move more into part time and casualised hiring in the next few years.[53]

Having made US$1.68 trillion in profits in the last quarter of 2010 and sitting on piles of cash, US corporations are doing fine while job numbers languish and more Americans struggle.[54] As a matter of fact, the jobs that are currently being created in the United States are those relatively low-skilled and low-paid that cannot be replaced either by offshoring or job-killing technologies. Since 2000, indeed, as the United States lost 5 million manufacturing jobs, which was about a third of what was left, the country gained 4 million jobs in healthcare.[55]

In short, the middle-skilled jobs that once formed the ballast of the world's wealthiest middle class are disappearing and a growing share of whatever job the American economy is still managing to create is in the least productive areas. Of the five occupations forecast by the Bureau of Labour Statistics to be the fastest growing between now and 2018, none requires a degree. These are registered nurses, "home health aides", customer services representatives, food preparation workers and "personal home care aides". If there is an explanation as why middle-class incomes have stagnated in the past generation, it is: Whatever jobs the US is able to create

[52] Rana Foroohar, "What ever happened to upward mobility?", *Time*, 14 November 2011.

[53] Edward Luce, *op. cit.*

[54] Roger Cohen, "America, awaken", *International Herald Tribune*, 28 June 2011.

[55] Edward Luce, *op. cit.*

are in the least efficient sectors — the types that neither computers nor China have yet found a way of eliminating.[56]

These corporations (and their managers), it is worth saying, are the same that in the case of the United States have being arguing against tax increases calling them "class warfare" and are massively evading taxes at home and lobbying for tax benefits. General Electric is a good example of "good corporate citizenship". In 2010, the company reported worldwide profit of US$14.2 billion of which US$5.1 billion came from its operations in the United States. Nonetheless, they claimed a tax benefit of US$3.2 billion.[57] In David Kocieniewski's words:

> Its extraordinary success is based on an aggressive strategy that mixes fierce lobbying for tax breaks and innovative accounting that enables it to concentrate profit offshore ... While G.E.'s declining tax rates have bolstered profits and helped the company to continue paying dividends, some taxpayers question what taxpayers are getting in return. Since 2002, the company has eliminated a fifth of its work force in the United States while increasing overseas employment. In that time, G.E.'s accumulated offshore profits have risen to US$92 billion from US$15 billion.[58]

Moreover, instead of laying the foundations for future growth by building new plants or investing in research and development in the Unites States, American corporations are investing massively in buy-backs of their own stocks. The principle behind this awkward use of money is simple: with fewer shares in the market, earnings per share tend to rise and by investing in their own stocks, the company benefits from short-term jump in stock prices that reflects well in its quarterly reports. And, of course, given the fact that executives are normally important shareholders of the companies under their control, they stand to benefit from such short-term jump. This has

---

[56] Edward Luce, "Is America working?" *Financial Times*, 11 December 2011.

[57] Edward Luce, *op. cit.*

[58] "G.E.'s tax strategies", *International Herald Tribune*, 26–27 March 2011.

helped senior management to collect millions in cash and stock incentive payments by meeting earnings-per-share goals.

Drug companies like Pfizer and Zimmer have been buying huge amounts of their own shares at the expense of developing new products that could increase their competitiveness. Pfizer spent more than US$20 billion repurchasing shares from 2005 to 2010 while Zimmer is on track to repurchase US$1 billion of its shares this year after having bought 500 million last year. "After diving in the wake of the financial crisis, buybacks have made a remarkable comeback in recent years, with US$445 billion authorised this year, the most since 2007, when repurchases peaked at US$914 billion. But spending on capital investments like new plants and infrastructure has stagnated more broadly in corporate America."[59]

One of the most striking results of the aforementioned state of affairs has been a historically high inequality level. Three facts underscore such inequality in the United States: the 400 wealthiest Americans have a greater combined net worth than the bottom 150 million Americans; the top 1% of Americans possess more wealth than the entire bottom 90%; and in the Bush era expansion from 2002 to 2007, 65% of economic gains went to the richest 1%.[60]

Not surprisingly, the United States is seeing growth in two types of jobs. On the one side, there are the 10% of Wall Street financiers, Silicon Valley developers, corporate managers and doctoral engineers and physicists, who continue to do extremely well. On the other side, there are the low-end service jobs, constituted by nurses, domestic aides, food preparers, call centre workers, janitors, auto repair workers, nutritionists, and the like, whose numbers grow while their incomes drop. David Autor, an MIT economist, has described this phenomenon as the missing middle. The result is exemplified by Walmart, whose CEO earns more in two weeks than the company's employee does in a lifetime.[61]

---

[59] Nelson D. Schwartz, "In U.S., stock buybacks win out over jobs", *International Herald Tribune*, 23 November 2011.

[60] Nicholas Kristof, "'Occupy Wall Street' and inequality", *New York Times*, 15 October 2011.

[61] Edward Luce, *op. cit.*

The above-mentioned process, on the other hand, does not seem to have done much for America's productivity. According to Jeff Faux and Larry Mishel: "... there is little evidence that the neo-liberal policy mix, which has generated this inequality, has also generated a more efficient economy. In fact, through the period of opening markets, productivity growth in the USA has not improved, being a sluggish 1%. Such productivity growth is slow both by historical standards and by comparative international standards."[62] Under such circumstances, the tremendous burden and sacrifices imposed upon the country's middle class would have served no other purpose than making the rich much richer.

The combination of a shareholder-value-driven capitalism and official passivity has been responsible for the situation we just described. That implies corporations lacking in any sense of stakeholder mentality in relation to their own workers or societies while ready to feed future competitors with their own technology and know-how if that improves their next quarterly gains. Also implies governments that elude long-term structural considerations amid a "*laissez faire*" attitude that fails to promote research and development, infrastructural development, public education, protection for the manufacturing base or support for start-ups companies. The race to technological leadership by China and the weak response to such a challenge by the United States, exemplifies well the difference between the industrial policy of the former and the market-oriented approach of the latter.

The United States lagging behind

China's well-defined technological strategy has taken hold through seven steps. First, by concentrating efforts, investments and synergies in 17 specific productive sectors as well as in a group of key state companies (the so-called "national champions" like Lenovo, Huawei, Sunzone, Chery, etc.). Second, by massively investing in research and development, which has grown at an average rate of 21% during the last 10 years, and it is estimated to reach America's level in 2016.

[62] "Inequality and the Global Economy" in Will Hutton and Anthony Giddens, edit., *Global Capitalism* (New York: The New Press, 2000).

Third, through a stick and carrot policy that promotes technological transfer from foreign corporations with presence in China. Fourth, by buying abroad corporations that possess useful technologies. Fifth, by attracting back Chinese scientists residing in other countries through generous incentives. Sixth, by investing US$250 billion a year in education and in the formation of technological cadres that includes, among others aims, putting its main universities among the global top 10 in a decade. Seventh, by setting up high-technology incubators that provides finance, physical facilities and advisory services to technology starts-up companies.[63]

The United States goes in a totally different direction. First, public financing for research and development has remained stagnated in real terms since 1995. Second, such investment not only lacks a strategic vision but also has been concentrated in short term (funding is usually limited to one or two years) and poorly interconnected programs. Third, American corporations where the bulk of technological innovations reside, have massively transferred the result of its research and development to China in order to access its market. Fourth, since the crisis of the so-called "New Economy", at the beginning of the new millennium, the United States has witnessed passively the exodus of an important part of its foreign technological establishment. Fifth, restrictions to the H1B visa for highly qualified professionals, have denied access to the country to some of the world's best brains (a good part of which have obtained their science and technology degrees in US universities, where more than 70% of PhDs in physics are awarded to foreign students). Sixth, even though the top American universities are among the global best (seven of the world's 10 more reputed according to the *Times Higher Education Supplement*) its educational system is in

[63] *China-USA Business Review*, Vol. 7, No. 1 (January 2008); Anil K. Gupta and Haiyan Wang, *op. cit.*; Thomas M Hout and Ghemawat Pankaj, "China vs. the world", *Harvard Business Review* (December 2010); James Kynge, *China Shakes the World* (London: Phoenix, 2006); "China buys up the world", *The Economist*, 11 November 2010; Joseph Stiglitz, "The Party's Over", BBC, December 2011; Howard Yu and Ben Lin, "When state capitalism meets bamboo entrepreneurship", *Today*, 30 January 2012; Kerth Bradsher, "China pushes for degrees for the masses," *International Herald Tribune*, 18 January, 2013.

shamble. According to the 2011 OECD's Programme for International Students Assessment, American students ranked 32 in mathematics proficiency (Shanghai students' ranked No. 1). Seventh, even though venture capitalism finances start-up firms in high-tech areas, government provides little incentives for spurring such start-ups — (nonetheless, venture capital fund financing has diminished substantially since the "New Economy" bubble burst and since the financial meltdown of 2008: in 2000, Silicon Valley venture capitalists raised US$200 billion while since 2008 they have been raising no more than US$20 billion a year; even more, part of that amount goes to American start-ups in Bangalore or Shanghai).[64]

Not surprisingly, then, the United States now shares the lead in aerospace and satellite with Asia and Europe while it has given up the chase in many other high-tech areas, including, robotics, flat panel displays, lithium ion batteries, nuclear power, most fields of clean energy, memory chips and high-speed trains. Even in computing, America's edge is beginning to be contested. In the late 1990s, the United States had a US$30 billion annual trade surplus in advanced manufactured goods while it now has a US$40 billion deficit. In 2000, it ranked first in the world in terms of its ability to innovate while in 2010 it had moved down to sixth. In 2010, the United States came last out of 40 countries in improvements to its climate for innovation.[65]

The problem of losing the innovation edge under the current circumstances is obvious as only through high technology can the United States successfully face China's competition. If nurses, domestic aides, food preparers, call centre workers, janitors, auto repair workers and nutritionists are the bulkhead to defend its economy against foreign competition, they have already lost the battle. Only through education and technological innovation will the

[64] Thomas M Hout and Ghemawat Pankaj, *op. cit.*; Alfredo Toro Hardy, *op. cit.*; Fareed Zakaria, *op. cit.*; Eric Hanushek and Paul Peterson, "Why can't American students compete with the rest of the world", *Newsweek*, 5 September 2011; Fareed Zakaria, "Are America's best days behind us?, *Time*, 3 March 2011; Edward Luce, *op. cit.*

[65] Edward Luce, *op. cit.*

United States retain a leading role in the international economy. While this happens, China is on the brink of becoming the largest supplier of college-educated workers to the global labour force as reported by Reuters on 14 June 2012. Moreover, according to the World Economic Forum's Global Competitiveness Index, the United States slipped to fifth place in 2011–2012, from fourth place the previous year, continuing a general downward trend evident since 2005.[66]

American short-sightedness, though, has other roots besides shareholder capitalism. Let us go back to 1979 when three fundamental historical events took place. That year, Deng Xiaoping began the economic reform in China, laying the foundations of the dizzying economic expansion of the country. It marked as well the triumph of the Islamic Revolution in Iran, putting in motion a transformational movement in the Middle East. Finally, it saw the invasion of Afghanistan by the Soviet Union, propitiating the formation of an anti-soviet Islamic jihad that would gather 35,000 radical Muslins from 40 different countries, planting the seed of Al Qaeda which was to become a highly disruptive phenomenon a couple of decades later.[67] That year represented a fork between two different processes and directions. On the one hand, a spectacular economic growth that was represented by China. On the other hand, a political radicalisation process that was represented by Islamism.

The obsessive attention that the United States brought to the latter made it lose sight of the former. In Kishore Mahbubanis's words:

> If you look at it objectively, the world's greatest power should always be focused on the world's greatest emerging power. That is a logical thing to do. Therefore, the United States should be spending 90% of its resources focused in China. Instead, the United States is spending 90% of its time focused on the Islamic world, fighting unnecessary wars in Iraq and Afghanistan.[68]

---

[66] Stephen Roach, "America's other 30 per cent offers hope", *Today*, 8 August 2012.

[67] Samuel Hungtinton, *The Clash of Civilizations and the Remaking of the World Order* (New York: Simon & Schuster, 1996).

[68] "The seesaw of power: a conversation with...", *op. cit.*

What was happening in China was indeed much more relevant than Islamism. China's emergence represented a true game changer and a fundamental challenge to the American leadership in the 21st Century. While Islamism, as highly relevant and even disruptive of Western societies as it may be, cannot be considered as a threat for America's global predominance. Hence, the attention of the leading superpower was not directed to the emerging rival power, as common sense would have advised, but to a secondary scenario.

While the United States spent more than 1.3 trillion dollars in the Afghan war and in the utterly unnecessary war in Iraq, carries forward an immensely costly drone war in Pakistan and Yemen, bombarded Libya and threatens Iran, its infrastructure and its educative system languishes in decay while its industrial base is vanishing.

Indeed, America's infrastructure ranks 23rd in the world, investing just 2.4% of its GDP in infrastructure versus 5% in Europe and 9% in China. The result is that the country's bridges, roads, schools, electricity grid, waterways, rail system, air traffic network, and levees have dropped to second world level. Notwithstanding that situation, the American Society of Engineers concluded that the country would need to spend US$450 billion a year for the next five years simply to maintain infrastructure in its current status.[69] Its high-tech infrastructure, on the other hand, is not in a much better position: in 2009, its broadband access ranked 15 worldwide and its broadband download speed ranked 19th, with over 100 million Americans lacking broadband in their homes.[70]

As for the state of its educational system Fareed Zakaria is clear:

> As American education has collapsed, the median wages of the American worker have stagnated, and social mobility — the beating heart of the American dream — has slowed to a standstill ... While we have been sleeping, the rest of the world has been upgrading its skills. Countries in Europe and Asia have worked hard to increase their college graduation rates, while the US's — once the world's

[69] Edward Luce, *op. cit.*

[70] Arianna Huffington, *op. cit.*; Fareed Zakaria, "Are America's best days behind us?", *op. cit.*

> highest — has flatlined. Other countries have focused on math and science, while in America degrees have proliferated in 'fields' like sports, exercise and leisure studies.[71]

In just one generation, indeed, the United States has fallen from first to 12th in the proportion of its young people with graduate degrees. More than a quarter of American students drop out of high school and a third drop out of college, while almost half fail to complete their college degree in the allotted time.[72] According to Edward Glaeser, professor of economics at Harvard University, the recently OECD Programme for International Student Assessment (PISA)'s international maths scores put the US in the middle of the pack and in par with Portugal.[73] As Arianna Huffington puts it:

> Our high schools have become dropout factories. We have one of the lowest graduation rates in the industrialised world: Over 30% of American high school students fail to leave with a diploma. And even those who do graduate are often unprepared for college. The American Testing Program, which develops the ACT college admission test, says that fewer than one in four of those taking the test met its college readiness benchmark in all four subjects: English, reading, math, and science ... Even the top 10% of American students, our best and brightest, ranked only 24th in the world in math literacy.[74]

More than a fifth of American adults have a reading age of fifth grade, which corresponds to 11 years old, or below. Not surprisingly then as reported by Edward Luce in a 2010 poll a small majority of Americans revealed that they did not realise that humans and dinosaurs never coexisted or, even more incredibly, another poll showed that almost half of Americans thought the sun revolved around the earth. Perhaps not in the same dimension of the two previous polls but

---

[71] "When will we learn?", *Time*, 14 November 2011.

[72] Edward Luce, *op. cit.*

[73] "Republicans must embrace education not tax cuts", *Bloomberg*, 25 October 2011, <http://www.blomberg.com/news/2011-10-25/republicans-must-embrace-educatio-not-tax-cuts-edward-glaeser.html>.

[74] *op. cit.*, pp. 114, 115.

nonetheless relevant is the fact that 49% of Americans believe that the President has the power to suspend the US Constitution.[75] As for the country's manufacturing base, the United States President's Council of Advisors on Science and Technology stated the following:

> Although the US has been the leading producer of manufactured goods for more than 100 years, manufacturing has for decades been declining as a share of GDP and employment. Over the past decade, it has become clear that this decline is not limited to low-technology products, but extends to advanced technologies invented in the US ... Moreover, it is increasingly apparent that technology innovation is closely tied to manufacturing knowledge. We cannot remain the world's engine of innovation without manufacturing activity.[76]

Moreover, the President's Council of Advisors on Science and Technology continues referring:

> The loss of US manufacturing jobs is not limited to 'low-tech' products. The trend of production migrating abroad has expanded to high-tech manufacturing. The nation's share of the global market of exports from high-technology industries declined from around 20% in the late 1990's to about 11% in 2008. The trade balance in advanced technology manufactured products — long a relative strength of the United States — shifted from surplus to deficit starting in 2001, and the trade deficit of US$17 billion in 2003 further widened to US$81 billion by 2010. At the same time, China's global trade position in high-technology products moved to surplus starting in 2001, and increased from less than US$13 billion in 2003 to almost US$130 billion in 2008 — led by trade in information and communications goods. We have not simply lost low-value jobs, such as assembly, but sophisticated and advanced manufacturing activities.[77]

---

[75] Edward Luce, *op. cit.*

[76] "Report to the President on Ensuring American Leadership in Advanced Manufacturing", Washington D.C., June 2011, <http://www.whitehouse.gov/sites/default/files/microsites/ostp/pcast-advanced-manufacturing-june2011>, p. 1.

[77] *ibid.*, pp. 2, 3.

Indeed, according to a report by the American National Science Board, the United States lost more than a quarter of its high-tech manufacturing jobs during the past decade. Most of it went to China, whose rapid expansion of science and engineering capabilities "... poses an ever more formidable economic challenge to the US".[78] Moreover, again in the words of the President's Council on Advisors on Science and Technology: "... the United States might be shut out from competing altogether in certain industries as knowledge and inventions are increasingly produced abroad in addition to the products that result from them."[79]

As China advances at an exponential speed, even threatening its technological leadership, the United States seems oblivious of its growing lack of competitiveness. As Paul Krugman has said not without a grain of exaggeration: "... the United States has lagged in everything except in financial services ..."[80] Obsessively focused in the Taliban, Al Qaeda, Saddam Hussein, the Iranian ayatollahs and other real or imaginary foes of that region of the world, the United States simply lost track of what was really meaningful. The 2011 Legatum Prosperity Index that provides a global assessment of national prosperity based in eight sub-indices, ranked the United States well behind China in the Economy sub-index. The latter measures the performance of countries in four areas that are essential to promoting prosperity: macroeconomic policies, economic satisfaction and expectations, foundations for growth and financial-sector efficiency. According to this sub-index ranking, the United States is in the 18th position whereas China is in the 10th.[81]

Consumed by its conflict in Flanders in the 17th century, Spain lost its economic supremacy to much more focused economic competitors. It would seem that the United States, consumed in its own contemporary Flanders, lost economic competitiveness to more

---

[78] "U.S. losing high-tech jobs to Asia", *The Washington Post with Bloomberg Business*, 18 January 2012.
[79] *op. cit.*, p. 5.
[80] "Losing their immunity", *International Herald Tribune*, 18 October 2011.
[81] *PRNewswire*, London, 8 November 2011, <http://wwwprosperity.com/downloads/2011ProsperityIndexPressRelease>.

focused rivals. And of course, as it happened with Spain then, the erosion of economic power leads to that of the imperial eagles as well. By looking in the wrong direction, Washington created the conditions for its falling behind.

The contrast generated by the presence of President Hu Jintao from China and President Obama at the G-20 economic summit meeting, at the beginning of November 2011, was a clear testimony of that. While all the regards where fixed towards the former, the latter was received with plain indifference: "The two contrasting appearances at the Group of 20 economic summit meetings that begins on Thursday look like the perfect example of weakening US influence, a stark portrait of an empire in decline."[82] By the same token, a Pew Research Center global survey, made public on June 2012, showed that 41% of people considered that China was the world's top economic power while 40% favoured the United States.[83] To be fair, though, President Obama has captured the seriousness of the situation and in its 2011 Discourse of the Union made reference to a new Sputnik moment.

Sputnik was the name of the first Soviet orbit satellite, whose launching so profoundly impacted the Americans and gave rise to the space race between the two countries. On that occasion, President Eisenhower, later followed by President Kennedy, assumed the challenge of not falling behind the Soviets in this area and mobilised the creative energy of its nation towards such aim. Obama's reference to a Sputnik moment addresses an inflexion point in America's decline that forces upon the country the need for a concerted response.

The conditions have changed, though. When Eisenhower and Kennedy responded to the Soviet challenge, they were able to count on the extraordinary capacity to build domestic political consensus that characterised their time. Moreover, they had at their disposal the necessary capital, labour and technological resources to advance such purpose. The current Sputnik moment not only is much broader in

---

[82] Helene Cooper, "U.S., out of money, leaves the G-20 limelight", *International Herald Tribune*, 3 November 2011.

[83] Agencies, "China now seen as top economic power", *Today*, 14 June 2012.

content, but the tools that both American Presidents had then at their disposal are clearly lacking now.

Consensus building around a big national objective is unattainable nowadays, amid an utterly and bitterly polarised Congress and society. Economic resources are lacking as the country is confronted with a public debt that surpasses US$16 trillion and a fiscal deficit that reached US$1.35 trillion in 2010. Labour has been systematically downgraded within a corporative mentality that emphasises brands and patents at the expense of all the rest that has become offshorable. Werner Von Braun, the German scientist that headed the American Space project, would probably not have been able to work in the United States nowadays due to the H1B visa restrictions. According to Michael Bloomberg's "Partnership for a New American Economy", even though immigrants play a relevant role in three out of four patents at America's top universities, foreign born innovators face today "daunting or insurmountable immigration hurdles that force them to leave and take their talents elsewhere".[84] Public funding for research and development that gave birth to a huge proportion of some of the most critical technologies faces today a market-oriented scepticism against federal research budgets. Moreover, incentives to private sector have shrunk and in spite of having invented the R&D tax credit, the United States is now only the 18th most generous in the world.[85] America's high-tech know-how, finally, is currently been massively transferred to its main strategic rival, China, by quarterly-oriented corporations focused on short term gains.

It appears to be too late thus for a new Sputnik moment. Notwithstanding President Obama's insightfulness with its "Winning the Future" agenda and its "Race to the Top" educational program, his country does not seem to be able or prepared to follow his lead on this matter. *That Used to be US* is the title of a book by Michael Mandelbaum and Thomas Friedman that laments America's decline.

---

[84] Andrew Martin, "Immigrants are crucial to innovation, study says", *The New York Times*, 25 June 2012.

[85] Edwar Luce, *op. cit.*

The Sputnik moment represents well what the United States could attain then, but cannot any more.

Obama's response to a rising China

To president Obama's credit, he has recognized the need to confront China's rise. To that aim he has given shape to an Asia-Pacific security and prosperity area for the 21st century. But, is it the right strategy? This project is supported by two broad aims. The first is to seek sustainable security by counterbalancing China's emergence through the gathering together of the United States and its traditional allies in the region. The second objective is to promote what he has called "our shared prosperity", essentially through an enlarged trans-Pacific trade and economic liberalisation agreement: the so-called Trans-Pacific Partnership. Hugh White, professor of strategic studies at the Australian University of Canberra talks of an Obama containment doctrine to China, describing it as "America's most ambitious new strategic doctrine since Truman committed America to contain the Soviet Union".[86]

This issue requires some background. According to Aaron L. Friedberg, American policy towards China, since the first of the two Bush presidents, contained two main elements: engagement (trade, cooperation, etc.) and balancing (avoiding that China's emerging power overruns the *status quo*). At the same time, China's strategy towards the United States since the times of Deng has been based in three points: building national power, advancing incrementally and avoiding confrontation.[87]

Since 2010, China's brashness with several of its neighbours, in relation to the disputed South China Sea and the Senkaku/Diaoyu islands, has represented a very serious drawback not only to the precept of advancing national power in an incremental way but also to the country's soft power strategy. According to Joshua Cooper Ramo, in the spring of 2004 several dozens of Chinese scholars and intellectuals gathered at the island of Hainan, with the purpose of giving

[86] "Contain China?", *The Straits Times*, 26 November 2011.

[87] *A Contest for Supremacy: China, America and the Struggle for Mastery in Asia* (New York: W.W. Norton & Company, 2011).

form to a China "brand" that could be successfully promoted internationally. It was there that the concept of "peaceful emergence" was coined.[88] It was a brilliant soft power marketing strategy that provided China with huge goodwill dividends. Nonetheless, the year 2010 and to a lesser extent the following years have threatened with derailing all that had been attained previously.

For a country like the United States, whose influence in the Asia-Pacific region had been waning for a long time, this meant a very important come back opportunity. And the best way to take advantage of such an unexpected overture was by presenting itself as the indispensable counterbalance to China's new regional might. That meant emphasising balancing over engagement in its relation to China. Needless to say, though, that "balancing" is a polite word whose meaning is none other than containment. To have forgotten Deng's aphorism of concealing its own capacity and winning time was clearly a serious mistake for such a skilful international operator as China.[89] "Taoguangyanghui" — the Chinese word for low profile — had indeed served them quite well until the aforementioned muscle flexing.

Nonetheless, the American announcement that it would deploy an important contingent of marines at an Australian base in Darwin, and subsequent policy statements regarding its military presence in the Asia-Pacific region, have touched a sensible nerve in many countries of the region. This has brought back memories of the time when South East Asia was at the epicentre of the East-West confrontation.

The sensibility of the subject is clearly reflected in the following words of Singaporean former Deputy Prime Minister and former Minister of Foreign Affairs, Wong Kan Seng:

> "The Cold War bisected the world ... The geopolitical landscape comprised two distinct blocs, with the rest of the world littered with 'proxy wars' of great power rivalry and pervaded mutual suspicion. Vietnam itself had seen two decades of bloody warfare before US troops pulled out in 1973, with the fall of Saigon coming

---

[88] *Brand China* (London: The Foreign Policy Centre, February 2007).
[89] Xulio Ríos, *op. cit.*

> shortly after. It was against this backdrop that our region and many of the countries of our region began to take their first steps as independent nations ... It was in this context that Singapore and four of our neighbours — Indonesia, Malaysia, Thailand and the Philippines — formed ASEAN in 1967 ... The grouping had as implicit *raison d'être* to provide a political framework to manage our political differences. All the founding ASEAN members had their own histories of suspicions and disputes to overcome. It was a long and slow process for ASEAN members to build confidence and feel at ease with one another."[90]

Not surprisingly, there was an immediate reaction to an American military presence that could undermine years of confidence building in the region. Several South East Asian countries expressed concern that the marines could fuel mistrust and affect regional security. Singapore's Foreign Minister K. Shanmugam explained that ASEAN nations did not want to get "caught between the competing interests of major powers", while Indonesia's Foreign Minister Marty Natalegawa expressed that such presence could "create a vicious circle of tensions and mistrust".[91]

Even in Australia, considered as one of the United States closest allies in the region, the reaction to an American military presence was highly polemical. Peter Leahy, former Australia Chief of the Army from 2002 to 2008 argued: "By substantially increasing its close relationship with the US, Australia may unduly complicate its relationship to China. As a sovereign nation, Australia should maintain its ability to say no to the US and separate itself from its actions." Australia's former Prime Minister and Foreign Minister Kevin Rudd has called for a Pax Pacifica that acknowledges China's legitimate aspirations while former Prime Minister Paul Keating wrote: "The future of Asian stability cannot be cast by a non-Asian power — especially by

---

[90] "Lessons for Singapore's Foreign Policy: The Cambodian Conflict", S. Rajaratnam Lecture 2011, MFA Diplomatic Academy, Singapore.
[91] *The Straits Times*, 21 and 23 November 2011.

the application of US military force. The key to Asian stability lies in the promotion of strategic cooperation."[92]

At the end of the day, the success or failure of the American security initiative will depend on the cleverness with which both Washington and Beijing play their cards. But, of course, the military encirclement of China is by no means the proper strategy to deal with its tectonic economic emergence. To respond to China's challenge through aircraft carriers, submarines, troop deployments and regional defensive alliances, as more and more seems to be the case, would be the biggest American short-sightedness of them all.

The more economically attuned 'Trans-Pacific Partnership', on the other hand, goes in the opposite direction to the Asia-Pacific economic strategy purposefully followed by China for many years. Hence, the natural reaction of the latter: "'If the rules are decided by one or several countries, China does not have the obligation to observe them', Chinese diplomat Pang Sen said last week at the Asia-Pacific Economic (APEC) summit".[93] East Asian countries are being thus placed amidst a balance that has China on the one side and the United States on the other: "Security analyst Yukio Okamoto warned 'The TPP raises the question of whether the region should aim for a US-style free trade area or to co-exist with China'."[94]

The countries of the region will have to choose between the two sides by calibrating several considerations. Should they aim to grow closer to a regional power that has shown an articulated and continuous strategy towards the region during the last decade or to a superpower that until recently seemed to have forgotten them? Should they look to a China-led East Asian integration process, that has reach momentum through its expanding free trade agreement with ASEAN (plus Japan and South Korea), or to an American-led trans Pacific deal that may take years of complex negotiations and subsequent approval by the United States Congress? Should they rely on a booming

---

[92] David C. Kang, "Balancing US, China interests in East Asia", *The Straits Times*, 24 October 2012.

[93] Grace Ng, "Pacific trade pact a wake-up call for China?", *The Straits Times*, 23 November 2011.

[94] Kwan Weng Kin, "Japan's balancing act", *The Straits Times*, 23 November 2011.

economy synergistically integrated to them (that in 2014 will become the world's largest importer) or should they aim towards a contracting economy whose deficits are so vast and its budget so out of balance that sooner or later will have to defect to its Asia-Pacific commitments?

Answers to the above appear to be obvious. As in the case of the "Sputnik moment", this economic initiative seems to be arriving too late. As a matter of fact, China seems to have anticipated this situation and in Kishore Mahbubani's words acted preemptively:

> China is acutely aware that this steady rise (its own) could one day alarm America...If America one day 'woke up' and decided to contain a rising China just as it contained the Soviet Union, it could have used ASEAN countries (many of whom were American allies or friends in the Cold War) to encircle China. Hence, in a strike against any possible American encirclement, China shared its prosperity with its ASEAN neighbors.[95]

It appears, indeed, that we are witnessing the sunset of the United States and by extension that of the West. While globalisation is evolving in Asia's direction, history is bending towards the emerging economies. And even if a new economic hegemony seems to be out of context within the multicultural approach represented by the "prism", the fact that the West does not call the shots anymore is crystal clear. According to Niall Ferguson: "The financial crisis that began in the summer of 2007 should therefore be understood as an accelerator of an already well-established trend of relative Western decline."[96]

2008: The American decline

In order to properly understand the nature and implications of that economic crisis, we have to bring some perspective into the matter. In 1986, Margaret Thatcher deregulated Great Britain's financial market. It was the so-called "big bang" of London's Stock Exchange that was to be followed around the world, particularly in the United

[95] *op. cit.*, p. 231.

[96] *Civilization: The West and the Rest* (London: Allen Lane, 2011), p. 308.

States. This new era of deregulation coincided not only with a deflated period in commodity prices but also with a 'global sea of liquidity'. This global excess of liquidity derived basically from two sources. On the one hand, from the surcharge paid by Chancellor Helmut Kohl for the German reunification and on the other hand from the US official stimulus cast in order to recover from the huge losses incurred by the savings and loans crisis of that country. The combination of these factors provided a tremendous boost to an economy of intangible goods, that is, a paper economy.[97]

The consolidation of vast investment reservoirs generated a great competitive pressure for obtaining short-term financial profits; short, indeed, as to allow that those investments could produce ripe benefits. This was symbiotically combined with corporate America's quarterly financial mentality. The result tended to be none other than the abandonment of productive investments by way of formulas that allowed the creation of money without the simultaneous creation of value. This implied that the anchor, which held together the financial economy and the real economy, was loosened.

Derivatives became the perfect instrument for such purpose. Breakthroughs in destock computing and an influx of mathematics PhDs to Wall Street enabled new investment technologies. Such technologies resulted in broad new classes of complex structured investment instruments that revolutionised wholesale banking.[98] But as the master of this new game George Soros observed, those instruments could become so esoteric that not even the most sophisticate investor would really understand how they worked.[99]

The United States was the natural place for the perfect storm to emerge, as shown by the fact that its detonator was a "... small equilibrium fracture in a particular sector of the American financial system:

---

[97] Jim Rogers, "A global sea of liquidity", *Time*, 13 March 1995; Alfredo Toro Hardy, *El Desorden Global* (Caracas: Editorial Panapo, 1996).

[98] Charles R. Morris, *The Two Trillion Dollar Meltdown* (New York: Public Affairs, 2008).

[99] Byron Wien e Kriztina Koenen, *George Soros* (Rio de Janeiro: Editora Nova Fronteira, 1995).

the real estate financing".[100] Such small equilibrium fracture produced a chain reaction clearly explained by Niall Fergusson:

> When house prices began to decline in 2006 ... those who had borrowed more than the value of their homes, stopped paying mortgage interests; those who had invested in securities backed by mortgages suffered large losses; banks that had borrowed large sums to invest in such securities suffered first illiquidity and then insolvency; to avert massive bank failures governments stepped in with bailouts; and a crisis of private debt mutated into a crisis of public debt.[101]

The underlying causes though lay in the lax financial and monetary regulations that allowed for all kind and shapes of excesses to be committed. Such deregulation process accelerated when the Glass–Steagall Law was repealed in 1999. The law had emerged as a result of the Great Depression of 1929 with the aim of providing guarantees to the banking system and its abolition threw down the fence that separated commercial banks from other activities. That allowed commercial banks to enter into the investment banking business and promoted their off-balance-sheet activities. Nonetheless, real problems were not the result of the excesses committed by deregulated commercial banks, but from those other institutions that have never been submitted to regulations: the shadow banks.

The so-called shadow banking system was constituted by a group of institutions (hedge funds firms, private equity firms, etc.) that acted as banks without being so and that were involved in high-risk financial instruments (hedge funds, auction rates, repo-tripartite, bonds with options, structured investment vehicles, etc.). Without any kind of supervision, shadow banks simply went wild. Some like Brooksley Brown, head of the Commodity Futures Trading Commission, issued loud warnings in the late 1990's about the consequences of failing to regulate the financial derivatives. Nonetheless, the Commodity Futures Modernisation Act, passed by Congress in December 2000

---

[100] Jacques Attali, *Survivre aux Crises* (Paris: Fayard, 2009), p. 34.
[101] Ferguson 2011, *op. cit.*, pp. 276, 277.

under the auspices of the Secretary of the Treasury Larry Summers and the Chairman of the Federal Reserve Bank Alan Greenspan, banned any attempt to regulate derivatives and new investment instruments.[102] The "*laissez faire*" environment that allowed the uncontrolled expansion of that system, particularly during the Bush Administration, was perfectly symbolised by a 2003 photo session in which representatives of different federal regulatory bodies cut piles of regulations with power saws and pincers.[103]

According to the prevailing dogma of the day, indeed, markets could self-regulate themselves. As Dambisa Moyo points out:

> In the US, Chairman Greenspan, as a convert and proselytiser for self-regulation, oversaw the rise of what came to be termed the shadow banking system. This was the network of hedge funds, private equity firms and off-balance-sheet entities that where outside the purview of the Fed. ... Such was the byzantine nature of the derivative complex that no one actually appreciated the size and indeed the whereabouts of this labyrinth of debt.[104]

And, of course, a natural by-product of the above was the tendency to under fund the regulatory agencies, rendering them totally unable to fulfil their tasks. A typical case was the Securities and Exchange Commission, which remained light-years behind the algorithmic software of the financial players that it was supposed to regulate.[105] But such extremes could not have been reached without low interest rates and the underestimation of risk that comes when money keeps entering easily. In C. Fred Bergsten words:

> Its role as the dominant international currency has made it much easier for the US to finance and, thus run up, large trade and current account deficits with the rest of the world over the past 30

[102] Edward Luce, *op. cit.*
[103] Paul Krugman, *The Return of Depression Economics and the Crisis of 2008* (London: W.W. Norton & Co., 2009).
[104] *How the West was Lost* (London: Allen Lane, 2011), pp. 66, 67.
[105] Edward Luce, *op. cit.*

> years. These huge inflows of foreign capital, however, turned out to be an important cause of the current economic crisis, because they contributed to the low interest rates, excessive liquidity, and loose monetary policies that brought the overleveraging and underpricing of risk ...[106]

The result of all of these was none other than the world's biggest financial crisis since 1929 that lead to the destruction of approximately US$40 trillion in equity value in the global economy; the nationalisation of America's largest mortgage lenders; the largest bankruptcy in history, that of Lehman Brothers; the disappearance of the investment bank and the issuance of bailouts and stimulus packages around the world that amounted up to trillions of dollars.[107]

As for the social costs involved, Elizabeth Warren, Chair of the Congressional Oversight Panel charged with monitoring the Troubled Asset Relief Program, listed the following: one in every five Americans is unemployed or underemployed; one in every nine families cannot make the minimum payment on their credit cards; one in every eight mortgages is in default or foreclosure; more than US$5 trillion in pensions and savings were wiped off and more than 120,000 families are filling for bankruptcy every month.[108] Moreover, some 100 million Americans are now below or close to the poverty line.[109] The political consequences of such state of things are obvious as conflict between rich and poor now eclipses racial strain and friction between immigrants and native-born as the greatest source of tension in American society, according to surveys.

But in addition to the huge financial crisis and the socio-political implications therein involved, the aforementioned excesses also led to a major debt crisis. In September 2008, the tipping point of the financial crisis, the United States public debt amounted to US$9.7 trillion,

[106] "The Dollar and the Deficits", *Foreign Affairs*, Vol. 88 (November/December 2009), p. 24.

[107] Fareed Zakaria, *op. cit.*

[108] Arianna Huffington, *op. cit.*

[109] Roger Cohen, "Decline and fall", *International Herald Tribune*, 22 November 2011.

being the result of an annual increase of 500 billion since 2003. Nevertheless, from September 2008 until mid 2011, such debt increased from US$4.5 trillion to reach US$14.2 trillion. The three Economic Stimulus Acts passed by Congress to overcome the crisis, in 2008 and 2009, had without any doubt a lot to do with that increase. Joining the financial and the debt crisis was also the fiscal deficit. According to the Congressional Budget Office, the annual deficits might well average more than US$1 trillion every year for a full decade after 2009 and, of course, the greater the debt, the higher will be the cost of servicing it. That cost was estimated to reach 19% of the total federal budget in 2011 and will represent 17% of total revenues by 2019.[110] As a matter of fact, in 2012 the country's budget deficit had been exceeding US$1 trillion for the fourth year in a row.[111]

In August 2011, the richest economy in the world was in the brink of defaulting payment on its debt. As a result, Standard & Poor took the unprecedented measure of downgrading the United States credit rating. The latter was the combined result of the amount of the debt itself and of the Washington bickering surrounding political negotiations for raising the debt ceiling. This brings us to another of the American features: its institutional shortcomings in dealing with the economy.

In a country characterised by the dispersion of political power like the United States, the decision-making process is closely associated with the coalescence of different interests. The so-called "iron triangles" have become the best expressions of such coalescence as they represent the joining of forces of a regulatory federal agency, a congressional committee or subcommittee and one or more pressure groups. In such a triangle we find: (a) the agency that regulates a certain economic sector; (b) the congressional committee that funds that agency and supervises its activities, and (c) the pressure

[110] Michael Mandelbaum, *The Frugal Superpower* (New York: Public Affairs, 2010), p. 8.

[111] Reuters, "US budget deficit tops $ 1 trillion for 4th year", *The Sunday Times*, 14 October 2012.

groups — within that particular economic sector — that finance the political campaigns of the members of the congressional committee or subcommittee.

This convergence of vested interest, where each of its three parties can satisfy the need of the others, can become totally immune from external pressure, leading to political autarchy. And even though the outcome of such decision-making process tends to be self serving and at odds with the general interest, the procedure itself tends to be fluid.[112] Not surprisingly in 2008, 80% of Americans surveyed told the Program on International Policy Attitudes that they believed the government was controlled by "a few big interests, looking for themselves".[113]

Needless to say that iron triangles thrive in opacity while fade in public light. And in matters of national relevance, the decision-making process changes its nature involving the two Chambers of Congress and the White House. In such cases, risk becomes the opposite of what is found within iron triangles with fluidity disappearing and deadlock showing its face at every corner. As the American political system functions upon the basis of opposed but shared powers, counter balances are call to promote cooperation and avoid power grabbing. Cooperation is the fuel that keeps the decision-making machine in motion: "The US system is one of shared and overlapping powers. No one person or party is fully in control; everyone is checked and balanced. People have to cooperate for anything to get done."[114]

During the last decades, though, polarisation has become entrenched in American politics and the overlapping moderates of

[112] Alfredo Toro Hardy, *El Desafío Venezolano: Cómo Influir las Decisiones Políticas Estadounidenses?* (Caracas: Universidad Simón Bolívar, 1987); John E. Chubb, *Interest Groups and the Bureaucracy: The Politics of Energy* (Stanford: Stanford University Press, 1983); Thomas R. Dye and Harmon Zeigler, *The Irony of Democracy* (Monterrey, Cal.: Brooks/Cole Publishing Company, 1987); Kenneth J. Meier and John Bohte, *Politics and the Bureaucracy* (Belmont, Cal.: Wadsworth Publishing, 2006).

[113] Arianna Huffington, *op. cit.*, p. 129.

[114] Fareed Zakaria, "The debt deal's failure", *Time*, 15 August 2011.

both parties that used to build compromises are no longer there. Meanwhile, Congressional party majorities in line with the White House have become the exception. It did not happen, indeed, during the eight Reagan years or Bush Senior four years or during six of the Clinton eight years. It happened during six of the Bush Junior eight years or two of Obama's first four years. In other words, during only eight of the last 32 years White House and Congress have been in hands of the same party. Not surprisingly, once and again the decision-making process gets blocked.

How can a superpower function with a minimum degree of rationality when its decision-making system fluctuates between fluidity for special interest politics and deadlock and nightmarish horse-trading in matters of national interest? As the case of the debt ceiling negotiations shows, economic crisis can be substantially worsened by institutional shortcomings. Indeed, the fiscal and economic irrationalities being dealt with by the political system can be overshadowed by the irrationality of the political system itself. The end of 2012 scheduled blast of tax increases and spending cuts facing Congress and the White House, known as the fiscal cliff, reverberated through the whole year hampering growth and wiping out nearly one million jobs. The contrast with China's professionals and technocrats, who have ruled the country pragmatically and with a self-effacing and collegial style, cannot be bigger. Especially so when political legitimacy in their case derives not from the ballot boxes but from a "mandate from the heaven" sustained in good results. According to Edward Luce, America's economy and political system are both in worse shape than they had been in a very long time, and their dysfunctions seem to feed on one another in a synchronised way. This combination makes decline all the more inevitable.[115]

The generalised and immense loss of confidence in American leadership, provoked by all of the above-mentioned factors, has indeed confirmed the impression that an era is coming to an end. Great Empires stop being so not because they want to, but simply

---

[115] *op cit.*

because they lose the capacity to continue being it. Normally, the economy is the Achilles' heel that breaks them down as Paul Kennedy explains: "There is a casual relationship between the shifts which have occurred over time in the general economic and productive balances and the position occupied by individual powers in the international system."[116]

From Portugal to Spain, from the Netherlands to Great Britain, the imperial will has reached as far as the capacity of their respective economies to support it. As Niall Ferguson explains:

> It is important to remember that most cases of civilisational collapse are associated with fiscal crises as well as wars. All the examples of collapse discussed above were preceded by sharp imbalances between revenues and expenditures, as well as by difficulties with financing public debt. ... From 2001, in the space of just ten years, the US federal debt in public hands doubled as a share of GDP from 32 percent to a projected 66 percent in 2011. According to the Congressional Budget's Office 2010 projections (using the 'Alternative Fiscal Scenario', which the CBO regards as more politically likely than its 'Extended Baseline Scenario'), the debt could rise above 90 percent of GDP by 2021 and could reach 150 percent by 2031 and 300 percent by 2047. Note that these figures do not take account of the estimated US$100 trillion of unfunded liabilities of the Medicare and Social Security systems. Nor do they include the rapidly growing deficits of states, nor the burgeoning liabilities of public employee's pension schemes ... These numbers are bad, but in the realm of financial stability the role of perception is in many ways more important. ... But one day, a seemingly random piece of bad news — perhaps a negative report by a rating agency — will make the headlines during an otherwise quiet news cycle. Suddenly, it will be not just a few specialists who worry about the sustainability of US fiscal policy but also the public at large, not to mention investors abroad. It is this shift that is crucial, for a complex adaptive system is in big trouble when a critical mass of its constituents loses faith in its viability.[117]

---

[116] Paul Kennedy, *The Rise and Fall of Great Powers* (London: Fontana Press, 1989), p. xxiv.

[117] Ferguson 2011, *op. cit.*, pp. 309, 310.

Collapse of course is too big a word to be used in the current context but decline is certainly an accurate one. That was how the United States received the torch of hegemonic leadership in the 20th century, when the United Kingdom proved to be impotent to continuing keeping that role. But times move much more rapidly nowadays as Zbigniew Brzezinski points out: "... the combined effect of the global political awakening and of modern technology contributes to the acceleration of political history. What once took centuries now takes a decade, what took a decade now happens in a single year. The paramountcy of any power will henceforth come under mounting pressure for adaptation, alteration and, eventual abolition."[118]

Indeed, Sebastian Mallaby put things in context when he says:

> The Suez humiliation marked the end of Britain's imperial pretentions. As the historian Niall Ferguson has written 'It was at the Bank of England that the Empire was effectively lost'. Harold McMillan, then British Chancellor of the Exchequer, confessed that Suez had been 'the last gasp of a declining power', adding that 'perhaps in 200 years the United States would know how we felt'. But today, a mere 55 years later, the question for Americans is whether those 200 years are up already.[119]

But it is not only the United States who is in a phase of manifest decline. Europe is in an even worse situation. The Euro Zone combined debt burden in 2012 was the highest since the euro was launched in 1999. It reached 87.3% of the region's GDP, in spite of the fact that the European Union debt-to-GDP limit was fixed in 60%.[120] Portugal, Ireland, Greece and Spain reminded the financial markets that not only banks might go bankrupt, but nations as well. The result was the pejorative term 'PIGS' coined by the specialised press on the basis of the initials of these four countries. Latter on a new 'I' was added to the acronym to include Italy. These countries

---

[118] *Second Chance* (New York: Basic Books, 2007), p. 206.

[119] "You are what you owe: Why power built on debt is no power at all", *Time*, 9 May 2011.

[120] Bloomberg, Agence France-Presse, 23 October 2012.

unleashed a fear spiral regarding the solvency of the Euro zone sovereign debt, as a good share of its members accumulates important structural deficits and high public debt. Investors fearing a possible default began demanding higher interests, which in turn raised the burden of the debt service, making defaults even more likely.

The Euro zone's nightmare

This self-fulfilling prophecy process is particularly worrisome as it is easy to anticipate which ones will be the first domino pieces to fall but not which one would be the last. Indeed, in 2011, Germany's public debt reached 83.96% of its GDP while France reached 82.32% of its own.[121] Not surprisingly German President Christian Wulff, noting his country's elevated public debt, asked who would "rescue the rescuers?".[122] How to avoid that the sensation of fragility projects itself over the whole domino line when the President of the Euro zone's main economic power publicly expresses such concerns? World markets have thus gone from their distrust for financial institutions to the distrust for sovereign States, but not those of the Southern Hemisphere or Eastern Europe as in the past, but First World nations.

A bit of background information is again necessary to put this into context. In December 1991, the Treaty of the European Union was approved in the Dutch city of Maastricht. Its reason was evident. With the collapse of the Soviet Empire and the reunification of Germany, the delicate balance of power upon which the European Economic Community had been built was upset. Germany threatened to become too powerful and the nationalistic instincts of that country, which had always been latent, presaged a new resurgence.

To deal with this danger, Helmut Kohl and François Mitterrand came up with the same answer: to redefine the terms of the European

[121] International Monetary Fund, *World Economic Outlook Database* (Washington D.C.: September 2011).

[122] Ambrose Evan-Pritchard, "Germany fires cannon shot across Europe's bows", *The Telegraph*, 26 March 2012.

community. Nevertheless, their reasons differed. Kohl wanted to strengthen his country's links with Europe in order to keep the nationalistic feelings of his fellow-citizens in check, while Mitterrand wanted to strengthen Europe in order to keep Germany in check. It was upon such basis that the Maastricht Treaty came to exist.

Maastricht established three central pillars for the European Union structure: a common currency, a joint foreign policy and a common system of justice. The creation of a single currency, the euro, was the fundamental step of the process. According to Jean-Michel Quatrepoint, the euro was born as a result of "volition and impotence". Volition to prevent a reunified Germany from becoming too powerful or alternatively, distancing itself from Western Europe. Impotence in the face of Europe's diminished status as a result of the collapse of the Communist bloc and the emergence of the United States as the world's sole super-power.[123] In short, the euro was visualised as an adequate formula to ensure the continuity of the European integration in the mist of the challenges that had arisen since the end of the Cold War.

Towards that goal, a set of concrete requirements was established, which had to be met by all signatory parties within a precise compliance time framework. European Union members who wanted to be part of the euro system had to adopt rigid policies of fiscal austerity. Controlling public budget turned into the battle cry of most European governments. The day established for the entering into force of the initial phase of the euro was January the first 1999, even though it was not until January the first 2001 when bills and coins denominated in euro began to circulate.

Two conflicting visions expressed the polarisation that marked the introduction of the new currency. For some, the euro would unleash an era of prosperity, creative energy and economic power for Europe that would lead it to rival the United States. For others, it would open an era of profound uncertainty, unemployment and cultural disarray, liable to lead to great social and political upheavals. Indeed, within fixed exchange rates values, the only way to regain competiveness was

[123] *Le Nouvel Economiste* (24 Avril–6 May, 1998), pp. 12–21.

through painful wage cuts and cost cutting measures that would bring with it innumerable tensions. Among the former were European political leaders and union bureaucrats. Among those who thought that the euro would be the source of endless problems were the European trade unions.

Economist and intellectuals were also divided and that included, as well, names from the other side of the Atlantic. Important American economists, such as C. Fred Bergsten Director of the Institute for International Economics and Lester Thurow from the Massachusetts Institute of Technology, thought that the new European currency would be the starting point for the decline of the American economy as a strong rival to the dollar was emerging. Others like Harvard economist Martin Feldstein, warned that the euro could set off a stage of great national conflicts. French sociologist Emmanuel Todd and British economist Bernard Conolly were probably the most pessimistic of them all. The first asserted that the euro was the biggest strategic error that Europe had made since the signing of the Versailles Treaty in 1919, while the second insisted that the foisting of a common currency upon so many disparate countries would end in ruin.[124]

The 1992–1993 European monetary crisis has been seen as a precursor of the current one. In their route to the euro, countries had to tie their exchange rate to the European Currency Unit (ECU) (antecedent to the euro) and in practice also to the German mark. The latter because Germany was the strongest economy and its economic policy was the most credible one. If the mark revalued, other currencies had to follow suit. It happened though that speculators knew that those other currencies were weaker and less credible than the mark.

Hence, when the Bundesbank increased interest rates, projecting the impression that a revaluation was in the pipe, hot money began to abandon weaker currencies and run into the German mark. In the process, George Soros sold more than 10 billion sterling pounds,

---

[124] Alfredo Toro Hardy, *The Age of Villages: The Small Village vs. The Global Village* (Bogota: Villegas Editores, 2002).

obtained 1 billion in gains and unleashed the fall of the British currency. The Bank of England lost US$50 billion in an unsuccessful attempt to defend the pound. Many reached the conclusion that being tied to the German monetary discipline was not only too big a risk but also a ringing bell alert against the straitjacket that the euro will bring with it. As a result, Britain decided to abandon altogether the so-called Exchange Rate Mechanism-II, considered as the "waiting room" for joining the euro. Bernard Conolly one of the euro's most vocal critics wrote in 1995 a book called *The Rotten Heart of Europe* in which he lambasted the European Exchange Rate Mechanism.[125]

As for the potential benefits and troubles to be brought by such currency, only time could have given an answer and what it is saying now definitively is not good. Indeed, the global economy has been lead to the brink of disaster courtesy of the euro. Several reasons are responsible of the fact that the Euro zone has created such a mess.

The first was projecting a wrong impression regarding the nature of its members' sovereign debt. According to Gordon Brown: "Financial markets assumed from the outset that the European Central Bank was ready to accept at its discount window the sovereign debt of all member countries on equal terms, thus fostering the impression that all euro sovereign debt was of equal quality."[126] It should have been obvious though that if both the German and the Greek debts were seen in equal footing, the result would be low interest rates as well as happy borrowing by the weaker economies of the zone. For peripheral counties of the zone to borrow in the same conditions than its core members became a temptation difficult to resist. That created a transference mechanism between central and peripherical economies within the Euro zone, according to which the former, which accumulated important economic surpluses, were *de facto* subsidising the external deficits of the latter. Not surprisingly, French

[125] Paolo Pesenti, "Back to the future: Revisiting the European Crisis", 17 October 2011, Federal Reserve Bank of New York, <httpl://libertystreeteconomics.newyorkfed.org/2011/10/back-to-the-future-revisiting-the-european-crisis.html>.
[126] *Beyond the Crash* (London: Simon & Schuster UK Ltd, 2010), pp. 183, 184.

and German banks' exposure to Greece alone reached US$125 billion.[127]

The second is the macroeconomic straitjacket that the euro imposes on its member countries. Again, in Gordon Brown's terms: "It was a risk ... because Europe's countries did not appear to have the flexibility necessary to adjust their economies to crises or even the very tough discipline of a single currency."[128] The rigid "one size fits all" approach becomes as illogical as the absolute lack of individual room of manoeuvre when facing a crisis. As Paul Krugman has explained, countries like Britain, Japan and the United States, which have large debts and deficits, retain their ability to borrow at low interest rates simply because they retain their own currencies. Investors know that they could finance their deficits by printing more of those currencies.[129]

The third was the limited role played by the European Central Bank. Instead of enjoying an ample mandate to deal with the different problems that its currency may have experienced, its mandate was primarily focused on keeping inflation under control. The euro became thus the only international currency that did not have a lender of last resort. So the only institution that could have acted unilaterally and decisively to avert the crisis, by buying the sovereign bonds of the affected economies, was incapable to do so. According to John Quiggin: "Unlike any previous central banks in history, the bank has disclaimed any responsibility for the European financial system it effectively controls, or even for the viability of the euro as a currency. Instead, it has focused entirely on the formal objective of keeping inflation rates to a 2% target."[130] It must be added though that under the increasing pressure of the crisis and thanks to the lead-

---

[127] Sistema Económico Latinoamericano, "La crisis en la Zona Euro, su impacto en el proceso de integración europeo y en las relaciones birregionales entre América Latina y el Caribe y la Unión Europea. Líneas de acción desde la perspectiva latinoamericana y caribeña" (Caracas 17 al 19 de octubre 2012).

[128] *op. cit.*, p. 186.

[129] "The hole in Europe's bucket", *The Straits Times*, 25 October 2011.

[130] "Enabling the euro crisis", *International Herald Tribune*, 11 October 2011.

ership of the Italian Mario Draghi the institutional boundaries of the bank have been pushed. It began by becoming a lender of last resort to European banks and then went on to propose a bond-buying plan, working in tandem with the European Stability Mechanism whose ratification by the 17 members of the Euro zone was completed in September 2012. Nonetheless, vital time had already been lost, letting free the mistrust beast.

The fourth was the indiscriminate expansion of the Euro zone. In Gordon Brown's words: "This risk has been amplified by the growing breadth of the membership which spreads across Europe from Ireland in the West to (beginning in January 2011) Estonia in the East."[131] The decision-making process became thus much more cumbersome.

The fifth is the unavoidable domino effect imposed by a common and extremely rigid discipline. This was loosely anticipated by the 1992–1993 European monetary crisis. Contagion becomes easy when individual room of manoeuvre is substituted by inflexible macroeconomics. When deepening the austerity measures becomes the only alternative to the lack of manoeuvrability, a vicious cycle of economic contraction begins to affect everybody, beginning by the most vulnerable. Nonetheless, in October 2012 even Germany, Europe's powerhouse, was being sucked into the region's economic quagmire as reported by Reuters.[132] And as economies weaken, a self fulfilled prophecy of mistrust on their sovereign debts begins to take hold.

Moreover, as in the case of the United States, the institutional shortcomings in the decision-making process have contributed to substantially amplifying economic problems. Indeed, when Maastricht put in motion the monetary union, it failed to create at the same time a fiscal union. As a result the common ship of the Euro zone has to be commanded by 17 different captains with probably as many destinations to direct the vessel to. Such kind of institutional disparity can only work in calm waters, when a sense of shared condominium over the ship can be developed. But the decision-making process tends to get blocked when contradictory points of view are in line, which

---

[131] *op. cit.*, p. 186.
[132] 24 October 2012.

normally happens when problems arise. The result being then that the ship cannot move in any discernable direction. A disentanglement of the crisis would just require that Europeans could reach reasonable agreements. Nonetheless a "prisoners' dilemma" takes hold, making consensual decisions an extremely heavy task. Decisions are only taken when the situation becomes unsustainable, which naturally makes them delayed and utterly insufficient.

As a result, Europe's influence in the global scene has shrunk. According to Walter Russell Mead, in a sentence that Kishore Mahbubani could well have written himself, "Asians increasingly think of Europe as a kind of big Italy — a charming place with beautiful architecture, glorious cultural monuments, delicious foods and some wonderful consumer products — but not as a serious factor in world politics."[133] The United States and the European Union face thus immense problems. Two of them are fundamental. The first is the huge gap between the financial timing and the political timing. The second is the Catch 22 situation between austerity and economic growth.

Timing incompatibility and incompatible objectives

While the financial timing moves at the electron speed and identifies itself with the mood fluctuations of the market when in contact with the flood of instantaneous information, the political timing oscillates between animated suspension and slow motion. They represent two parallel universes that can never touch each other. How can the financial markets coupled with a checks and balance system paralysed by polarisation as it is the case in the United States or with the procrastination that the European Union leaders showed during the development of its crisis? Moreover, even when a clear course of action is decided at the political level, the time frame required for its implementation bears no correlation to the financial markets timing. A good example of the latter was found in December 2011 when the

[133] "The Euro's global security fallout", *The Wall Street Journal*, 18 June 2012.

European Union members (Britain excluded) agree to sign a "fiscal pact" to curb budget deficits.

"Governments will pledge themselves not to borrow further. National Constitutions will have to be amended to ban this practice, budgets will be submitted to the approval of the EU before they are adopted and countries which violate these provisions will be fined."[134] How can anyone harmonise the implementation of these objectives with fluxing moods that can express themselves instantaneously through the simple touch of a digital screen or a PC keyboard? Not surprisingly, the financial markets remained utterly unimpressed by this huge political initiative. And what to say about Angela Merkel's contention that in order to proceed with euro bonds more political and economic union is needed? That would imply among other things constitutional change in several member countries, including France. How to proceed with such a huge institutional undertaking when the market's time frame is moving at light speed? The gap between the financial and the political timings is not new, of course, but never before had it acquire its current magnitude as technology has leaped forward while the political processes has, if anything, become more complex and cumbersome.

Moreover, timing incompatibility is complemented by incompatible objectives. According to Cyril Aydon, the publication of *The General Theory of Employment, Interest and Money* by John Maynard Keynes in 1935 "did for economics what Copernicus´ *On the Revolution of the Heavenly Globes* did for cosmology".[135] For Keynes, the natural remedy for overcoming recessions was to stimulate consumption through public expenditure. Indeed, the level of output determined the level of employment which, in turn, was determined by the level of effective demand, that is, the level of purchases of goods and services. And in order to stimulate the latter, government action was necessary. The implementation of his ideas was decisive for overcoming the Great Depression of those days. Henceforward,

---

[134] Jonathan Eyal, "New Europe won't be in from the cold", *The Straits Times*, 12 December 2011.

[135] *History of Mankind* (London: Running Press, 2007), p. 327.

everything seemed to point out that economy counted with the appropriate medicine for such disease. The problem is that recession can be accompanied by another illness: debt.

Living for many years beyond their real means led both the United States and Europe to accumulate a staggering public and private debt. The combination of recession and debt makes evident the strong systemic crisis currently experienced by these economies, as none of these two ailments can be cured without worsening the other. More economic stimulus means debt increase and hence loss of confidence by the private sector and the financial markets. Austerity, on the other hand, means economic contraction. And economic contraction is indeed a problem, particularly for the Euro zone that according to the IMF's October 2012 Report is expected to have a negative growth of 0.3% in 2012 succeeded by an additional negative growth of 0.4% in 2013. Nonetheless, you can have austerity and lack of confidence at the same time as Paul Krugman has pointed out in numerous occasions.

Krugman' arguments were clearly demonstrated by the reaction obtained when the duo Merkel–Sarkozy induced the rest of the European Union members, with the exception of Britain, to sign a "fiscal pact" that would curb each country's budget deficits, with "automatic consequences" for breaches. Instead of welcoming the merits of the proposal, many financial commentators began to alert that the fundamental problem in troubled European countries was that the debt burden was growing at a faster rate than their economies. Hence, more austerity and discipline would only make more difficult to grow quickly, which in turn would jeopardise debt repayment. Conversely when the Euro zone's members initially agreed to lend 100 billion dollars to Spain, for the rescue of its crumbling banking system, the markets reacted negatively because that implied an increase of its national debt. In other words a typical Catch 22 situation or, as the IMF Chief Economist Olivier Blanchard puts it, a "damned if you do, damned if you do not" situation.

How then overcoming the risk of recession when faced to timing and objectives that are impossible to harmonise? The truth is that it is extremely difficult, if not outright impossible, to put the mistrust beast back in its cage after so much irresponsibility, confusion, rigidity and procrastination. And, as long as the beast is on the loose, no one is safe. Roger Cohen's superb irony captures the prevailing mood: "Everyone's so glum and gloomy. I suppose this is what decline looks like … It puts me in mind of Rome circa 475 A.D., Visigoths on the prowl."[136] But where does Japan stand in all this mess?

Japan's three "D"s

Japan on its part, submitted to the rigour of its two "d", deflation and debt, faces a profound systemic crisis as well. Deflation means that prices for almost everything fall steadily as there is little incentive to buy today when it will be cheaper tomorrow. Moreover, in Gordon Brown words:

> With his invention of the term balance sheet deflation, Richard Koo of Nomura Research has described such an economic trap in which credit stops growing, not because banks do not want to lend, but because companies and households do not want to borrow. The conclusion is that when the private sector has surplus that it will not invest, the government has to become the borrower of last resort. With such a combination of corporate surpluses and low demand, only running a public-sector deficit can stop a recession from becoming a depression. As I look back, the biggest lesson I have learned from Japan's long-running recession is to never allow an economy to sink so far that a recovery becomes more elusive.[137]

And public-sector deficit is becoming indeed a problem as serious as deflation itself as it is already twice the size of its US$5 trillion economy. According to Naoyuki Shinohara, Deputy Executive Director of the International Monetary Fund, Japan's public debt which in 2011 was in course to exceed 200% of its GDP, had become "unsustainable".[138] It should be added that if deflationary tendencies

---

[136] "Decline and fall", *The International Herald Tribune*, 22 November 2011.
[137] *op. cit.*, p. 75.
[138] "Japan's public debt and fiscal deficit 'unsustainable' warns IMF", MercoPress, 27

keep maintaining growth at bay there is only one way that debt can go: up. This upstart trend of its debt may present a serious long-term problem to Japan as its population is both declining and getting older. The size of Japan's economy is hampered by its shrinking population and its ability to pay off its debt is limited by its aging. A Euromonitor International report states the following: "Japan's ballooning senior population has already caused significant changes to the country's demographic makeup ... Declining birth rates and smaller families have led to a population that is not only shrinking, but growing increasingly older ... By 2020 people aged 65 and older will make up nearly 30% of the population."[139] Not surprisingly, Standard and Poor's reduced Japan's bond rating to AA — in January 2011.

Nonetheless, a near term disruption in the government debt market remains unlikely as a result of three considerations: stable domestic savings (Japanese investors hold about 95% of government bonds), current account surplus and control over its own currency. Not having to depend on foreign bond holders and having sovereignty over its own currency is, indeed, a blessing. But were Japan to run a current account deficit, it would mean trouble as it would be unable to keep financing its huge public debt without recurring to overseas funds. The fact that in 2011 Japan logged its first annual trade deficit in 30 years means that the time when Japan may be running out of savings is coming closer.[140]

A third "d" seems now to be appearing in Japan's economic scenario: delocalisation. Indeed, Fukushima may be transforming itself in a highly disruptive economic factor as it has shattered Japan's traditional trust in nuclear energy and promoted the search for alternative energy sources which, in turn, has given rise to the phantom of higher

---

March 2012, <http://en.mercopress.com/2011/02/10/japan-s-public-debt-and-fiscal-deficit-unsustainable-warns-imf>.

[139] Elizabeth Friend, "Japan's greying population leads to new foodservice demand", <http://blog.euromonitor.com/2011/10/japans-graying-population-leads-to-new-foodservice-demand.html>.

[140] "Japan's first trade deficit since 1980 raises debt doubts", *Reuters*, 25 January 2012, <http://www.reuters.com/article/2012/01/25/japan-economy-trade-idUSL4E8CO5N420120125>.

energy costs. Such phantom together with a resilient strong yen seems to be pushing Japanese production base overseas. According to Naoyuki Haraoka, Executive Managing Director of Japan Economic Foundation:

> Japanese manufacturing companies now intend to earnestly engage in consolidating their overseas affiliates' business. The sharp increase of DI's for physical investment and employment in particular seems to imply that they are interested in relocation of their business bases, including production bases, since both are core factors of a production base. This interpretation of the statistics is thus that in the future the Japanese manufacturing industry could hollow out due to increasing relocation of its production bases from Japan to overseas. Since March disaster ... Japanese industries seem to have already started to think about relocation of their production bases overseas, possibly due to a continuing strong yen and a concern over a possible rise in energy costs.[141]

This "hollow out" of Japan's manufacturing industry may have dire consequences for employment in the country while benefiting overseas recipients of their investments and offshored jobs. China and the ASEAN countries would presumably be the main beneficiaries of this process in yet another example of transference of wealth and employments into emerging economies.

Unfortunately for Japan its political system is not better suited for dealing with its economic problems that those of the United States and the European Union. According to Charles A. Kupchan: "Policy making has ground to a halt even on urgent issues: It took more than 100 days for the Diet to approve reconstruction funding for the victims of the tsunami and nuclear disaster ... Japan is stuck in a political

---

[141] "The Economic Outlook for Japan in 2012 and Beyond — How can the Japanese Economy help the Global Economy to avoid falling into a Great Depression?", (Institute of Southeast Asian Studies Regional Outlook Forum, Singapore, 5 January 2012), p. 9.

and economic no man's land, exposed to the dislocations of a globalised economy."[142]

As the feeling in the South goes, after Lehman there was nothing to look for in developed economies regarding economic lessons or paradigms. And, of course, after all the bickering that surrounded the American debt ceiling negotiations and the European Union debt crisis soap opera, as well as Japan's inability to emerge from its long recession compounded with its ineffective management of the aftermath of its 2011 natural disasters, a generalised loss of confidence in their leadership qualities has taken hold. The prevailing impression is "the end of an era". And that impression is rapidly becoming conventional wisdom.

The West's lonely band

While the dynamic of world economy comes from emerging economies, the risks, problems and instability comes from advanced economies. According to Cornell's economist Eswar Prasad, advanced economies are responsible for 90% of the increase of debt in the world.[143] It is not clear, though, how emerging economies may avoid the undesirable effects of crisis, actions or inactions emanating from the North. The re-launching of the G-20 with increased status and influence, after the 2008 crisis, certainly represents a very important step in the right direction. Nonetheless, it is an insufficient one as the instrumental capacities vested in multilateral economic bodies still eludes emerging economies. Within these institutions their voting power bears no correlation to their actual strength. A single case can exemplify the above. While China accounts for 13.6% of the global economy, its voting power at the IMF is only 3.8%. "John W. Snow, a former US Treasury Secretary, said, 'Comprehensive, fundamental reform is needed if the IMF is to remain legitimate and relevant to its

---

[142] "Refounding good governance", *The New York Times*, 19 December 2011.

[143] "The future of the international monetary system", Tolani-National University of Singapore Business School-Lee Kuan Yew School Public Lecture, Shangri-La-Hotel, Singapore, 13 June 2012.

membership ... For this effort to succeed, members need to look beyond their immediate narrow interests'."[144]

Nonetheless, when China offered to provide US$100 billion to ease the Euro zone crisis, and in return asked for European support in obtaining more influence at the International Monetary Fund (or alternatively market economy status at the World Trade Organisation), the European Union spurned Beijing's demands. According to Benjamin Lim and Nick Edwards, Reuters' correspondents in Beijing:

> The IMF route would have been the simplest diplomatically, especially after European Union leaders last month laid out a plan to leverage up the resources of its crisis-fighting fund through an IMF-backed investment vehicle. But the sources in Beijing said this option was abruptly closed to China when it became clear to EU politicians that any investment from China would be contingent on gaining a greater say in IMF decision making and a more rapid path to inclusion of China's Yuan in the IMF's special drawing rights (SDR) currency unit. Increasing China's say at the IMF would mean reducing EU representation and possibly diluting the influence of the United States, which enjoys veto-power status given its voting rights at the IMF.[145]

So embedded is the notion that such institutions "belong" to developed economies that even a common sense proposal like the above-mentioned was rejected. This responds to the arrogance divide that separates countries, which hang to the glories of the past from those who are building the future. As Kishore Mahbubani has pointed out, "the European tendency to treat non-Europeans cultures and societies with disdain and condescension is something deeply rooted in their psyche."[146]

---

[144] Kishore Mahbubani, *op. cit.*, p. 256.
[145] "Politics stymie China's EU aid offer", *Reuters*, 11 November 2011, <http://www.reuters.com/article/2011/11/11/us-china-europe-f-idUSTRE7AA2DU20111111>.
[146] *op. cit.*, p. 266.

The irony is that China's civilisation not only predates that of Europe but has also shown a continuum that the latter lost during the long Middle Ages. Circa 700 A.D., the city of Chang'an in China counted with 1 million inhabitants. Not much later, during the Chinese literary golden age, millions of books were been printed in wood prints. Around 1000 A.D., an economic revolution was added to the cultural explosion and paper money was introduced in the country. A century later, China was producing the same amount of iron that Europe would produce in 1700. Between 1405 and 1433, Admiral Zhen He was moving his fleet of 300 gigantic ships and 27,870 sailors around the Pacific and Indian oceans, well ahead of Columbus initial voyage to America with three small caravels and 90 sailors.[147]

In Josep Stiglitz words: "To maintain a cabal among developed countries, whereby the US appoints the World Bank president and Europe picks the International Monetary Fund's head, seems particularly anachronistic and perplexing today, when the bank and the fund are turning to emerging-market countries as a source of funds."[148] Indeed, both the elections of Christine Lagarde from France as the head of IMF and Jim Yong Kim from the United States as chief of the World Bank were seen as expressions of times gone by. The fact that the latter was confronted by two obviously better qualified candidates from Nigeria and Colombia, that stood no chance as a result of the prevailing situation, made the iniquity even bigger.

It would seem to be in the best interest of developed economies to recognise the relevance of China, India and the rest, as otherwise they may end up conducting a lonely band while the party moves somewhere else. As Kishore Mahbubani has clearly stated, it is futile for the 12% of the world's population who live in the West to imagine that they can determine the destinies of the remaining 88%, many of whom feel newly energised and empowered. However, if the West

---

[147] Ian Morris, "Por qué aún domina Occidente", *Vanguardia Dossier*, No. 42 (March 2012).

[148] "Picking the next chief: Whose World Bank is it?", *The Straits Times*, 12 April 2012.

tries to continue its domination, he says, a backlash will become inevitable.[149]

It will probably take some time before Western economies discover the obvious, which Daniel W. Drezner clearly describes:

> But unless rising powers such as China and India are incorporated into this framework, the future of these international regimes will be uncomfortably uncertain (....) If China and India are not made to feel welcome inside existing international institutions, they might create new ones — leaving the United States on the outside looking in (....) Global institutions cease to be appropriate when the allocation of decision-making authority within them no longer corresponds to the distribution of power.[150]

Not surprisingly, in their Summit and the end of March 2012 the leaders of the BRICS member countries agreed to move towards creating a new development bank that would improve access to capital for developing nations, while agreeing as well to do deals with one another in their local currencies. As Radhika Deasi clearly explains, without fanfare the main emerging economies are bypassing the economic institutional architecture of the West:

> The BRICS and emerging economies have already set in train a wider set of changes in the institutional architecture of the world order. Since Western powers maintain their grip on its major institutions, these rising powers have simply side-stepped them, setting up new institutions and using old minor ones in new ways. The result is a decentralised institutional structure that does not look like a rival to Western-dominated centralised and worldwide institutions at first sight. But it is. For example, it bypasses US dollar-cantered world monetary and financial regime ... Over this period, the International Monetary Fund's influence fell and it had to compromise key policy prescriptions — pre-eminently on capital controls — as regional

[149] *op. cit.*, p. 126.

[150] "The New New World Order", *Foreign Affairs*, Vol. 86 (March/April, 2007), pp. 34, 36, 39.

> developments banks and arrangements between two or more developing economies to conduct trade in their own currencies undermined its monopoly ... As the rising profile of the BRICS reshapes geopolitical economy and its institutional architecture, backing this or that candidate for president of an unreformed World Bank hardly matters.[151]

The facts, indeed, are speaking for themselves and the Global South is increasingly going its own way in relation to the developed world. Jim O'Neill who invented the acronym BRIC began using the term "decoupling" to refer to such process, which became evident during the 2008 economic crisis.[152] Nonetheless, a year before the crisis an International Monetary Fund working paper already attested the existence of such phenomenon. According to the paper, it was possible to have both decoupling and globalisation at the same time. Such study referred that growth had become more synchronised among developed economies and also among emerging ones. Economic activity in emerging economies had indeed decoupled from the developed ones during the last two decades. Consequently the impact of developed economies in the growth of the emerging ones had fallen in a significant way:

> Similarly, the growth rates of output and industrial production of the Emerging South economies have become more strongly associated with those of their emerging southern trading partners. Surprisingly, cross-group correlations of growth fluctuation suggest that the Emerging South economic activity has appeared to diverge (or decouple) from that of the North in the globalization period. ... Moreover, both the North and the Emerging South economies have started to exhibit more intensive intra-group growth spillovers.[153]

---

[151] "The West must wake up to the growing power of the brics", *The Guardian*, 2 April 2012.

[152] Niall Ferguson, *The Ascent of Money* (New York: Penguin Books, 2008).

[153] Cigdem Akim and M. Ayhan Kose, "Changing Nature of North-South Linkages: Stylized Facts and Explanations", International Monetary Fund, Working Paper WP/07/280, Washington D.C. (December 2007), pp. 5, 6.

Decoupling

As said, the facts speak by themselves and oil consumption is a good example of it. According to Liam Halligan:

> In 2011, the world economy was sluggish, with global GDP growth of 3.8%, down from 5.2% the year before. Yet world oil use rose almost 1% in 2011, with crude averaging US$111 a barrel. The International Energy Agency (IEA), the energy think tank funded by oil importing Western governments, tells us that crude demand is 'declining remorselessly thought the OECD (countries)'. Given that the Western economies remain weak and the Euro zone is heading for recession, the 'advanced economies' are consuming less crude. The fine prints shows, though, that even IEA demand projections ... show OECD oil use falling just 0.9% this year. Demand among the non-OECD countries, meanwhile, including the emerging giants of the East, is forecast to rise 2.8%. Total global crude consumption, then, is still set to increase by another 1% this year, mimicking the trend of last year.[154]

In November 2011, Jim O'Neill predicted that the BRICS combined economies, now worth US$13 trillion, would double in the coming decade, surpassing the size of the economies of both the United States and the European Union.[155] Moreover, the Inter-American Development Bank estimates that the growing global demand has markedly shifted in favour of emerging markets, which currently account for 75% of growth in global demand, compared to 50% prior to the crisis. This trend is likely to continue in the foreseeable future given current medium-term growth projections for developed and emerging countries:

> In sum, the aftermath of the global financial crisis has two salient features. On the one hand, domestic demand in industrial countries

---

[154] "Soaring oil prices will dwarf greek drama", *The Daily Telegraph*, 26 February 2011.

[155] Jim Yardley, "For alliance, a sum less than its parts", *International Herald Tribune*, 29 March 2012.

> is weak, growth is anaemic, and unemployment high, resulting in an important deterioration of fiscal balances and, in some cases, explosive growth in public debt levels. On the other hand, emerging markets have faced increased domestic demand, faster growth, and a fall in unemployment levels and relatively comfortable fiscal positions.[156]

But jointly with demand we find exports. The United Nations Economic Commission for Latin America and the Caribbean pointed out that South–South exchange, headed by China, is currently the main driving force of global trade growth, since the volume of exports from developing countries grew by 17% in 2010 compared with 13% in developed countries.[157] According to Gordon Brown: "This weakening of the European, American and Japanese growth rate also reflects the fundamental shift taking place across the world in the location of production and the direction of trade ... And with China leading the growth of South–South trade, globalisation will no longer be dominated by trade between today's developed countries."[158] Moreover, even amid the European crisis, data showed that Asia's manufacturing sector was gaining strength at the beginning of 2012.[159]

Some good examples of the above are the trade expansions between China and Latin America, and China and Africa. The former went from US$8.3 billion in 1999 to US$178.6 billion in 2010 jumping to US$233.7 billion in 2011, while the latter grew from US$10 billion in 2000 to US$114.81 billion between January and

---

[156] Alejandro Izquierdo and Ernesto Talvi, coord., *One Region, Two Speeds?* (Washington D.C.:, Inter-American Development Bank, March 2011), p. 3.

[157] "Exports from Latin America and the Caribbean will increase in 27% in 2011", Economic Commission for Latin America and the Caribbean, Press Release, 31 August 2011, <http://www.caribbeanpressrelease.com/articles/8630/1/ECLAC-Exports-from-Latin-America-and-the-Caribbean-Will-Increase-by-27-in 2011/Page1.html>.

[158] *op. cit.*, p. 136.

[159] Martin Vaughan, "Asian manufacturing shows resilience", *The Wall Street Journal*, 2 March 2012.

November 2010. China has already surpassed the United States as the largest trade partner with Africa while its trade with Latin America is growing nearly twice the level than that of such region with the United States. Trade between China and India also went from US$1.8 billion in 2001 to US$60 billion in 2010, and should be reaching US$100 billion in 2015.[160]

The increase in trade between China and the Arab world has been so impressive that some experts are talking about the reconstitution of the Silk Road: "The door between the Arab world and China, which was shut for centuries, is now open again."[161] China's exports to Arab countries worth US$6 billion in 2000 reached US$60 billion in 2010. In the process, China overtook the United Kingdom in 2002, Germany in 2006 and the United States in 2008 as the larger exporter to this region. Conversely, China is importing 0.5 million oil barrels a day from Saudi Arabia, 0.3 from Oman and 0.1 from Yemen amidst a trend of increasing sales of oil by Arab producers.[162]

Trade between developing economies in Asia and Latin America grew seven times over the past decade reaching US$268 billion in 2010 while trade between India and Africa exploded from a mere US$1 billion in 2001 to US$50 billion in 2010 and trade between Brazil and Africa quadrupled since 2002 to US$20.6 billion in 2010. Actually both India and Brazil already export more to the fellow emerging markets than to the developed world. Almost half of

---

[160] John and Doris Naisbitt, *China's Megatrends* (New York: Harper Business, 2010); Ruth Morris, "China: Latin America trade jumps", *LBC Latin Business Chronicle*, 9 May 2011, <http://www.latinbusinesschronicle.com/app/article.aspx?id=4893>; CEPAL, *La República popular China y América Latina y el Caribe: Diálogo y Cooperación ante los Nuevos Desafíos de la Economía Mundial* (Santiago de Chile: Junio de 2012); "China, Africa trade increase in 2010", *Africa News.com*, <http://www.africanews.com/site/list_message 32503>; Chi Ravi Vellor, "India's passage to China", *The Straits Times*, 7 January 2011.

[161] Ben Simpfendorfer, *The New Silk Road* (New York: Pelgrave Macmillan, 2011), p. 160.

[162] *ibid.*

sub-Saharan African exports now go to developing markets compared with less than a quarter in 1990.[163]

Intraregional trade in Latin America grew 48.8% between 2009 and 2011 and in 2012 it is expected to reach almost US$210 billion.[164] As for Asia, 50% of its trade takes place within the region where 44 trade agreements are already in place and another 85 are on the way.[165] Let us just make reference to one of those treaties, which will be the largest free trade zone by population in the world. In Simon Morttake's words:

> Tariffs have been slashed on 90% of goods trade between China and the six largest economies in the Association of Southeast Asian Nations under a 2002 free-trade pact. The China–ASEAN Free Trade Agreement mandates tariff-free status on goods, with exemptions granted until 2015 on certain items. Four other, poorer ASEAN countries have agreed to follow suit in order to create the world's largest free-trade zone by population. In 2008, China–ASEAN trade hit a peak of US$231 billion before the global recession in 2009 led to an 8% contraction. Trade recovered last year and rose 50% in the first seven month of the year to US$161 billion.[166]

Consumption, the other side of the same coin, has also increased in a very impressive way. According to Pam Woodall:

> For the past couple of decades, emerging economies have grabbed a rising share of world manufacturing production and exports thanks to their lower wage costs ... But an important new milestone will

---

[163] Michael Schuman/Manzhouli, "Tading Up", *Time*, 7 November, 2011; Stuart Grudgins, "As rich world sputter, Brazil looks to Africa", Reuters, 17 November 2011, <http://www.reuters.com/article/2011/11/17/us-brazil-africa-newspro-idUSTRE7AG1KN20111117>.

[164] Sistema Económico Latinoamericano, "Informe sobre el Proceso de Integración Regional 2011–2012" (Caracas, agosto 2012).

[165] Gordon Brown, *op. cit.*

[166] "Southeast Asia embraces China trade, but how's the relationship? It's complicated", *The Christian Science Monitor*, 8 February 2011.

> be reached in 2012, when the upstarts will import more goods than rich economies. That is a dramatic change since 2000, when they imported barely half as much as rich countries did ... At the beginning of 2012, the total real GDP of the rich economies will be no bigger than it was at the end of 2007. In contrast, the output of the emerging economies will have jumped by almost a quarter over the same period. Their combined output will account for over two-fifths of world GDP at market exchange rates in the coming year, almost twice the share in 1990 ... Imports into emerging markets have grown twice as fast as those into developed ones over the last decade. ... But consumer spending is also rising rapidly. In 2012, emerging markets will account for nearly half of global retail sales. Even more important, the increase in their spending in absolute dollars terms will be twice as big as the increase in the developed world ... China will overtake America as the world's biggest importer by 2014.[167]

Of course, there would be a much larger space for domestic consumption growth in East Asian countries if it were not for the huge foreign exchange reserves held. Indeed, as mentioned before, the penalties imposed on the region by the IMF as a result of the 1997 economic crisis, led them to emphasise the accumulation of such reserves. East Asian countries have around US$8 trillion in reserves, which are imposing limits on their aggregate demand.[168]

Nonetheless, when we bear in mind, as previously mentioned, that middle class will encompass 700 million people in China in the year 2020 and 583 million in India in 2025, it is easy to foresee what the implications will be. Credit Suisse's *2010 Global Wealth Report* sees Chinese household wealth doubling to US$35 trillion by 2015, transforming China's new middle class in the leading driver of world growth. Already in 2010 China surpassed the United States in auto sales, as Chinese consumers purchased a record 13.9 million automobiles, versus 11.6 million sold in the

[167] "Hey big spenders", *The Economist: The World in 2012.*

[168] Gordon Brown, *op. cit.*

United States.[169] If successful, the shift to consumer spending currently taking place in China will become world altering. The numbers speak by themselves. China's 2011 GDP was around US$6 trillion. If consumer spending goes up from the current 36% and reaches the government stated goal of 45%, US$540 billion would flow into consumption of goods and services.[170] China has already overtaken the United States as the main world consumer of mobile phones, cars and personal computers.[171] At the same time, projections by Goldman Sachs show that over the next 15 years higher incomes will drive consumption upward in India, with India's consumers spending three and a half times more than they do today.[172] The Brookings Institution in Washington D.C. and Citigroup go even further with the former projecting that by 2030 India's middle class will spend more than that of the United States or China while the latter stating that Indians could become the planet's most important consumers.[173]

According to a recent report by IGD, the British grocery industry research group, China has overtaken the United States to become the world's biggest market for grocery shopping. The Chinese grocery sector is expected to continue its fast grow over the next few years to reach almost 1 trillion UK pounds by 2015. The report also predicts that all the BRIC countries will be in the top 5 grocery markets by 2015 when Indonesia will enter the top 10 list for the first time. Hence, five of the 10 largest grocery consumer markets will be in the developing world, including there the first five places.[174]

Moreover, as James McGregor from the Yale Center for the Study of Globalisation points out, China has a challenging reform ahead: fixing the "hukou", or housing registration system, enacted in the

---

[169] *Ibid.*; Edward M. Kerschener and Naeema Huq, *op. cit.*

[170] Michael Schuman/Manzhouli, *op. cit.*

[171] CEPAL, *La República popular China y América Latina y el Caribe: Diálogo y Cooperación ante los Nuevos Desafíos de la Economía Mundial* (Santiago de Chile: Junio de 2012).

[172] Gordon Brown, *op. cit.*

[173] Michael Schuman, *op. cit.*

[174] Agencies, "China now the world's biggest grocery market", *Today*, 5 April 2012.

1950's to prevent peasants from flooding the cities. The Chinese government estimates that more than a quarter of urban residents in major cities lack an urban housing registration. Such a "hukou" reform could transform 10 million migrant workers annually into the next wave of urban consumers, forming a potential new global market of unprecedented size that would boost the world economy.[175] This is an area where an important challenge could become a huge opportunity.

Thanks to the extraordinary momentum not only of China but also of India, Brazil, Turkey, Indonesia, South Africa, Thailand, Argentina, Malaysia, Nigeria, Vietnam, Angola, Saudi Arabia, the Philippines, Peru, Qatar, Chile, Ethiopia, Venezuela or Rwanda, to mention just a few, developing economies have been able to sustain a dynamism that, under current international conditions, would have seemed impossible just a few years ago. According to Michael Schuman and Manzhouli: "The consequences of that go well beyond the mere movement of goods. The more important trade and investment within the emerging world become, the less important the West becomes to the global economy, a trend accelerated by the Great Recession."[176] Meanwhile, the weight of developed economies in world trade has been reduced from 60% in 1985 to less than 40% in 2010.[177]

Decoupling does not mean, of course, that emerging economies have become immune to the European crisis or to the American sluggish growth, but it implies resilience in relation to such problems. Reference to China, the main turbine of the emerging world, becomes fundamental in order to understand the nature of this process. With a saving rate of 51% of its GDP, the country relies very little on foreign borrowing. Its growth is financed from resources derived from its own population. Its banks are highly liquid and their deposit

[175] "Threat posed by China's state-owned firms", *The Straits Times*, 13 October 2012.
[176] *ibid.*
[177] CEPAL, *La República popular China y América Latina y el Caribe: Diálogo y Cooperación ante los Nuevos Desafíos de la Economía Mundial.*

taking more than matches their loan making. Moreover, China has ample fiscal space to recapitalise any bank threaten with insolvency. Fiscal space that gives the government enough room of manoeuvre, to stimulate growth again if exports to Europe were to experience a dramatic fall.[178]

In 2011, amid the low economic growth shown by Europe and the United States, China's exports grew 9% whereas its imports did so in 10%. Even more, in May 2012, the country's exports and imports were still growing at 15% and 13%, respectively, in relation to May 2011.[179] In mid 2012, China was still facing a labour shortage which was a clear sign of its resilience in relation to the international situation: "Guangdong's job market is showing signs of withstanding China's slowdown as factory owners report that shortages of workers persist in the southern export hub ... Strength in the job market may encourage the ruling Communist party to limit the scale of the stimulus that is being rolled out to support the world's second-biggest economy."[180] And even if during the second half of the year China's economic situation became more problematic, in September 2012 Chinese exports grew 9.9% from a year earlier, roughly twice the 5% expected by investors. Exports to neighbouring emerging economies in ASEAN jumped to a 25.5% year-on-year growth in September 2012 versus 10.3% in August 2012.[181]

In as long as China can withstand the storms coming from the West so will the vast network of countries that have linked their economies to the Middle Kingdom. Their houses may undoubtedly be badly shaken but they will not fall down. In 2010, China was indeed the second most interconnected country in the world in terms of trade flows, ranking also second in terms of the size of its trade,

---

[178] How strong is China's economy?, *The Economist*, 26 May 2012.

[179] CEPAL, *La República popular China y América Latina y el Caribe: Diálogo y Cooperación ante los Nuevos Desafíos de la Economía Mundial.*

[180] Justina Lee, "China labor shortages in Guangdong show stimulus limits", *Bloomberg*, 6 June 2012.

[181] Reuters, Bloomberg, "China's trade picks up", *The Sunday Times*, 14 October 2012.

which that year reached US$3.2 trillion. That gave China the top rank in terms of overall systemic trade. The United States ranked first in size and 19th in terms of interconnectedness, which placed it in the sixth place in systemic trade importance.[182] The aforementioned derives from the fact that China has become the first or the second trade partner for 78 countries that represent 55% of the global GDP.[183] Not surprisingly, Martin Jacques talks about a Chinese economic world order.[184]

Even though some analysts in the developed world are projecting their own gloom over the emerging economies, the fact remains that the latter, with China in lead, have an arsenal of economic policies still intact to face an economic downturn. While interest rates are near zero in the United States, Europe and Japan, they average 6% in emerging markets. Fiscal stimulus, a luxury out of reach for the majority of advanced economies, is widely available in most developing economies. Banks from emerging economies have more capital and much less problem to obtain funding than their European counterparts. At the same time, foreign exchange reserves in the former are sufficiently ample so as to allow them protection against falling exports. And so on. By developed economies standards, the emerging economies are still doing exceedingly well and even though a deceleration of their economic growth is evident, part of it has been intentionally aimed with the idea of putting order in their own houses.[185]

Let us just take as example China's debt and foreign-exchange reserves. While American and European experts have been writing in highly pessimistic terms about local government debts in China, the

---

[182] Esward Prasad and Lei Ye, *The Renminbi's Role in the Global Monetary System* (Washington D.C.: Brookings, February 2012).

[183] Sistema Económico Latinoamericano, "Las relaciones entre China y América Latina y el Caribe en la actual coyuntura económica mundial" (Caracas, septiembre, 2012).

[184] "How China will Change the World", Lee Kuan Yew School of Public Policy Lecture, Singapore, 24 September 2012.

[185] "Emerging markets: The great slowdown", *The Economist*, 21 July 2012.

combined local and central government's debt of that country only amounts to 34% of its GDP a far cry from Japan's 220% or the US's 94%. Moreover, 80% of that debt was funnelled into infrastructural projects — ports, airports, rails, roads and bridges — which will yield important income in years to come.[186] As for foreign-exchange reserves, China has the world's largest which reached US$3.29 trillion in September 2012.[187]

As *The Economist* says: "None of the biggest emerging economies stands on the edge of a dramatic financial precipice, like their counterparts in the euro area, or a fiscal cliff, like America's. But their economic prospects have nonetheless started to head downhill."[188] It could not have been otherwise given the extent of the developed economies crises. Nonetheless, emerging economies are not only showing resilience but they are becoming increasingly entrusted with carrying on their shoulders the global economy. Just Asia represents 55% of the current world economic growth.[189]

According to the World Bank semi-annual report, released in 8 October 2012, East Asia and the Pacific region are forecasted to grow 7.2% in 2012, picking up to 7.6% in 2013.[190] True, it is not a brilliant performance, but is far from being a dramatic downfall. As for China, the International Monetary Fund report, released on 9 October 2012, forecast a 7.8% economic expansion in 2012 and 8.2% in 2013. Not so good in 2012, much better in 2013, but in any case not a hard landing at all. Emerging economies, on their part, are forecasted to grow four times as fast as advanced economies at 5.3% in 2012 and 5.6% in 2013. Conversely, the IMF report forecasts a 2.2% growth for the United States in 2012 and a 2.1% in 2013 and

---

[186] David Yeo and Philip Ng, "China's Twin Paradigm Shift: Beacons in a Sea of Change", *IE Insights*, International Enterprise Singapore (Vol. 1/July 2012).

[187] Reuters, Bloomberg, "China's trade picks up", *op. cit.*

[188] "Emerging markets: Dream on?", 21 July 2012.

[189] CEPAL, *La República popular China y América Latina y el Caribe: Diálogo y Cooperación ante los Nuevos Desafíos de la Economía Mundial.*

[190] Agencies, "East Asian growth at 11-year low?", *Today*, 9 October 2012.

a 0.4% contraction in 2012 and a growth of 0.2% in 2013 for the 17-country Euro zone.[191]

The Arc of History is bending to the emerging economies of the South and, as in the title of an old British song that was played after the Yorktown defeat in 1781, marking the end of an era, "The World Turns Upside Down".

---

[191] Blomberg, Agence France-Press, "IMF cuts global growth forecasts for 2012, 2013", *The Straits Times*, 10 October 2012; Agencies, "Dark clouds ahead", *Today*, 10 October 2012.

Chapter

3

A Dragon in Latin Lands

The dragon that appeared from nowhere

As seen in the previous chapter, the Global South is integrating its economies at a staggering pace. Within that context, the strong but complex economic partnership between China and Latin America epitomises well the shift that has taken place in the global economy. Their bilateral trade has increased exponentially during the last decade and their story has much to tell.

In 1990, only 0.6% of Latin America's total imports came from China while that country was listed at No. 17 for Latin American exports. In 2000, China was at No. 12 within Brazil's export markets while it was at No. 35 within Venezuela's export destinations.[1] Nonetheless, in 2011, China represented 9% of total regional exports, while it was the origin of 14% of its imports. In 2011, China became

[1] Sistema Económico Latinoamericano, "La crisis en la Zona Euro, su impacto en el proceso de integración europeo y en las relaciones birregionales entre América Latina y el Caribe y la Unión Europea. Líneas de acción desde la perspectiva latinoamericana y caribeña" (Caracas 17 al 19 de octubre 2012).

the first export market for Brazil, Chile and Peru and the second for Argentina, Cuba, Uruguay and Venezuela, while it is rapidly escalating the first positions for the majority of the countries of the region. In 2011, 14.7% of South American exports were shipped to China. Between 2006 and 2011, Latin American exports to China grew three times faster than its total exports while imports from there grew twice faster than the total.[2]

According to the International Monetary Fund, trade between China and Latin America reached US$178.6 billion in 2010 of which Chinese exports to Latin America represented US$88.3 billion and Latin America exports to China US$90.3 billion. Moreover, Latin America trade with China is growing at nearly twice the level of that of the region with the United States.[3] Bilateral trade between China and its largest economic partner in that part of the world, Brazil, represented US$56,379 billion in 2010 of which China exported US$25,593 billion and Brazil exported US$30,785 billion. Between 1999 and 2003, Brazil exports to China grew by 525%.[4]

The United States continues to retain its No. 1 position as regional trade partner (especially in the Northern part of Latin America) with the European Union as No. 2 and China as No. 3. According to 2011 projections of the Economic Commission for Latin America and the Caribbean, ECLAC, the European Union was to be displaced by China as Latin American second largest market for its exports in 2014 and as second largest importer in 2015.[5] Nonetheless, a 2012 report by ECLAC showed that in 2011 China had already slightly passed the European Union as source of regional imports. That year Latin America imported US$139.7 billion from

[2] CEPAL, *La República popular China y América Latina y el Caribe: Diálogo y Cooperación ante los Nuevos Desafíos de la Economía Mundial* (Santiago de Chile: Junio de 2012); Andre Loes, "Lat Am trade flows", HSBC Global Research, Economics Latin America, February, 2013.

[3] Ruth Morris, "China: Latin America trade jumps", *LBC Latin Business Chronicle*, 9 May 2011, <http://www.latinbusinesschronicle.com/app/article.aspx?id=4893>.

[4] Juan Miguel González Peña, "Una aproximación a las relaciones económico-comerciales entre China y América Latina y el Caribe", *Observatorio de la Política China*, 13 de septiembre 2011.

[5] *ibid.*

China versus US$137.5 billion from the European Union. In the opposite direction, Latin America exported US$94.0 billion to China and US$138.2 billion to the European Union. As for the United States, in 2011, it imported US$420.1 billion from Latin America while it exported US$304.0 billion to the region. Nonetheless, according to HSBC estimates, in 2030 China will be surpassing the US as the largest trade destination for the region.[6]

Which is relevant though is the fact that for Latin America the Chinese trade came from the blue. In 1999, trade with China represented only US$8.3 billion whereas Europe has been its oldest trading partner in a relation that dates back to 1492, when Europeans and Amerindians met for the first time.[7] Since then and until the end of the Second World War, when it was supplanted by the United States, Europe was consistently Latin America's fundamental trade relation.

Needless to say as well that China amply surpassed the two traditional Latin American trade partners in the Asia-Pacific area: Japan and South Korea. Those two countries that have been actively trading with the region since the beginning of the 70s are currently considerably below China. In 2008, trade with Japan amounted to US$68.1 billion whereas trade with South Korea reached US$43.8 billion in 2010.[8]

The sudden and unexpected appearance of such a huge market for its exports and source for its imports has had a game changing effect for the Latin American economies. Moreover, the implications of this dragon that appeared from nowhere have had not only a direct effect on their economies but a highly relevant indirect one as well. Indeed, as the price of commodities has risen substantially in the global markets, thanks to the Chinese demand, Latin America has benefited not only from the commodities that it sells to China but also from what it sells to the rest of the world.

---

[6] CEPAL, *La República popular China y América Latina y el Caribe: Diálogo y Cooperación ante los Nuevos Desafíos de la Economía Mundial*; Andre Loes, *op. cit.*

[7] John and Doris Naisbitt, *China's Megatrends* (New York: Harper Business, 2010).

[8] "Japan Latin America trade growth", *Latin Asia Business Chronicle*, 14 May 2009, <http://www.latinbusinesschronicle.com/app/article.aspx?id=3400>; "Latin America: Record Korea trade", *Latin Asia Business Chronicle*, 12 September 2011, <http://www.latinbusinesschronicle.com/app/article.aspx?id=5105>.

According to the World Bank: "This suggests that the robust growth observed in Latin American countries in the past decade is an important measure of its connections to China, both directly (via trade and increasingly also FDI channels) and indirectly (mainly via China's impact on the international prices of commodities)."[9] Between 2000 and 2006, indeed, 70% of the export growth in Latin America was explained by the growth in the export of commodities.[10] So, even if only Brazil, Chile, Venezuela and Peru have trade surpluses with China, most of Latin American countries benefit from the hike on the international prices of commodities.[11]

For China, the implications of this current new trade with Latin America have been much more modest, as they represent just a small percentage of a trade tsunami that has moved in every possible direction. In 2011, it accounted for 6% of China's total exports and 7% of its imports.[12] Nonetheless, it becomes relevant as Latin America has become China's most dynamic export market with an annual growth of 31% between 2005 and 2010, versus 16% for the rest of the world.[13] As stated by Premier Wen Jiabao on 26 June 2012, China is aiming to reach US$400 billion in trade with Latin America for 2017.[14]

The fact that in 2008 Beijing published a White Paper defining a strategic relation with Latin America that covers cooperation in a wide variety of areas, speak by itself. Moreover, China has shown a clear interest

---

[9] *Latin America and the Caribbean's Long Term Growth: Made in China?* (Washington D.C.: September 2011).

[10] Kevin P. Gallager and Roberto Porzecanski, *The Dragon in the Room* (Stanford: Stanford University Press, 2010).

[11] CEPAL, *La República popular China y América Latina y el Caribe: Diálogo y Cooperación ante los Nuevos Desafíos de la Economía Mundial.*

[12] *idem.*

[13] "Exports from Latin America and the Caribbean will increase in 27% in 2011", Economic Commission for Latin America and the Caribbean, ECLAC, Press Release, 31 August 2011, <http://www.caribbeanpressrelease.com/articles/8630/1/ECLAC-Exports-from-Latin-America-and-the-Caribbean-Will-Increase-by-27-in 2011/Page1.html>.

[14] Alicia Bárcena, "El salto de China en América Latina y el Caribe", *El Universal*, 5 de Julio 2012.

in participating as an observer in different multilateral organisations that covers Latin American affairs both from an economic and political perspective. That includes the Rio Group, the Inter-American Development Bank (IDB), the Latin American Integration Association (LAIA), the Economic Commission for Latin America and the Caribbean (ECLAC), the Organization of American States (OAS) and the Latin American Parliament.[15]

This new trade wave has also been accompanied by a current of investments and financing. In 2010, China became the third largest investor in Latin America, after the United States and the European Union. That year it invested US$15.3 billion. Conversely, investments on the opposite direction are also on the table as Venezuela, in association with Petro China, is in the process of building three refineries in Guangdong in order to process its heavy oil. At the same time, China has transformed itself in a very important financial source for the region: "Since 2005, China's Development Bank and other institutions have spent an estimate of US$75 billion on financial investments in South America, said Boston University professor Kevin Gallagher. This is, he points out 'more investment than the World Bank, US Export Bank and the Inter-American Development Bank combined'."[16]

But even if this emerging economic partnership has produced impressive results it does not flow easily, at least not from a Latin American perspective. Costs as well as benefits are involved in the process even for the winners, but together with the winners there are losers as well. The latter are those Latin American countries for whom the Chinese juggernaut only spells problems. It is thus a complex relation that entails winners and losers as well as costs and benefits. This is a normal occurrence within an economic relationship still in the making.

In order to understand the process in course we have to begin by the beginning which entails understanding what Latin America is all

---

[15] Juan Miguel Gonzalez Peña, *op. cit.*; Julio A. Díaz Vásquez "Relaciones económicas China-América Latina: ¿Oportunidad o amenaza?", El *Observatorio de la Política China*, 6 de agosto 2011.

[16] Chris Arsenault, "The dragon goes shopping in South America", *Aljazeera.net*, 21 December 2011, <http://www.aljazeera.com/category/person/chris-arsenault>.

about. From the basic notions onwards, we have to move step-by-step trying to preserve a sense of perspective all along the way.

What is Latin America?

In essence, Latin America is made up of those non-Anglo or Dutch components of the Americas formed in the common mould of the Catholic religion, the Latin cultural heritage and the romanic languages. Iberian America and Haiti would naturally fit into this mould; the former because of its Spanish and Portuguese ancestry, the latter because of its French one. However, if we were to take this argument to its logical conclusion, we would also have to include not only the catholic- and French-speaking provinces of Quebec in Canada, but also France itself by virtue of its overseas territories in the Americas. Indeed, the latter are not considered to be colonies but integral parts of the French State. Nevertheless, when the term Latin America is used, reference is made to a more restricted meaning. That is, the Iberian American countries. Why then the term Latin America?

The notion of "Latin America" originated in France. The term was coined in 1861 in an article published by the French scholar L.M. Tisserand in the magazine *Revues des Races Latines.*[17] Not gratuitously, it was the time when Napoleon III sought to give legitimacy to his conquest of Mexico and to that end wanted to highlight its common Latin heritage with France. Despite its military failure in Mexico, the France of Napoleon III bequeathed to the region the term by which it is mostly known. Notwithstanding its imperialistic origin the term was easily accepted, which derived from the fact that from the very moment in which independence from Spain was obtained, regional aspirations toward modernisation tended to affirm themselves by contrast to the inherited order.

Moreover, the end of the era of Napoleon III coincided with the emergence, all over Iberian American countries, of a powerful Positivist movement. This movement sought a break with Hispanic

[17] Leopoldo Zea, *Latinoamérica, Tercer Mundo* (México: Editorial Extemporáneos, 1977).

cultural and political matrixes, while establishing a direct parentage with Western civilisation skirting round Spain. A concept that accomplished precisely that objective had to be necessarily welcomed. So, it was that we came to be known as Latin Americans, obviating much more descriptive notions of our origins. Nonetheless, as aforementioned, to speak of Latin America means referring specifically to Iberian America.

Iberian America has its starting point at the Treaty of Tordesillas, signed between Spain and Portugal in 1494, which divided between them the recently discovered southern America. Both European countries were located in the Iberian Peninsula and so shared its old, rich and complex civilisation. This civilisation would be the result of many centuries of physical co-existence and fusion of cultures among Christians, Muslims and Jews and before that of the interaction with Greeks, Phoenicians, Carthaginians, Romans and Germans (Goths, Visigoths and Suevi). Spain and Portugal were part of the same Roman Province, Hispania, and could have evolved as a single State, but political and military factors in the 10th and 11th centuries decided otherwise. It has been said that the Iberian countries share with the Slavs the fact of being in the extremes of Western civilisation.

Starting with these joint denominators, Spaniards and Portuguese went through the same process of racial mixture and cultural fusion when they reached the New World, thus giving rise to a new human group of similar characteristics. Perhaps the most notable feature of this group is its eclectic mindset, which can move easily within Western parameters while at the same time being able to watch those parameters from the outside with a critical and even surprised perspective. Given the combination of its Iberian roots, its blood and cultural mix, the fact of being a region traditionally open to immigration and the distances imposed by its geography, Latin Americans are in the fringe of the West, equally able to position themselves in the outer of its gates or to cross inside. As a result, Latin Americans have an open and flexible attitude that excels in lateral thinking and tends to be at odds with rigidity. Not surprisingly, they lack in method and discipline but are very good in creativeness and improvisation.

Keeping these similarities aside, however, there are relevant differences between Portuguese and Spanish America. To begin with, Portuguese are more pragmatic and conciliatory when compared to the Spaniards. This is replicated as well in the differences between Brazilians and Hispanic Americans. The history of Brazil displays a process of moderate evolution, devoid of the epic deeds and sudden shocks so typical of their Hispanic Americans cousins. It has been correctly pointed out that the Brazilians fell asleep one night as a colony and woke up to find themselves an independent Empire and, some time later, woke up again to find themselves a Republic.[18] The history of Hispanic America, on the other hand, looks more grandiose and traumatic.

Hispanic America, for its part, also shows similarities and differences among its diverse components. There are many elements in common, but two in particular. To begin with there is a history of parallel events. That is, 300 years of colonial subjection to Spanish centralism and Catholic fundamentalism; a simultaneous awakening to the ideas of freedom and independence; an independence movement characterised by the cooperation between and the overlapping of their founding fathers and armies; an emergence into an independence life marked by the disorientation resulting by the sudden overthrow of the old established order and the rise of the "caudillos", that is, the strong men; a parallel stage of confrontations and civil wars between those who aspired to a modernisation of structures and those who clung to the vestiges of the order inherited from Spain; the simultaneous emergence of a positivist generation that sought a definitive break with Hispanic cultural moulds in order to impose "order and progress" in line with developments in other parts of Europe. And so on.

In the second place, we find a common language preserved from fragmentation and corruption thanks to the monumental grammar "destined for the use of Americans" that was published in 1847 by the Venezuelan humanist Andres Bello. In other words, a mixed but cultured Spanish language transformed into a powerful instrument of cultural homogeneity.

---

[18] *ibid.*

But beyond their many similarities, Hispanic Americans also show important differences. Two of them turn out to be of the utmost importance. The first are those which derive from their variety of latitudes, topography and climates, which range from the four seasons of the austral countries to the permanent summer of the tropics, from the altitude of the mountainous regions to the sea level. This is responsible for a variety of patterns of behaviour that goes from the introverted character of Chileans to the extroverted nature of Venezuelans, from the melancholic attitude of Bolivians to the joyful expressivity of Dominicans. And so on. But even within the same countries, we find variations deriving from geography with people from the coasts exhibiting a much more extroverted nature than those coming from the high plateaus.

In second place are the differences that emerge from the diverse racial mixtures or the lack of it. There is a Hispanic America of strong indigenous roots which, running down from Mexico and Guatemala, extends along the length of the basin of the Andean Pacific. Another strain, mostly white, is located in the Southern Cone of South America. A third, with African presence, starts in the Spanish-speaking islands of the Caribbean and extends towards Panama, Venezuela, Colombia and the coast of Ecuador and Peru. The diverse countries of Hispanic America give different connotation to this phenomenon.

Brazil, in itself the size of the rest of South America together, was able to assimilate its racial variables and the different patterns of behaviour deriving from its latitudes and climates, preserving a unitary sense of nationality. To that extent, Brazil with its almost 200 million inhabitants, has the diversity of many countries compacted in a single one. The unifying nature of its independent Empire, that was a natural continuation of its colonial period, allowed them to remain together during the formative years of the country, forging a common identity amidst their many differences. The lack of relevant traumas during its subsequent historical process made easy this coexistence.

Nevertheless, leaving aside the particularities of the different components of Iberian America, or to use the correct term Latin America, the truth is that there is a strong sense of common destiny and solidarity not only between Hispanic Americans but between them and

Brazilians. Both share a regional identity and are intermingled in a web of economic and political organisations. We could make reference to MERCOSUR, the Latin American Association of Integration, the Group of Rio or UNASUR, to mention just a few. It is a thriving community of 577 million inhabitants where a common tongue — the "portuñol" — is beginning to emerge as a result of the frequent use of a mixture of the two cousin languages: the Portuguese and the Spanish.

These countries are geographically located in North, Central and South America in addition to the insular Caribbean. Mexico is the only Latin American nation in North America. Guatemala, El Salvador, Honduras, Nicaragua and Panama are in Central America (even though Panama is normally referred as being located in the Isthmus). Venezuela, Colombia, Brazil, Ecuador, Peru, Bolivia, Chile, Argentina, Uruguay and Paraguay are located in South America, whereas Cuba and Dominican Republic are Caribbean island nations. In total, they represent 21,069,500 square kilometres which is tantamount to 14.1% of the Earth's land surface area. Of such amount Brazil has 8,514,877 square kilometres.

Latin American countries' GDP and their world rank according to its GDP is shown in Table 1.

Latin America plus the Caribbean

Even though Latin America has a distinct identity, frequently it is associated with the non-Spanish- or non-Portuguese-speaking countries of the Caribbean. As a result, the combined notion of Latin America and the Caribbean made its appearance. These last countries can be divided into three groups according to their mother tongue: English in the case of Trinidad and Tobago, Jamaica, the Bahamas, Guyana, Belize, Saint Lucia, Grenada, Saint Kitts and Nevis, Dominica, Montserrat, Saint Vincent and the Grenadines and Antigua and Barbuda; French in the case of Haiti; and Dutch in the case of Suriname.

Table 1 Latin American Countries' GDP and Its World Ranking

Brazil	US$2,087 billion (7)
Mexico	US$1,039 billion (13)
Venezuela	USS$387.8 billion (24)
Argentina	US$368.7 billion (27)
Colombia	US$288.1 billion (33)
Chile	US$203.4 billion (43)
Peru	US$153.8 billion (50)
Cuba	US$62.7 billion (63)
Ecuador	US$58.9 billion (68)
Dominican Republic	US$51.5 billion (71)
Guatemala	US$41.1 billion (78)
Uruguay	US$40.2 billion (79)
Costa Rica	US$34.5 billion (84)
Panamá	US$26.7 billion (89)
El Salvador	US$21.7 billion (96)
Bolivia	US$19.7 billion (101)
Paraguay	US$18.4 billion (103)
Honduras	US$15.4 billion (108)
Nicaragua	US$6.5 billion (138)

Source: World Bank, World Development Indicators Database, 1 July 2011.

With the exception of Belize, Guyana and Suriname, located in Central or South America, the rest are island nations. Curiously enough, the continental countries of Guyana and Suriname are not located in the Caribbean basin but facing the Atlantic Ocean. In that sense, they are neither Latin American nor Caribbean nations. Nonetheless, they are normally included within the Caribbean and within the notion Latin America and the Caribbean.

Except for Haiti which obtained its independence at the beginning of the 19th century, when most of Latin America did so as well, the rest had access to Statehood within the decolonisation process of the second half of the 20th century. For logical reasons, Haiti has been historically closer to Latin America than the rest of the non-Spanish-speaking Caribbean. Actually Simon Bolivar, the founding father of six Latin American republics, received an important help in his independence struggle from the already independent Haiti.

After the rest became independent States, they began to interact with Latin American countries, essentially within the framework of the Organization of the American States (OAS), which is the forum that deals with hemispheric political affairs. But they also mingled at extra hemispheric negotiations or organisations such as the GATT Uruguay Round, the Group of 77 or the Non-Aligned Movement. Coincidences between the developing countries of the hemisphere began to emerge in a very natural way.

Within the Americas, and besides the OAS, the two groups of countries also interacted in several regional organisations and mechanisms. In 1975, the Latin American and Caribbean economic System (SELA) was established with the aim of promoting economic cooperation and social development between Latin America and the Caribbean. The Caribbean Community (CARICOM) that initially gathered the English-speaking countries of the area and latter was expanded to include Haiti and Suriname has had a representation at the Latin American Group of Rio since 1990. Moreover, since 2005 several of the CARICOM member countries became integral members of the said Group of Rio. On the other hand, Mexico, Venezuela and Dominican Republic have been observers at CARICOM. In 1999, the Summit of Latin America, Caribbean and European Union took shape as an informal mechanism that gathers every two years the chiefs of State and government of these regions. In 2008, the Summit of Latin America and the Caribbean for Development and Integration was launched.

Finally, during the XXI Summit of the Group of Rio, in February 2010, the creation of a new association aiming at integrating these two regions in a more systematic way was decided. That gave birth to the Community of Latin American and Caribbean States which was formally established in Caracas, Venezuela, in December 2011 and is formed by 33 countries (all the Western hemisphere with the exception of the United States and Canada). This group aims at promoting a concerted Latin American and Caribbean position in the fundamental global issues of today, while strengthening economic integration among its members.

While these two groups of countries have attained a great degree of convergence, each has a distinct identity (with Haiti and Suriname having their own within the CARICOM). Not surprisingly, this is a subject where flux notions prevail. At times, reference is made to the joint concept of Latin America and the Caribbean while at other times just Latin America is mentioned. Even in the latter case, the Caribbean countries may be assumed to be included even if not mentioned specifically. Most of the references made to Latin America in this book, though, excludes the non-Spanish-speaking countries of the Caribbean as they are not labour-intensive manufacturing economies nor, with the exception of Trinidad and Tobago, natural resources producers. Hence, they mostly fall outside of the scope of this work.

From an economic point of view and with some exceptions, the non-Iberian countries of the Caribbean have a much smaller dimension. The GDP of such countries is shown in Table 2.

Latin America (and in this case we talk strictly about Iberian America) moved into the 20th century full steam ahead. Its raw materials provided important economic growth rates and some of the countries of the region were among the richest in the world at that time. Between 1870 and 1913, Latin American GDP grew 3.5% while the world GDP grew 2.1%.[19] Brazil generated 70% of the world's coffee exports with rubber also booming, while in terms of meat, cereal and wool, Argentinean exports had very few competitors worldwide. Uruguay, a much smaller country than Argentina, was also booming with the same export commodities. With the introduction of the cold-storage, during the first decade of the century, profits from meat exports multiplied four-fold. Silver export booms in Mexico, Peru and Bolivia had their equivalent in copper export booms in Chile and Peru. But there was also saltpetre in Chile and Peru. The latter also exported sugar and guano. Sugar exports were

[19] Claudio Loser, "The Impact of Globalization on Latin America Task Force", University of Miami, Center for Hemispheric Policy (11 June 2012).

Table 2 Caribbean Community Countries' GDP and Its World Ranking

Trinidad and Tobago	US$20.3 billion (100)
Jamaica	US$13.9 billion (111)
Haiti	US$11.09 billion (138)
The Bahamas	US$7.5 billion (133)
Suriname	US$3.2 billion (155)
Guyana	US$2.2 billion (159)
Belize	US$1.4 billion (173)
Saint Lucia	US$932 million (176)
Grenada	US$628 million (182)
Saint Kitts and Nevis	US$526 million (186)
Dominica	US$526 million (187)

Source: World Bank, World Development Indicators Database, 1 July 2011.
Note: The three smaller island States of the region, Montserrat, Saint Vincent and the Grenadines and Antigua and Barbuda, are not even listed within the World Bank indicators.

prevalent in tropical countries of the region more to the North as it was the case of banana as well. Within the second decade of the new century, oil exports boomed in Mexico with Venezuela and Colombia following behind.[20]

The import-substituting industrialisation process

The Great Depression of the 30s, though, showed the fragility of an economic world order to which Latin America had tried to incorporate itself not only as a reliable commodities supplier but as a relevant importer of manufactured goods. Indebted and in bad economic situation as a result of the global crisis, the primary productive sector had to be subsidised by the State while industrialisation began to be seen

[20] Tulio Halperin Donghi, *História Contemporánea de América Latina* (Buenos Aires: Alianza Editorial, 1997).

as the appropriate medicine to provide a firmer economic ground. A light industry began to take shape in the region in order to compensate for the import needs that the international crisis had left uncovered. The Second World War would give new impetus to this industrialisation process which, if relevant for Latin American standards, was still modest for international ones, especially due to the limitations of capital goods imports. In this case though the aim was to provide substitution for manufactured products that were not arriving and not to compensate for the shortcomings of a primary industry which, much to the contrary and thanks to the war, was booming again. The average Latin America GDP growth during the period 1913–1950 was 3.4% while the world GDP grew by 1.8%.[21] Already in 1947, the industrial sector had a bigger percentage of the Argentinean GDP than the primary sector. With the end of the war what was already a fact — an import-substituting industrialisation process — was to be duly conceptualised.[22]

Since 1948, indeed, the conceptual framework of that import-substituting industrialisation process began to be defined. Two economists and an organisation were basically responsible for that. The former were Raul Prebisch and Sir Hans Wolfang Singer. The latter was the Economic Commission for Latin America, ECLA. So if the first steps in import substitution industrialisation were largely non-theoretical and were based on pragmatic choices of how to face the limitations imposed by manufactured needs left uncovered, the second phase would have a strong theoretical foundation.

Prebisch, a well-known Argentinean economist who had been the first General Director of the Argentinean Central Bank and who in 1949 worked for ECLA, was requested by its Secretary General to write an analysis on the deterioration in the terms of trade of raw materials. After having written the first draft of a long text, he came to read Singer's recent paper "Post-War Relations between Underdeveloped and Industrialised Countries", which complemented his

[21] Claudio Loser, *op. cit.*
[22] *ibid.*

own ideas. Prebisch changed the first version and proceeded to print the fresh material extensively quoting Singer in his conclusions. The latter, a German, had been a protégé and a pupil of both Schumpeter and Keynes and at the time was one of the few economists at the new Economics Department of the United Nations. The result was a book called *The Economic Development of Latin America and Some of its Main Problems*, published in 1949. So, it was that without collaborating directly, and having come to similar conclusions separately, both economists gave birth to what was called the Prebisch–Singer hypothesis.

Such hypothesis was to be extensively spread through the region by ECLA an organisation dependant of the United Nations born in 1948. Since 1950 and until 1963, its Secretary General was Prebisch himself. Under its auspices, a group of outstanding Latin American economists followed suit to the Prebisch–Singer ideas elaborating on the need for developing a substitutive manufacturing base. In 1984, it is worth mentioning, the range of action of the institution was expanded to cover the Caribbean countries and its name was expanded as well to become the Economic Commission for Latin America and the Caribbean (ECLAC).

According to José Antonio Ocampo and María Angela Parra:

> The original formulation of this thesis combined two different yet clearly complementary hypotheses whose subsequent theoretical development in the economic literature was to follow parallel courses. One of these hypotheses regarded the negative effect of the income-inelasticity of the demand for commodities on developing countries' terms of trade, while the other dealt with the asymmetries in the functioning of labour markets in the world economy's 'centre' and 'periphery'.[23]

Hence, the so-called hypothesis was made up of two sub hypotheses. The first had to do with the fact that the prices of primary

[23] "The Terms of Trade for Commodities in the Twentieth Century", CEPAL Review No. 79 (April, 2003), p. 8.

products have a descending tendency over a period of time with low rates in terms of improvement of productivity. Countries specialised in their production were thus condemned to lag behind the industrial ones and the terms of trade between them would be detrimental to raw material producers. As for the second, Daniel Yergin and Joseph Stanislaw point out: "They argued that the world economy was divided into the industrial 'center' — the United States and Western Europe — and the commodity producing 'periphery'. The terms of trade would always work against the periphery."[24]

In order to face this double negative situation, ECLA's economists with Prebisch at their lead, would argue that the answer was to create a substitutive manufacturing base. In Daniel Yergin and Joseph Stanislaw words:

> So instead, the periphery would go its own way. Rather than exporting commodities and importing finished goods, these countries would move as rapidly as possible towards what was called 'import-substituting' industrialisation. This would be achieved by breaking the links to world trade through high tariffs and other forms of protectionism ... Currencies were overvalued, which cheapened equipment imports needed for industrialization; all other imports were tightly rationed through permits and licenses.[25]

To put in motion such a process, a set of objectives was indeed required: active industrial policies to subsidise and orchestrate the production of strategic substitutes; protective barriers to trade; overvalued currencies to help manufacturers import the capital goods they needed; promotion of domestic private sector investments and discouragement of foreign direct investments; etc. So unlike Asia, where an "outward-oriented industrial growth" would be emphasised since the 1960's, Latin America would visualise industrialisation as an "inward-oriented process". Products that would otherwise have to be imported were to be manufactured domestically.

---

[24] *The Commanding Heights* (New York: Simon & Schuster, 1998), p. 234.

[25] *ibid.*, p. 234.

Flaws, results and implosion

The import-substituting industrialisation presented though three important flaws. The first was to conceive the process as permanent in nature. So instead of proceeding like all major developed economies have done — using its interventionist economic policies to promote industrialisation and protect national companies until they were prepared to compete internationally — domestic industries were indefinitely isolated. The "industries in their infancy", a thesis conceptualized by Alexander Hamilton at the end of the 18th century, assumed a permanent character in the Latin America of the 20th century. In other words: "The infant-industry logic became the all-industry logic".[26] This implied creating a gap between highly competitive companies abroad and highly protected, and by extension frequently inefficient ones, inside. In as long as the latter were cut off from the former by thick walls there was no problem, but if those walls were ever to fall suddenly massacre would follow.

The second flaw was not to have given enough consideration to the fact that the unequal distribution of income generated small national markets, insufficient to sustain the industrialisation effort. With the exception of larger countries such as Brazil or Mexico, this flaw posed an important problem for the majority of the region. To overcome such difficulties and enlarge consumer markets, ECLA's economist suggested two alternatives. On the one hand, better income distribution within each country so as to bring the enormous disenfranchised population into the consumer market. On the other hand, regional or sub-regional economic integration that would allow the products of one country to be sold in the other countries. Thus, the "inward-oriented growth" evolved from a national to a regional or a sub-regional perspective. Unfortunately, insofar as Latin American countries had engaged in building the same type of industries, the scenario turned out to be more competitive than complementary, making integration a difficult task. Moreover, when each country

[26] *ibid.*, p. 234.

showed different levels of inflation or payment of its manpower or of exchange rates against the dollar, the competition tended to become destructive in many cases. Despite the great obstacles faced, though, advances were very important and integration never ceased to be a fundamental goal.

The third one was that the dependency on commodities continued to be fundamental, as they were the ones generating the currency that nurtured this whole process. Indeed, while manufactures were sold inside the protected trade area, commodities were sold abroad thus becoming the fundamental source of currency. In this manner, the descending tendency on their prices, or its volatility, not only continued to affect the terms of trade with "central" economies but generated an immense vulnerability for the whole import-substituting industrialisation structure.

Notwithstanding such important flaws the system provided results. Some qualified opinions can attest it. According to Kevin P. Gallager and Roberto Porzecanski: "It will be easy and tempting to look backward to the period roughly between 1940 and 1970. During that period, Latin America was indeed able to build innovation and industrial capabilities. Indeed, that period was certainly the 'golden age' of economic growth in Latin America that is yet to be matched."[27] Joseph Stiglitz opinion goes in the same direction:

> In earlier decades, Latin America had notable success with strong government interventionist policies ... focused more on the restriction of imports than on the expansion of exports. High tariffs were placed on certain imports, to encourage the development of local industries — a strategy often referred to as import substitution. While its success did not match that of East Asia, Latin America's per capita income still grew at an average of more than 2.5% annually from 1950 to 1980. Brazil, whose government intervened more aggressively in the economy, grew at an average of 5.7% ....[28]

[27] *op. cit.*, p. 140.

[28] *Making Globalization Work* (London: Allen Lane, 2006), p. 35.

Daniel Yergin and Joseph Stanislaw refer to the following: "Until the 1970s, the approach seemed to work. Real capital income nearly doubled between 1950 and 1970."[29] Columbia's professor Greg Grandin on his part adds: "If we take Latin America in its entirety, we find that between 1947 and 1973 (the state-dominance stage) the per capita income grew by 73% in real terms."[30]

The success of the model, based on the Keynesian doctrine, mirrored the unprecedented prosperity that such policies brought to the Western World between 1945 and 1975. Nonetheless, between 1950 and 1973, Latin America grew faster than the world average: 5.4% versus 4.9%. Moreover, in 1981, Latin American share of world GDP was 11% while its GDP per capita exceeded the world average by 10%.[31] The collapse of the import-substituting industrialisation model would be closely linked to the end of Keynesianism in Western economies, where a combination of inflation and stagnation, known as stagflation, would lift von Hayek's ideas from the dusted bookshelf.

The inherent vulnerabilities within the import-substituting industrialisation model were ready to concatenate when the right set of international conditions appeared. And they did as a result of the debt crisis. It all began during the 1970's when an international banking system overflowed with petrodollars, deriving from the sudden hike of oil prices, devoted itself to grant plentiful loans. This easy access to international credits, actively promoted by the lenders themselves, was seen by Latin American governments as an excellent opportunity to invest in infrastructure and the modernisation of its State industries. As a consequence, the region got massively indebted under the assumption, prescribed by the conventional wisdom of the day, that the interest rates would remain low for the foreseeable future.

But they did not. As Joseph Stiglitz points out: "In 1980, fighting its own problem of inflation, the United States initiated interest rate increases that climbed to over 20%. These rates spilled over to loans to Latin America, triggering the Latin American debt crisis of the

[29] *The Commanding Heights* (New York: Simon & Schuster, 1998), p. 234.

[30] *Empire's Workshop* (New York: Metropolitan Books, 2006), p. 198.

[31] Claudio Loser, *op. cit.*

early 1980s, when Mexico, Argentina, Brazil, Costa Rica, and a host of other countries defaulted on their debt."[32]

The debt crisis hit Latin America very hard and between 1975 and 1982 the regional debt increased from US$45.2 billion to US$333 billion.[33] Needless to say that this increase had much to do with the snow ball effect derived from interest rates over 20% and with short-term loans and International Monetary Fund credits to pay the old debt.

But at the same time that interest rates were speeding up the price of primary products was speeding down. The reasons were very much the same. Faced with the hike in the oil prices in 1979 the new governments of Ronald Reagan and Margaret Thatcher decided to fight inflation not only through monetary tools (such as interest rate increases), but also by reducing the fiscal expenditure. The result of those austerity policies was a recession that increased unemployment and precipitated the fall in the demand and consequently in the prices of commodities. Such unexpected downturn in the prices of primary products gravely affected the capacity of Latin American governments to meet their debts. While the sources of currency income were dropping significantly, the external debt began to grow exponentially as a result of the interest rates hike.

This period of extreme weakness was combined with the appearance of a new economic paradigm brought in, again, by the duo Reagan–Thatcher: the neoliberal model. Just when Latin American governments were faced with the need to renegotiate their debts and acquire new loans to pay the old ones, they were confronted to this ideological juggernaut. With its negotiating strength reduced to its minimum, the region was faced with the premises of the Washington Consensus and the directives of its executive arm, the International Monetary Fund.

Acceptance of their terms became unavoidable given the confluence of several factors. Firstly: "As part of the rescue packages, the International Monetary Fund became ... a sort of international bankruptcy receiver."[34]

---

[32] *op. cit.*, p. 36.
[33] Daniel Yergin and Joseph Stanislaw, *op. cit.*
[34] *ibid.*, p. 132.

As such, indebted countries willing to renegotiate their debts had to accept the IMF conditions. Secondly, because of the credibility or ostracism parameters that were imposed among nations, according to their acceptance or rejection of the neoliberal credo, as referred in Chapter 1. Thirdly because of the influence of the so-called "Chicago boys", or University of Chicago trained technocrats (but more frequently applied to Ivy League graduates imbued with market economy ideas), in leading economic positions within Latin American governments (a consequence of the previous two factors).

Opening of the gates

The above led to the sudden and widespread opening of Latin American markets forcing the protected industrial sector to compete with the most efficient companies of the world. The impact of such a measure upon jobs is clearly described by Joseph Stiglitz: "It is easy to destroy jobs, and this is often the immediate impact of trade liberalisation, as inefficient industries close down under pressure from international competition. IMF ideology holds that new, more productive jobs will be created as the old inefficient jobs that have been created behind protectionist walls are eliminated. But that is simply not the case."[35] As for the impact on industries Rubens Ricupero, Secretary General of the United Nations Commission for Trade and Development (UNCTAD), pointed out that this resulted in an accelerated and premature disappearance of an important part of the Latin American industrial base.[36]

Transforming the infant-industry logic into an all-industry logic that indefinitely isolated local industries from outside competition was indeed a huge mistake. But the corrective medicine should never have been the sudden opening of trade barriers. As Joseph Stiglitz remarks: "The most successful developing countries, those in East Asia, opened themselves to the outside world but did so slowly and

---

[35] *op. cit.* 2002, p. 59.

[36] Foreword to Alfredo Toro Hardy, *Tiene Futuro América Latina?* (Bogotá: Villegas Editores, 2004).

in a sequenced way. These countries ... dropped protective barriers carefully and systematically."[37] No one doubts that Latin America had an important catch-up process ahead; nonetheless, the reform process should have been guided by common sense and not by ideology. If there was much to be dismantled, there was much to be preserved as well and the dismantling process should have been more gradual. What happened though was the equivalent to the brutal throwing down of the protective walls to let Genghis Khan hordes in. Companies that had thrived under the old system began to be slaughtered *en masse*.

On the other hand, and also under the ideological commands of the Washington Consensus, an irrational privatisation process of state-owned companies took shape. Again, in Joseph Stiglitz words: "Unfortunately, the IMF and the World Bank have approached the issues from a narrow ideological perspective — privatisation was to be pursued rapidly ... those who privatised faster were given the high marks."[38] The very same State companies and public utilities, whose expansion had indebted the governments of the region, started to be sold at laughable prices as a result of this fast paced logic. Usually, the beneficiaries of this process were transnational corporations.

None of the textbook requisites in this matter were fulfilled. Indeed, according to Ha-Joon Chang, those requisites are the following:

> ... the privatised firm should be sold at the right price. Selling at the right price is the duty of the government, as the trustee of the citizens' assets. If it sells them too cheaply, it is transferring public wealth into the buyer ... In addition, if the wealth transferred is taken outside the country, there will be a loss of national wealth ... In order to get the right price, the privatisation process must be done at the right scale and with the right timing. For example, if a government tries to sell too many enterprises within a relatively short period, this would adversely affect their prices.[39]

---

[37] *Globalization and its Discontents* (London: W.W. Norton & Company, 2002), p. 60.
[38] *Ibid*. p. 54.
[39] *Bad Samaritans* (London: Random House Business Books, 2007), p. 117.

So, while Latin American governments were facing a foreign debt that had grown out of all proportion in relation to the originally granted loans, the assets that benefited from such loans were bargained to the transnational capital. This involved a net and massive transfer of wealth overseas. In this regard, it is worth mentioning the case of Spanish companies, which took biggest advantage from the privatisation wave in Latin America. The smaller size of these companies had kept them marginalised from the European scene, which is precisely the reason why they went to Latin America. However, after a few years of extraordinary capitalisation of their regional investments, these same corporations were able to return to the European stage. But this time, as major players. That, of course, was attained at the expense of Latin American wealth.

Additional part of the problem had to do with the fact that privatised companies were frequently disconnected from its traditional domestic suppliers and reconnected with intra corporative chains of supply. This applied as well to many local private companies that could not stand on their own feet and had to be sold to foreign corporations. The result in both cases being that the national productive chains were totally disrupted and supplanted by foreign chains of supply. Big local companies, precisely those bought by foreign corporations, ceased to be the turbines of industrial development that they had been until then and became disconnected islands within our economies. And amidst these islands, numerous medium- and small-sized enterprises that had hitherto been linked to them began to disappear.[40]

So the impact was double. On the one hand, there were the local companies that could not compete and simply went broke. On the other hand, the local suppliers of disappeared, privatised or sold companies were also swept away. Not surprisingly, the effects of the neoliberal policies were devastating for the Latin American industrial base, which between 1980 and 2002 suffered a significant contraction. In Argentina, the industrial participation in the country's GDP went

---

[40] Alberto Arroyo Picard, "El TLCAN 5 Años Después: Contenidos, Resultados y Propuestas", Comisión de Comercio de la Cámara de Diputados, México (LVII Legislatura, 2000).

down from 29% to 15%; in Brazil from 31% to 19.9%; in Uruguay, from 28.6% to 17%; in Peru, from 29.3% to 14.4%; in Colombia from 21.5% to 13.5% and in Ecuador from 20% to 7%.[41]

But, there was not only the shrinkage of the industrial base but also of the technological capabilities that had been associated with it. During the import-substituting industrialisation phase, a great effort in research and development had been made as the industrial development strategy required building endogenous technological capacities. With the implementation of the Washington Consensus policies not only most of the regional R&D efforts were abandoned but the whole idea of generating local technology began to be seen as useless. Henceforward, imported technology became the aim and it was assumed that this would naturally come by way of trade or foreign direct investment and that the market would automatically allocate such capabilities.[42] Mexico's case epitomises this process. According to Kevin P. Gallager and Roberto Porzecanski:

> Built-up during the ISI [import-substituting industrialization] period, Mexican electronic firms were virtually eliminated after trade liberalisation and replaced by a foreign enclave economy with few linkages, minimal R&D, and limited partnerships with universities... Mexican endogenous capacities for high-tech were seeded and cultivated by ISI policies from the 1940s to the 1980s. Mexico's larger size allowed it to promote the development of the domestic high-tech sector during the ISI period, a sector that became relatively vibrant by the 1980s (....) The domestic high-tech industry is nearly extinct ... Between 1985 and 1997, the number of indigenous electronics firms in Guadalajara (former hub of Mexico's high-tech industry) declined by 71%, and 13 of the 25 indigenous electronics firms that were still in existence at the end of 1997 had been closed by 2005 (....) Moreover, the FDI-led innovation and growth strategy created an 'enclave economy', the benefits of which were confined to an international sector and not connected to the wider

---

[41] Emir Sader, Ivana Jinkings *et al.*, coord., *Latinoamérica: Enciclopedia Contemporánea de América Latina y El Caribe* (Madrid: Clacso-Ediciones AKAL, S.A., 2009).
[42] Kevin P. Gallager and Roberto Porzecanski, *op. cit.*

> Mexican economy (....) The assessment characterises Mexico as having a 'maquila innovation system'. This is a system that imports technology and equipment and hosts networking activities by MNCs [multinationals] in a manner divorced from the broader economy.[43]

It is crystal clear that Guadalajara could not have expected to survive unharmed in the era of Silicon Valley, but joint ventures could have been established between these two clusters in order to preserve as much as possible of Mexico's R&D establishment. Instead more than 40 years of sustained technological efforts were swept away and supplanted by an "enclave" assembly sector.

At the beginning there was the impression, though, that the Washington Consensus policies were working. But it was just a mirage as Joseph Stiglitz points out:

> When price stability was restored and growth resumed, the World Bank and the IMF claimed credit for the success; the case for the Washington Consensus had been made. But, as it turned out, the growth was not sustainable. It was based on heavy borrowing from abroad and on privatisation, which sold off national assets to foreigners ... Growth was to last a short seven years, and was to be followed by recession and stagnation. Growth for the decade of the 1990s was only half what it had been in the decades prior to 1980, and what growth there was went disproportionately to the rich.[44]

Nevertheless, the most serious impact of these reforms was the social one. In Greg Grandin's words:

> If we take Latin America in its entirety, we find that between 1947 and 1973 (the state-dominance stage) the per capita income grew by 73% in real terms. By contrast, during the era of the free market fundamentalism, the average per capita income stagnated at 0%. By the late seventies, 11% of Latin Americans could be considered as poverty-stricken ... By 1996, the number of indigents rose to a third of

[43] *ibid.*, pp. 109, 111, 112, 114, 115.
[44] *op. cit.* 2006, p. 36.

its total population. That is, 165 million people. And by 2005, 221 million people lived below the poverty line, an increase of 20 million in just a decade.[45]

Indeed, during the 90s, and as a result of the ideologically oriented reforms in place, inequality skyrocketed arriving at a percentage of 53.9% in a scale from 0 to 100, where 100 represents total inequality. At that time, world inequality average was 38% and Africa's inequality was lower than that of Latin America. According to the World Bank, the richest 10% of Latin American population received 48% of the total income whereas the poorest 10% received only 1.6%.[46] Moreover, during the 90s poverty reached 44% of the region's population with 20% under the extreme poverty line.[47]

Neoliberal policies had a profoundly regressive effect for Latin America, both economically and socially. Had Latin America followed a commonsensical approach to reform, as was the case in China during the same period, the history of the region would have evolved in a very different direction. If instead of applying a shock therapy the river had been crossed by feeling the stones, many good things could have been preserved, while inefficiencies within the system could have been purged in a rational way. But that was not possible as neoliberals, with their "level playing field" notion, rejected as unfair competition the natural tools of industrial policies. As Kishore Mahbubani clearly points out in relation to the market economy model: "The first error was to regard capitalism as an ideological good, not a pragmatic instrument to improve human welfare."[48]

While Latin America witnessed, during those years, an accelerated descendant tendency, both economically and socially, China showed a spectacular ascendant one. And these reverse tendencies would become evident when China and Latin America roads crossed each

[45] *op. cit.*, p. 198.
[46] Christopher Patten, "Speech of Commissioner Patten at Canning House Gala Dinner", London, Canning House, 4 February 2004.
[47] Luis Paramio, "Perspectivas de la izquierda en América Latina", Documentos del Real Instituto Elcano de Estudios Internacionales y Estratégicos (Madrid, 2003).
[48] "Western capitalism in crisis", *The Straits Times*, 9 February 2012.

other at the beginning of the new millennium. When the latter's industries were beginning to redress from the impact caused to them by the neoliberal tsunami, the avalanche of the Chinese low-cost products came along. It was a second shock that pushed Latin American industries back to the corner.

China's redeeming virtue

It happened though that trade with China had a big redeeming virtue that the Washington Consensus never had. China was indeed a voracious consumer of commodities. According to the International Monetary Fund, between 2002 and 2006, the general index of commodities worldwide, excluding oil, was increased 60% in real terms. Moreover, in the areas of oil and metals such increase was 150% and 180%, respectively. This phenomenon was attributed to China whose imports of commodities multiplied by 20 during the last two decades. Conversely, before China's led boom and for the five previous decades, the price of commodities had been falling at an annual rate of 1.6% in relation to manufactured goods.[49]

A World Bank Report allows us to properly understand the meaning of the term commodity:

> Commodities are defined as traded, non-branded, bulk goods with little processing — their quality and characteristics can be objectively established, and they are supplied without qualitative differentiation across a market. Under our definition, then, commodities are natural resources (minerals, oil, gas) or goods produced directly by exploiting natural resources (as in agriculture). So, we use these terms interchangeably.[50]

So while the regional industrial base got hammered, the commodities sector began to blossom in an unexpected way. For the latter, a gigantic market suddenly appeared from the blue, generating

---

[49] Bernardo Kosacoff y Sebastián Campanario, *La Revalorizacion de las Materias Primas y sus Efectos en América Latina* (Santiago de Chile: CEPAL, mayo 2007).
[50] Emily Sinnot, John Nash and Augusto de la Torre, *Natural Resources in Latin America and the Caribbean: Beyond Booms and Busts?* (Washington D.C.: The World Bank, 2010), p. 2.

benefits not only as a result of its direct sales to China but also from the generalised increase in world prices produced by the Chinese demand. In Kevin P. Gallager and Roberto Porzecanski words:

> In the recent boom, Latin American export growth, which was considerably faster than GDP growth, was being driven by a commodities boom. Indeed, 70% of the growth in Latin American countries exports was due to growth in commodities exports, and commodities exports comprised 74% of all Latin American countries growth. China had both indirect and direct effects in this trend. Directly, Latin American countries exports to China have increased 370% since 2000 ... Indirectly, Chinese consumption of global commodities was making them scarcer and boosting global prices and leading somewhat to more Latin American countries exports.[51]

As a result, growth rates soared in countries that represent 69% of Latin America's GDP, which are precisely those increasingly connected to China or dependent on commodities. Regional growth between 2004 and 2007 was more than 5% and forecasted to grow at 4.5% during the period 2011–2012. Moreover, and much to the contrary to what happened during the Washington Consensus years, there have been tangible social benefits deriving from it. According to a 2011 World Bank report between 2002 and 2011, a period in which sales to China grew exponentially, GDP per capita in the region increased by almost 25%. Poverty rates in the region declined steeply between 2002 and 2008, with more than 50 million Latin Americans having been lifted out of moderate poverty.[52] In a speech delivered shortly before leaving the World Bank presidency, Robert B. Zoellick went even further when he said: "Between 2003 and 2010, the income of the average Latin America increased by more than 30% ... About 73 million Latin Americans have been lifted out of poverty since 2003."[53]

---

[51] *op. cit.*, p. 37.

[52] World Bank, *Latin America and the Caribbean's Long Term Growth: Made in China?*, *op. cit.*

[53] "Globalization: Made in the Americas", 30th Anniversary Celebration of the Inter-American Dialogue, Washington D.C., 7 June 2012.

Unfortunately, there was a price tag attached to this bonanza, with the region having had to redefine its role within the international distribution of labour. That has implied going back in time, markedly so, to the beginning of the 20th century when the region was a well-known producer of commodities. Eighty years of industrialising efforts made are in the process of disintegrating.

This state of affairs generates two consequences. Firstly, the pendulum of economic influence in most of Latin America is swinging from the United States to China. The well being of China's economy is becoming as important as or even more so for many Latin American countries than that of the United States. Secondly, the relation between China and Latin America is a complex one, which entails benefits as well as costs and that engenders winners as well as losers.

The first of those considerations has not gone unnoticed in Washington. The possibility of being displaced from the access to commodities that have always been within its reach, due to a factor exogenous to the hemisphere, is a cause of concern. At the end of the day, the United States may have global sources of natural resources to choose from, but the ones that have been traditionally considered as secure, even strategic, were those located in its own neighbourhood. As China rises in the percentage of primary products' world demand, competition in its own hemisphere becomes a new fact of life for the United States. "China could be said to have jumped the fence into the United States' backyard in an attempt to capitalise on the impressive inventory of natural resources that the region has to offer."[54]

However, it is when oil enters onto the stage that the situation becomes sensitive. According to the 2004 projections of the US Department of Energy, both China and the United States would be importing around 70% of their oil requirements in 2025.[55] These estimates have changed in relation to the United States, though, thanks to new technologies like horizontal drilling and fracking (the blasting of water, chemicals and sands through rock), that allows to

---

[54] Lauren Paverman, "China looks to Venezuela for energy security", *Worldpress.org*, 11 October 2011, <http:/worldpress.org/Americas/3820.cfm>.
[55] Alfredo Toro Hardy, *Hegemonía e Imperio* (Bogotá: Villegas Editores, 2007).

tap the huge oil and gas reserves in existence in the shale and other tight rock fields in Texas and North Dakota. In Robert B. Zoellick words: "In 2008, imports supplied 70% of US oil demand. By 2020, PHC Energy estimates that imports could be down to 40% of US oil demand."[56] Nonetheless, as the United States Geological Survey is suggesting, methods like fracking may explain a sharp increase in earthquakes in the midsection on the country, which could make them quite unpopular with public opinion in general and with the affected communities in particular.[57] Indeed, as Fareed Zakaria commented, "Fracking remains controversial and arouses great passion".[58]

Be as it may, though, imports will still represent an important percentage of American oil consumption for years to come. And those imports will be faced to the realities of a "Peak Oil" or "Plateau Oil" era. In other words, the point in time when the maximum rate of global petroleum is reached and the rate of production enters into a progressive but terminal decline. Indeed, despite new major oil finds such as North Dakota or off Brazil's coast, fresh supplies of oil are just enough to offset the production decline from older fields. Since 2005, as estimated by the International Energy Agency, the world is living off an oil plateau.[59] Moreover, in David G. Victor and Linda Yueb words: "After a long era of excess capacity, since 2001, prices for oil and most energy commodities have risen sharply and become more volatile ... Governments in nearly all the large consuming nations are now besieged by doubts about their energy security like at no time since the oil crises of the 1970s."[60]

American hegemony in the region is not only being challenged by China though within the commodities producing countries. In the non-Spanish Caribbean countries, where it has little to look for in

---

[56] *op. cit.*

[57] "Rise in quakes 'man-made': Study", Associated Press, 9 April 2012.

[58] "The new oil and gas boom", *Time*, 29 October 2012.

[59] David Biello, "Has petroleum production peaked, ending the era of easy oil?", *Scientific American*, 25 January 2012.

[60] "The New Energy Order: Managing Insecurities in the Twenty-first Century", *Foreign Affairs*, Vol. 89 (January/February 2010), p. 61.

terms of raw materials, Beijing has been more than generous in providing billions of dollars in loans, grants and other forms of economic assistance. At the end of 2011, China announced that it would lend US$6.3 billion to Caribbean governments. It has been said that the reason behind these initiatives is to acquire "potential new allies that are relatively inexpensive to win over".[61] Nonetheless, the fact that several countries in the region still maintain diplomatic relations with Taiwan is to be seen as an important strategic consideration for China. According to W. Alex Sanchez and Lynn Tu from the Council on Hemispheric Affairs: "China relationship with the Caribbean is complex, as this region is particularly important to Beijing's foreign policy goals regarding Taiwan ... Several Caribbean states currently recognise Taiwan as an independent republic instead of maintaining the 'one-China' position that has been endorsed by the mainland government."[62]

So one way or the other the United States previously uncontested supremacy in the region is being tested to its limits by China. This in itself is a remarkable historical event if we just considered that one of the two main reasons (together with isolationism) why Washington was unwilling to accept the collective security represented by the League of Nations, before War World II, was because it collided with its hegemony in Latin America as expressed by the Monroe Doctrine. In Henry Kissinger words: "The League was believed to be incompatible with the Monroe Doctrine because collective security entitled, indeed required, the League to involve itself in disputes within the Western Hemisphere".[63] And that indeed would have created serious problems for the United States which, since 1903 (when it propitiated the separation of Panama from Colombia) and for the next three decades, invaded 34 times the Caribbean Basin countries (including

[61] Randal C. Archibold, "Beijing makes presence felt in the Caribbean", *International Herald Tribune*, 9 April 2012.

[62] "China vs. Taiwan: battle for influence in the Caribbean", Council on Hemispheric Affairs, 13 March 2012, <http://www.coha.org/china-vs-taiwan-battle-for-influence-in-the-caribbean/>.

[63] *Diplomacy* (New York: Simon & Schuster, 1994), p. 372.

Mexico and Central American nations), to impose its will upon them. Needless to add that after World War II, and for many decades, Latin America was seen by Washington as its undisputed fief. So from a Latin American and Caribbean perspective, there is much to be thankful to China for introducing a new element of counterbalance in the region.

Of course, not all Latin American countries are on the same footing from a Washington perspective with Mexico, Central American nations (Nicaragua excluded), Dominican Republic, and Panama representing the core of its hegemony over the region. Colombia, Peru and Chile are also close (specially the first of them) but in their cases the footprint of China has been accepted as a fact of life. The rest of South America, with Brazil and Venezuela representing the two heads of this process, are a totally different story. Their drifting away from Washington seems to have been digested as inevitable. The countries linked to Beijing seem to have done better economically, these last few years, than those associated with Washington, with those in the middle ground like Chile, Peru and Colombia benefiting more from its relation with the former than with the latter. So, as it seems, the showcase effect has not worked on the United States benefit.

But, of course, what really matters for Latin Americans is the second consideration. That is: Who is harmed and who benefits within Latin America from China's sudden appearance in its neighbourhood? And the answer is not simple. For some countries and sectors of the region, China just means trouble as it not only subtracts export markets but also foreign direct investments. For others, though, China represents the opportunity of a high and sustained economic growth within a framework of clear complementarities. For them, China is becoming an important market and a significant source of investment and financing. Amid these two clear cut positions, we find the in-betweens: countries that benefit in certain areas and are affected in others. To be classified in one group or another, or in the middle, depends on the respective export items.

The Inter-American Development Bank refers to Mexican-type countries and Brazilian-type ones. The former are mainly net commodity importers and highly exposed to trade in goods and services with the United States. The latter are commodity exporters with lower dependence to developed countries in terms of exports of goods and services. The Mexican group includes Central American, Dominican Republic and, of course, Mexico itself. The Brazilian group contains all South American countries plus Cuba in the Caribbean. Within those two groups, the first is badly affected while the second benefits.[64]

The Mexico–Brazil distinction refers to two different elements. The first one involves countries that export commodities and hence benefit from the high prices attached to it and countries that export manufactures and are harmed by Chinese competition. The second one mirrors, on a Latin American context, Ian Bremmer's categorisation between "pivot states" and "shadow states". The former are those that have been able to build profitable relationships with multiple economic partners without becoming overly reliant on any of them, while the latter are those that have tied their economic possibilities almost entirely to a single powerful partner. As a consequence "pivot states" can be more resilient and strong, given the diversity of its options, while "shadow" ones simply follow the fortune of its dominant partner.[65] While South American countries in general with Brazil and Chile in head have diversified their economic partners, Mexico, Central America and Dominican Republic have become overly reliant on the United States. And even though Mexico has signed 15 free trade agreements, in addition to NAFTA, 79% of its exports as well as the bulk of its currency remittances and direct foreign investments are related to a single partner: the United States

The Inter-American Development Bank, distinction, though, brings into consideration as well exports in services. This would include, by instance, a reduction in Mexico's airlines ticket sales or Costa Rica's call centres incomes as a result of the economic contraction in the United States. For the time being, this is something aside of our focus of analysis. The rest is perfectly valid for our purposes.

---

[64] Alejandro Izquierdo and Ernesto Talvi, coord., *One Region, Two Speeds?* (Washington D.C.: Inter-American Development Bank, March 2011).

[65] *Every Nation for Itself: Winners and losers in a G-Zero World* (New York: Portfolio, 2012).

Mexico, Dominican Republic (an island country in the Caribbean) and the Central American nations, excluding Panama, were negatively affected not only as net importers of commodities but also as exporters of manufactures to the American market. It has been estimated that between 2009 and 2011, Latin America ceased to export US$250 billion to the United States as a result of the latter economic contraction.[66] The hardest hit by this situation were clearly the Mexican-type countries.

On the other hand, Brazil and the rest of South American countries not only benefited from its condition of net exporters of commodities but by their wider access to other markets, with particular reference to China. Even if not a South American country, Cuba must be added in this group as it is, together with Chile, Brazil, Peru, Venezuela and Argentina, one of the main beneficiaries of this new trade wave with China. Moreover, in terms of percentage of its exports to China, Cuba is at the top of the group.[67] So, whenever reference is made to Brazilian-type economies (or commodity exporting South American nations), Cuba should be understood to be in the group even if not mentioned specifically. But, this clear cut distinction between net winners and losers is not straightforward as Brazil and other South American countries not only export commodities but manufactures as well. So, even if the overall economy of such countries benefits from the hike in the price of commodities, their industrial sectors are damaged as a result of the Chinese competition in its export and domestic markets.

Mexican-type economies

Let us begin with the losers. In the United States, the imports from China grew by 1.600% between 1990 and 2005.[68] The most affected

---

[66] Secretaría Permanente del Sistema Económico Latinoamericano y del Caribe, "Relaciones Económicas de Estados Unidos con los Países de América Latina y el Caribe en Época de Transición", Caracas (Mayo, 2012).
[67] CEPAL, *La República popular China y América Latina y el Caribe: Diálogo y Cooperación ante los Nuevos Desafíos de la Economía Mundial.*
[68] *Newsweek*, 9 May 2005.

Latin American countries were those in the direct line of fire of China: "Today, China is seen as most threatening to countries that rely mainly on labour-intensive manufactures and low wages for their export advantage."[69]

After the massacre caused in the industrial base of the region by the Washington Consensus policies, the so-called maquila system took hold in some of their countries. Such system is based in labour-intensive assembly lines that depends on foreign technology and supply chain and whose production goes to export markets. This is the case of Mexico, Central American countries and the Dominican Republic. Given the devaluation of Mexico's currency in 1994 and the North American Free Trade Agreement, it made very good sense to locate maquila factories in this neighbouring country. On the other hand, the proximity and the special access to the American market that benefited the Caribbean Basin Initiative member countries and, since 2005, the approval of the Dominican Republic and Central America Free Trade Agreement (with the United States), were the reasons for investing in maquila factories in those countries.

Countries heavily involved with the maquila system were hit harder than anyone else by Chinese competition: "China has significant comparative advantages in the product categories that are crucial to Mexico and countries in Central America (textiles, apparel, and electronics), in particular, because these countries specialise in the labour-intensive parts of the production chain in which China has an important comparative edge."[70] Mexico and Costa Rica standout in the high-tech exports sector. El Salvador, Nicaragua, Guatemala and the Dominican Republic specialise in the apparel, textile or shoes sectors in which Mexico and Costa Rica are also involved.

High technology as used in this case is a deceiving concept, though, as we talk of import parts of devices classified as high tech, that are simply assembled in labour-intensive production facilities, and then exported as final high-tech product. In the case of Mexico, more

---

[69] Inter-American Development, *The Emergence of China: Opportunities and Challenges for Latin America and the Caribbean* (Washington D.C.: March 2005), p. 69.
[70] *ibid.*, p. 96.

than 95% of all high-technology firms are just foreign assembly plants.[71] "Moreover, Mexico remains a low-wage assembly haven for US products and is not showing much of an increase in the sophistication of high-tech exports."[72] According to Kevin P. Gallager and Roberto Porzecanski:

> Between 2000 and 2006, 65% of Mexico's high-technology exports were under direct threat, amounting to 32% of all Mexico's exports. About 16.6% of Mexico's high-technology exports are under partial threat and represent 8.2% of total exports. Combined, 82% of Mexico's high-technology exports are under some sort of threat from China, comprising 40.1% of all Mexican exports .... In Costa Rica, 93.1% of its high-tech exports are under threat, representing almost 30% of the country's exports.[73]

Personal computers are a good example of such situation as Mexico's market share in United States imports went from 14% to 7% between 2001 and 2006, whereas China's share grew from 14% to 45% during the same period.[74]

In the apparel industry sector, countries such as El Salvador, Nicaragua, Guatemala and the Dominican Republic have experienced a significant decline not only in its sales to the United States but also in foreign direct investments. The model which is based on proximity, low wages, tax incentives for export-processing zones and special access to the United States, is being challenged to the bones by China.[75]

In 2003, China displaced Mexico as United States' second commercial partner and, according to the Latin American and the

---

[71] Kevin P. Gallager and Roberto Porzecanski, *op. cit.*

[72] *ibid.*, p. 81.

[73] *ibid.*, p. 68.

[74] Enrique Dussel Peters, "The Mexico-China Economic Relationship in Electronics: A Case Study of the PC Industry in Jalisco", in *The Impact of China's Global Economic Expansion on Latin America*, edited by Rhys Jenkins (Norwich: University of East Anglia Press, 2008).

[75] Inter-American Development Bank, *op. cit.*

Caribbean Economic System, "Mexico and China are rivals in the United States market where both countries are the second and first surplus's trade partners of the United States".[76] The reason why Mexico fell behind was clearly explained in a report prepared by the consulting firm McKinsey & Co at the end of 2003: a worker in a Mexican assembly line earned US$1.47 an hour, in comparison with US$0.59 for a worker in China. Not surprisingly, between 2000 and December 2003, 850 factories, whose production was directed to the United States, closed down in Mexico.[77] Moreover, not even the geographical proximity has been able to compensate for the difference in costs between Chinese and Mexican-type countries' products:

> China's shipping costs per kilogram are much higher than Latin America's. Unfortunately for Latin America, China's *ad valorem* cost (shipment cost per value) is comparable to or even lower than Latin America's, with the weight/value ratio for the goods playing the key role. In the aggregate, goods from China are 10 times lighter per dollar shipped than Central American goods, and 20 times lighter per dollar shipped than South American goods. In other words, any proximity advantage that Latin America enjoys in terms of shipping costs is completely lost as a result of its specialising in heavy, low-value products.[78]

But there is nonetheless a line of defence in heavy high-value products as Kevin P. Gallager and Roberto Porzecanski point out: "Mexico is losing out in sectors abundant in unskilled labour where value-to-transport costs are cheap. It is holding steady, instead, in assembly sectors such as trucks and autos, where transport costs are more significant and NAFTA's rules of origin serve as local content rules mandating that production stay in North America".[79]

---

[76] Sistema Económico Latinoamericano, "Las relaciones entre China y América Latina y el Caribe en la actual coyuntura económica mundial" (Caracas, septiembre 2012), p. 4.

[77] "Mexico: Was NAFTA worth it?", *BusinessWeek,* 22 December 2003.

[78] Inter-American Development Bank, *op. cit.*, p. 77.

[79] *op. cit.*, p. 93.

In 2006, 80% of all Mexican exports to the United States market (which represents 85% of total Mexican exports) were constituted by maquila manufactured products, which are the more affected by China's competition.[80] Conversely, 11 of the 20 products that comprise their most dynamic exports to the United States market are commodities, with oil and its derivatives playing a protagonist role here.[81] Exports from crude oil and its derivatives represent 16% of Mexican total exports.[82] In this area, Mexico differs from the Central American countries and from the Dominican Republic and approaches more to South America's export patterns, which is why it has not been as negatively affected as the rest of its group.

Unfortunately for Mexico, though, oil exports may not be there for much longer. The country depends heavily on oil revenues, which provide 30% to 40% of the government's fiscal revenues, but oil production in Mexico is declining rapidly. According to experts, Mexico could begin importing oil within 10 years.[83] "Mexico, the third largest supplier of foreign oil to the United States, could lose the capacity to export crude altogether within a decade ... The country's shift from exporter to importer would deal a severe blow to Mexico's federal government, which depends on oil sales for roughly a third of its budget... Production by Pemex, the national oil company, has fallen 25% from its peak in 2004, while internal demand has climbed, sharply curtailing the amount of crude available for export."[84] Recent discoveries in the Gulf of Mexico seem, nonetheless, to be challenging these assumptions. The potential of such discoveries has been estimated in a range that goes from 4.000 to 13.000 million barrels. They would have to be added to the 12.352 million barrels of proven,

---

[80] Juan Miguel González Peña, *op. cit.*

[81] Kevin P. Gallager and Roberto Porzecanski, *op. cit.*

[82] Mejía Reyes Pablo y Carbajal Suárez Yolanda, "Comportamiento de las exportaciones mexicanas ante la desaceleración estadounidense", *Revista Trimestral de Coyuntura Económica*, México D.F., (Julio-Septiembre 2008.)

[83] M. Angeles Villarreal, "The Mexican Economy after the Global Financial Crisis", Congressional Research Service, Washington D.C. (9 September 2010).

[84] John Collins Rudolf, "Mexico oil exports could end within a decade", *New York Times*, 29 April 2011.

possible and probable reserves (the so-called 3Ps) that Mexico has today, giving the country a few additional years as an oil exporter.[85]

So, even though oil revenues are a fundamental part of Mexico's economy, the bulk of its exports are represented by manufactures. These are the most affected by China: "99% of Mexico's manufacturing exports are under some kind of threat from China, representing 72% of Mexico's entire exports."[86] It would be interesting to add that Mexico has been overflowed in recent years by Chinese products while its exports to China have been modest. In 2010, Mexican imports represented US$41.409 million while Mexican exports to China were just US$8.396 million.[87] In 2011, China represented less than 2% of total Mexican exports while 15% of its imports came from this Asian country. As a matter of fact, Mexico's trade deficit with China is responsible for an overwhelming majority of Latin America's trade deficit with the latter. Otherwise, trade equilibrium between China and Latin American economies would be the case.[88]

It seems thus that Mexico is been negatively affected in many fronts: by the loss of imports from the United States, by the concomitant loss of foreign investments that have been redirected to China and by the loss of parcels of its domestic market to the Chinese competition. Moreover, it is also been hurt by the need to import commodities whose prices have experimented important hikes as a result of China's demand. Having had to sacrifice a big share of its agricultural sector, as a trade off for the American Congress to approve the NAFTA agreement, Mexico finds itself in the need to import many food requirements that it once produced. In 2011 Mexico was the world's second-largest importer of corn and the third-largest importer of soy. At the end of the day, there is just one area where Mexico indirectly benefits from China's emergence: the price of oil. Not surprisingly, Mexico's relations with China are currently at its lowest level since they opened diplomatic relations 40 years ago.[89]

---

[85] EFE, "Hallazgo de pozo petrolero confirma 'enorme" potencial en el Golfo de México", 5 de octubre 2012.

[86] Kevin P. Gallager and Roberto Porzecanski, *op. cit.*, 51.

[87] Juan Miguel González Peña, *op. cit.*

[88] CEPAL, *La República popular China y América Latina y el Caribe: Diálogo y Cooperación ante los Nuevos Desafíos de la Economía Mundial.*

[89] Sistema Económico Latinoamericano, "Las relaciones entre China y América Latina y el Caribe en la actual coyuntura económica mundial", *op. cit.*; Andre Loes, *op. cit.*

Some analysts believe, though, that as China's salaries increase the attractiveness of Mexico for American investors will also do so, favouring what has been called as "near-shoring". The important increase in exports and investments in the flat screen and in the mobile device sectors in Mexico have been mentioned as good examples in this direction. Nonetheless, according to the Economic Commission for Latin America and the Caribbean, the advantage of China is not only related to salaries but also to its highly developed and flexible chains of production and clusters as well as to its superb infrastructure.[90] Moreover, as we shall see later on, Asia's chains of productions, posses a tremendous challenge to any Latin American economy wanting to compete in terms of low salaries. Within them the different components of any given product are manufactured where the lowest wages for that particular segment can be found and later assembled were export logistics is better.

There are, nonetheless, two main industrial areas where Mexico is little affected by China: natural resources' processing industries and manufacturing sectors where transport costs from East Asia become relevant (heavy-high-value products). The former includes petrochemical and steel products, cement, beer, spirits or food-processing industries, while the latter includes the automotive, airplane or electric power equipment industries, where direct foreign investments in assembly lines is very important. In those sectors, foreign investments and manufacturing exports have remained unchallenged in Mexico.

As for Mexican-type economies' exports to China, there is not much to be said. Less than 2% of Mexico's exports, as already mentioned, go to that market. For the rest of the countries of that group, opportunities are very small. The only exception is Costa Rica that benefits from having diplomatic relations with China, which is not the case for most of the others that still recognise Taiwan. As a consequence, this country is able to export some electronic parts and components to the Asian giant. Nonetheless, trade balance between two of them clearly benefits China whose exports to Costa Rica amounted to US$3.107 million in 2010, while in the opposite direction they only amounted to US$688 million.[91]

[90] *idem*.

[91] Sistema Económico Latinoamericano, "Las relaciones entre China y América Latina y el Caribe en la actual coyuntura económica mundial", *op. cit.*

Brazilian-type economies

On the other side of the fence, we find the winners from China's sudden appearance in the neighbourhood. The convergence between two giants: a commodities consumer and a commodities producer, makes this relation a very particular one. On the one hand, the consumer giant represented by China was responsible in 2011 of the percentage of world demand shown in Table 3.

Among the many commodities of which China is the world's largest consumer we can mention copper, lead, zinc, tin, nickel, aluminium,

Table 3. China Percentage of World Demand in Commodities

Coal	49.9%
Iron ore	47.7%
Pigs	46.4%
Steel	45.4%
Lead	44.6%
Zinc	41.3%
Aluminium	40.6%
Copper	38.9%
Eggs	37.2%
Nickel	36.3%
Rice	28.1%
Soybeans	24.6%
Wheat	16.6%
Chickens	15.6%
Oil	10.3%
Cattle	9.5%

Source: China's Demand, World Commodity Prices and the Australian Economy.[92]

[92] *Connect the Dots*, 4 July 2011, <http://ctdtoday.com/2011/07/04/chinas-demand-world-commodity-prices-and-the-australian-economy/>.

meat, soy, rice, wheat, tea, rubber, raw wool, cotton, oil seeds and coal, while it is the second largest consumer of oil and corn.[93]

According to the International Energy Agency, in 2035, China will be consuming a fifth of the global energy, which would represent a 75% increase in relation to 2008.[94] There is also the need to feed a population of 1.3 billion human beings whose living standards are rapidly escalating. And, of course, there is a gigantic infrastructure and urbanisation development process in course which James Kynge describes as follows:

> In China, the urbanisation is still an infant. There are approximately 400 million people living in big and small cities at this moment, but by 2050 it is expected this number will rise to 600 or 700 millions to reach a billion or 1.1 billion people. The investment required to accommodate so many people in an urban environment is impossible to calculate precisely, but it is clear that the global demand of steel, aluminium, copper, nickel, iron, oil, gas, carbon and many other raw materials and resources will remain strong as long as urbanisation in China reaches its limits.[95]

Between 2002 and 2005, China was responsible for almost all the global growth in the demand of nickel, as well as 50% of the global growth of copper and aluminium.[96] In 2004, China became the largest coal consumer in the world and surpassed Japan as the second largest oil consumer after the United States.[97] Between 2005 and 2011, commodity prices, pushed in large extent by China's consumption, increased in the following percentages: rubber 330.8; cotton 280.8; tin 250.0; sugar 248.0; palm oil 212.7; corn 210.1; copper 199.7; coconut

---

[93] The Economist, *Pocket World in Figures: 2012 Edition* (London: Profile Books Ltd., 2012).

[94] Niall Ferguson, "El Reino del Centro vuelve al foco del escenario", *Vanguardia Dossier*, No. 42 (Marzo 2012); CEPAL, *La República popular China y América Latina y el Caribe: Diálogo y Cooperación ante los Nuevos Desafíos de la Economía Mundial.*

[95] *China Shakes the World* (London: Phoenix, 2006), p. 29.

[96] Bernardo Kosacoff and Sebastián Campanario, *op. cit.*

[97] Juan Miguel González Peña, *op. cit.*

oil 197.2; soya oil 186.1; wheat 169.7; soybeans 159.7; coffee 149.5; lead 144.0; oil 116.3; tea 103.2, cocoa 98.8; rice 89.2; nickel 69.1; lamb 66.7; beef 31.7; aluminium 30.9.[98]

South America, on the other hand, is a commodity producer giant that expresses its might in several fields. The first of them is food where it is becoming the "Farm of the World." As Mariano Turzi explains:

> America's economic power, in particular, rested on a secure and steady supply of oil from the Middle East ... And countries like Saudi Arabia, Iran and Iraq became important to US foreign policy. An underappreciated parallel is developing in the world's political economy today — but this time, grain replaces oil, China stands in for the United States, and South America plays the Middle East's role. Indeed, as climate constrains and demographic imperatives make food security an ever more critical issue, agricultural resources may become the new linchpin in international relations. In a world where soil trumps oil, South American agricultural producers, with their vast amounts of fertile land and water, might see their geopolitical positions greatly improved.[99]

Since 1990, the productivity of the farming sector in Latin America has grown faster than that of the United States and East Asia. Latin America represents 40% of global agricultural exports while, according to the General Director of the Inter-American Institute for Agricultural Cooperation, Victor Villalobos, 42% of the world's potential for growth in agriculture lies in Latin America.[100] Good example of this is Brazil which ranks No. 1 worldwide in the production of coffee, sugar and orange juice and No. 2 in soy products, and which is the second largest exporter of corn and the third largest exporter of soybean in the world.[101] But, food in South America is not only agricultural products as the region also tops the world in several animal exports items.

---

[98] The Economist, *op. cit.*

[99] "Grown in the Cone: South America's Soybean Boom", *Current History*, Vol. 111, No. 742 (February 2012), p. 50.

[100] Sunny George Verghese, "The Latin America-Asia Partnership", Latin Asia Business Forum 2012, Singapore, 3 October, 2012; "Latinoamérica reúne el 42% del potencial de expansión agraria", Agencia EFE, 2 de junio, 2012.

[101] "It's only natural", Special Report: Latin America, *The Economist*, 11 September 2010; Andre Loes, *op. cit.*

In poultry export ranking, Brazil occupies the No. 1 global position.[102] The same is true in the case of beef where Brazil is the world's leading exporter, having expanded its national herd 24% and its exports up over 450% in volume and 385% in value since 1994. As for Argentina, most sources estimate that its herd volume is around 50 to 55 million heads with exports reaching 720,000 tonnes in 2006.[103]

Regarding oil, Venezuela's proven oil reserves surpassed those of Saudi Arabia in 2010 when 296.5 billion barrels in reserves where certified.[104] Nonetheless, the estimates of those reserves are substantially bigger, doubling those of Saudi Arabia: "Scientists working for the US Geological Survey say Venezuela's Orinoco belt holds twice as much petroleum as previously thought. The geologists estimate the area could yield more than 500 billion barrels of crude oil. The USGS team gave a mean estimate of 513 billion barrels of 'technically recoverable' oil in the Orinoco belt".[105] It should be added that those are reserves with minimal exploration and geological risk involved. But it is not only Venezuela. According to some experts, Brazil's gigantic off-shore oil reserves could reach up to 100 billion barrels of oil. Moreover:

> Colombia's oil production is climbing so fast that it is closing on Algeria's and could hit Libya's pre-war level in a few years. Exxon Mobil is striking new deals in Argentina, which recently heralded its biggest oil discovery since the 1980s. For the first time in decades, the emerging prize in global energy may be the Americas ... As said by Amy Myers Jaffe, associate director of Rice University's Energy Program in Houston 'This should make the world's megasuppliers nervous, since the pendulum has already begun to move in this direction'.[106]

---

[102] Luiz Sesti, "Brazilian broiler production", <http://www.polutrymed.com/Poultry/SendFile.aspDBID=1&LNGDID=1>.

[103] Carlos Steiger, "Moder beef production in Brazil and Argentina", *Choices: The Magazine of Food, Farm and Resources Issues* (Second Quarter 2006).

[104] Benoit Faucon, "Venezuela's oil reserves topped Saudis in 2010", *The Wall Street Journal*, 18 July 2011.

[105] "Venezuela oil may double Saudis", *BBC News*, 23 January 2010, <http://news.bbc.co.uk/2/hi/8476395.stm>.

[106] Simon Romero, "The Americas regain the title of oil titans", *International Herald Tribune*, 21 September 2011.

Indeed, the bulk of oil reserves are beginning to shift from the Middle East to the Americas (which include as well the huge Canadian oil sands reserves and the U.S. oil shale and offshore reserves). As Andrés Cala clearly explains: "So while the US is preoccupied with containing Chinese surging ambitions in Asia ... the biggest contributors to oil production in the future, are just south of its border."[107] In addition to oil, there are also other sources of exportable energy where South America enjoys a very relevant position. Brazil is the international leader and the largest world exporter of ethanol, while with 7,001 million tonnes it also has the 10th largest coal reserves in the world. Within South America, Colombia follows in world coal reserves with the number 12 position representing 6,672 million tonnes. As for gas proven reserves, Venezuela is in the number 9 world position with 178,860 billion cubic feet.[108]

As for mining, few regions can compete with South America. Chile is the No. 1 copper producer in the world while Peru is at No. 3. At the same time, the latter is the world's largest producer of silver, the second of zinc, the fourth of lead and the sixth of gold. Brazil, on its part, ranks third in the world in the production of iron ore, manganese, aluminium and ferroalloys, fourth in tin, sixth in gold, eighth in steel and represents 92.4% of the world's production of columbium. Cuba ranks sixth in the world in nickel production and accounts for 8% of the global cobalt production. And so on.[109]

This gathering of the commodities giants (consumer and producer) is proving to be of fundamental importance for both parties.

---

[107] "Should the US worry about China's Latin American inroads?", *Energy Tribune*, 31 October 2011.

[108] Fabiana Frayssinet, "Biocombustibles luego de la euforia", *IPS*, 12 de febrero, 2012; World Energy Council, *2010 Survey of Energy Resources* (London: 2010); "Countries with the largest coal proven reserves", aneki.com: rankings and records; "World's top 22 natural gas proven reserves holders", *Petroleum Insights*, 1 January 2011, <http://petroleuminsights.com/2011/03/worlds-top-22-natural-gas-proven.html>.

[109] Leia Michele Toovey "Copper mining in Chile", *Copper Investing News*, 3 February 2011; Leia Michele Toovey, "Copper mining in Peru", 13 February 2012; "Brazil mining and industry", *Zimbio*, 14 November 2011; *MBendi Information Services*, 22 November 2011; Andre Loes, *op. cit.*

Since 2004, China exceeded the United States as the largest world consumer of grain and meat, when it reached a demand of 382 million tonnes of grain and 64 million tonnes of meat.[110] In just one decade, China turned into the largest soybean importer in the world, consuming 35 million tonnes a year and since 2006 Brazil became China's first international provider of soybean, exceeding 10 million tonnes of annual exports to that market.[111] Brazil and Argentina together represent 45% of the global exports of soy. Not surprisingly, Brazil and Argentina exports to China were multiplied by 10. At the same time, those two countries account for 20% of the Chinese import of meat, while Peru fulfils 45% of China's animal food consumption.[112]

In relation to oil, Thomas L. Friedman says: "If current trends hold, China will go from importing 7 million barrels of oil today to 14 million a day by 2012. For the world to accommodate that increase it would have to find another Saudi Arabia."[113] As seen, Venezuela, Brazil and the other South American producers will be in position to provide such additional oil with Venezuela alone probably duplicating Saudi Arabia's reserves.

Not surprisingly, between 1999 and 2003, Brazilian exports to China grew 525% while the export percentage for the rest of the world was 52%. While in 2000, Brazil exported US$1,000 million to China in 2010 it exported US$30,785 million. Of such amount 83.7% corresponded to commodities.[114] As for total Latin American exports in 2010, those directed to China grew 51% which doubled the average of the regional exports grow that year.[115]

In conclusion and as well-known Spanish scholar Xulio Rios clearly points out: "Beijing requires huge amounts of natural resources to nurture its amazing growth rates. It cannot pass over the fact that

[110] Juan Miguel González Peña, *op. cit.*

[111] *International Herald Tribune*, 6 April 2007.

[112] Bernardo Kosacoff and Sebastian Campanario, *op. cit.*

[113] *The World is Flat* (London: Penguin Books, 2006), p. 500.

[114] Juan Miguel González Peña, *op. cit.*

[115] Julio A. Díaz Vásquez, "China-Latinoamérica: relaciones económicas 2010", *Jiexi Zhonguuo: Análisis y Pensamiento Iberoamericano sobre China*, Número 2 (Primer Trimestre 2012), pp. 16–22.

Latin America possesses 15% of the world oil reserves, 25% of the world agricultural lands, 30% the world water and 40% of the world gold and copper reserves".[116]

Given its low per capita income, China has much to catch up with. This country will surpass in size America's GDP when its per capita income becomes a quarter of that of the United States. Hereafter, as mentioned before, its population dimension would allow China several additional decades of sustained economic growth at high rates. According to many economists, this guarantees an expansive cycle for Latin American commodities similar to the one that took place at the end of the 19th century and beginning of the 20th century. A cycle supported by structural conditions and, therefore, likely to continue for a sustained period: "... the connection with China for many of the Latin American countries has been dominated by the complementarities between the region's natural resource abundance and China's commodity-intensive growth pattern. The connection to China has thus raised expectations that Latin American countries may achieve ... high long-term growth in the future".[117]

And, of course, it is not just China's direct demand of Latin American commodities which is relevant, but also the fact that the international prices of such commodities have been boosted by China's demand. It has been argued that in 2006 just 10 sectors in six countries comprised 91% of all Latin American exports to China.[118] Since then, Latin American commodities' exports to China have expanded significantly, but even if that were still the case, it would not matter much in as long as the prices of commodities were in the rise thanks to that country.

For the Latin American group of commodities exporters to China, this nation is also becoming a source of investment with enormous potential. This reached new momentum on 9 March 2007, when the Chinese government announced the creation of a special agency, the China Investment Corporation, with the intention of investing abroad an important part of its international reserves whose

[116] "Crédito y descrédito en América Latina", *Jiexi Zhonguuo: Análisis y Pensamiento Iberoaméricano sobre China*, *ibid.*, p. 23.
[117] World Bank, *op. cit.*, p. 43.
[118] Kevin P. Gallager and Roberto Porzecanski, *op. cit.*

amount had already reached US$2.45 trillion in 2010. "Analysts say that the agency could assign hundreds of billions of dollars to acquire strategic assets around the world, particularly in developing countries of Africa and Latin America. 'They are not looking for financial assets, but for assets of energy, minerals and natural resources, things that China desperately needs', pointed out J. Ulrich of J.P. Morgan".[119]

China's investments and loans

According to the Economic Commission for Latin American and the Caribbean, total foreign investment in Latin America grew by about 40% in 2010 to US$113 billion with China representing the fastest growing investor with an amount of US$15.3 billion. China's investment in that year accounted for 9% of the total, becoming the region's third largest investor. Moreover, it was expected that China would increase substantially its investments in subsequent years. About 90% of China's confirmed investments in Latin America targeted the extraction of natural resources.[120] According to Andrés Cala in October 2011, China was likely becoming the top tnvestor in Latin American for that year with the lion share of such investments directed to the energy sector.[121]

In the near future, investments are planned to expand to more areas as well as more countries: "More Latin American countries will obtain foreign direct investment from China, said Zhu Xinqiang, Vice-governor of the Export-Import Bank of China ... At the same time, more investment will be put into infrastructure, construction, high tech and agricultural projects in Latin America. In the past three years, China's investment in Latin America mainly centred on natural resources."[122] This widening of the investment scope responds to the

---

[119] Jim Yardley and David Barboza, "China acts to become a huge global investor", *International Herald Tribune*, 10 March 2007.

[120] *Foreign Direct Investment in Latin America and the Caribbean 2010* (Santiago de Chile: ECLAC, 2010).

[121] *op. cit.*

[122] Su Zhou, "China to diversify Latin America investment", *Chinadaily.com.cn*, 13 September 2011, <http://usa.chinadaily.com.cn/business/2011-09/13/content_13678038.htm>.

demands of several Latin American governments unsatisfied with the current trend of trade and investments, labelled by some critics as neo-colonial. A good example of this was the request by Brazilian President Dilma Roussef during her April 2011 trip to Beijing to obtain from China infrastructural investment, transfer of technology and creation of local employment.[123]

But, at the same time, this results from the need to become more creative when confronted with investments' limitations in the commodity sector: "Due to stricter regulation of foreign land ownership in Brazil and Argentina, China has changed its investment model, investing in infrastructure rather than land ... Chinese investors have changed their model to one in which deals are structured as infrastructure investments in exchange for crop offtake, rather than direct investment into farmland".[124]

A good example of the above would be the lease of 320,000 hectares (877.120.000 acres) for a 20 year period by the Argentinean Province of Rio Negro to China's Heilngjiang Beidahuang State Farms Business Trade Group. According to this deal, China has agreed to invest in infrastructure development such as irrigation system and similar in exchange for a land lease whose aim is producing crops to be sold exclusively to China.[125] Needless to say that even though land acquisition may not be involved in these cases, the possibility of land grabs investments is very much present. That is why this is an area where national legislations should define the limits to what can be lease (or sold) to foreign companies.

It should be added that thanks to the revalorisation in the price of commodities, in which China's demand played such an important role, important investments from other sources have also materialised. According to London's Institute of International and Strategic Studies, Latin America received US$113.000 million in direct foreign

---

[123] *El País*, 8 de noviembre 2011.

[124] "Rabobank Report: China's increasing investments in South American Agribusiness", *Bloomberg*, 28 July 2011.

[125] Mariano Turzi, *op. cit.*; Fernardo Glenza, "Argentina: La Soberanía en jaque", Agencia Periodística de Mercosur, 11 de junio 2011.

investments in 2010, 90% of which were directed to natural resources extraction.[126]

But not only through investments but also through credits, is China's presence felt in the commodities producing countries of the region. The rationality behind those credits is again to gain access to such commodities: "Debts owed to China by these Latin American countries will be paid back in commodities, especially in oil shipments."[127] In that sense, credits become tantamount to investments:

> Chinese firms are adapting quickly and deal structures are getting more creative. A notable example is 2009's Sinopec/China Development Bank's US$10 billion loan to Brazil's Petrobras. The Brazilian firm found world-class offshore deposits and needed large amounts of capitals to finance the extraction. Unlike other transactions, the deal did not involve an equity stake in Petrobras. It was structured instead a standard off-take agreement. The Chinese will get 150,000 bbl/d of oil in year one and 200,000, bbl/d of oil for nine additional years. In return, Petrobras gets a low-interest 6.5% loan of US$10 billion. According to the contract, the oil will be sold to Sinopec at 'market prices' and paid in cash.[128]

As mentioned before, since 2005 China's Development Bank and other institutions have spent an estimated US$75 billion on financial investments in South America, which is more than the World Bank, the US Export Bank and the Inter-American Development Bank put together. According to the Inter-American Dialogue, a Washington D.C. think tank, in 2010 China lent to Latin America US$37 billion, which again was more than the US$30 billion that the World Bank,

[126] "Inversiones extranjeras directas en América Latina en 2010", *El Universal*, 6 de septiembre 2011.

[127] Bryan Le, "China's direct investment in Latin America a 'tipping point'", Associated Press, 8 June 2011.

[128] Erik Bethel, "Why is China investing in Latin America's natural resources", *Seeking Alpha*, 21 December 2011, <http://seekingalpha.com/article/315266-why-is-china-investing-in-latin-america-s-natural-resources>.

the Inter-American Bank and US Export and Import Bank combinedly lent to the region during that year.[129]

China's loans, it must be emphasised, come with no macroeconomic or ideological strings attached which, for a region that was ravaged by the impositions of the International Monetary Fund or the World Bank, is a refreshing situation. All that China is interested in is access to commodities. The only risks faced by South America's countries are those derived from an asymmetric power of negotiation and by China's toughness as a negotiator. As for the latter point, the following remarks by former German Minister of Foreign Affairs Joschka Fisher are enlightening: "China will become a largely inward-looking superpower, which — precisely for that reason — will pursue its foreign policy interests in a completely unsentimental manner."[130] In other words, its raw national interest precludes any other consideration, making it a very tough interlocutor. But, in as long as South American countries show clarity in identifying its own interests and resolution in defending them, China remains a better alternative than the traditional multilateral lenders or the private banking sector.

Venezuela, who enjoys of a strategic association for joint development with China, is a good example of this combination of investments and loans that has been translated in numerous development projects. Some of those projects are based in Venezuela while others, benefiting Venezuela as well, are based in China. Among the former, we find several Chinese joint ventures with Venezuela's counterparts: CNCP, SINOPEC and CNOOC participating in oil and gas developments in association with Venezuela's State oil company PDVSA (Junín 1, Junín 4, Junín 8, Boyacá 4 and MP3 blocks in the Orinoco heavy oil belt and offshore Mariscal Sucre gas project in the country's eastern coast); China's CTPDC and PDVSA creating a company for manufacturing oil drills in Venezuela; China's Chinalco and RPC investing in the aluminium sector and in agricultural infrastructural developments; China Railway Engineering Corporation building a

[129] "China presto más a América Latina que los entes multilaterales", *El Universal*, 17 de febrero 2012.

[130] "China a different type of superpower", *The Straits Times*, 7 October 2010.

speed rail line across the centre of the country; China Harbour Engineering Corporation building a new terminal in the Puerto Cabello harbour and projecting to build seven new thermoelectric facilities; China Construction Corporation planning to dredge the Orinoco river; Metallurgical Corporation of China going forward with the expansion of the Paula port; Wuhan Iron and Steel, Metallurgical Group Corporation and China Communications Construction Company engaging in mining related activities; China's ZTE, Huawei, Lanchao, Haier, Chery and XCMG, in joint ventures with Venezuelan companies, manufacturing mobile phones, personal computers, home appliances, automobiles and heavy equipment in Venezuela. As of end of 2011, Venezuela had a portfolio of over US$25 billion in projects being funded by China Development Bank.[131]

Conversely, other projects with Venezuela's economic participation are based in China. PDVSA has signed joint ventures with CNCP and Petro China for the construction of three refineries for processing the South American country's heavy oil and four 320.000 tonnes VLCC super tankers (the firsts of many others to come). The construction of the first of such refineries, which is already in motion, and that of the super tankers, takes place in Guangdong province. In another area, China launched two satellites in 2008 and 2012, respectively, whose construction was also co-financed by Venezuela. The agreements between the parties not only included building the satellites but also the transfer of technology and the training of technicians in the several disciplines involved for the direct control of operations by Venezuela.[132]

Many of the above-mentioned projects are been financed through a Chinese–Venezuelan investment fund that began operating in 2007

[131] Silvia Hernández Rada, "Venezuela y China: Relaciones económicas en el régimen de Hugo Chávez (1999–2011)", *Observatorio de la Economía y Sociedad China*, Universidad de Málaga, número 15 (Junio, 2011); Evan Ellis, "The Expanding Chinese Footprint in Latin America", *Asie Visions 49*, Institut Francais de Relations Internationales, Center for Asian Studies (Paris: February 2012).

[132] "Venezuela-China", Special Supplement celebrating the 38th Aniversary of Diplomatic Ties, *ChinaDaily*, 28 June 2012.

and whose aim is the development of joint projects. Until November 2011, China had committed US$32 billion to that fund.[133]

When companies like ZTE, Huawei, Lanchao, Haier, Chery and XCMG manufacture, through joint ventures with Venezuelan ones, mobile phones, personal computers and laptops, home appliances, automobiles and heavy equipment, the benefits for the host country are multiple: it does not have to import those products from China, local jobs are created, technology is transferred and the consumer enjoys of low priced products. If this model could be replicated around South America, the common complain of exporting commodities and importing manufactures, would certainly diminish.

The above-mentioned complain clearly relates to the third and intermediate position between the two clear-cut previous ones: countries that benefit in certain areas but are affected in others. Indeed, on the one hand, we have the so-called Mexico-type countries that have been negatively affected by China's emergence and, on the other hand, we have the Brazil-type countries that benefit not only from its commodities' exports but also from China's investments and loans. In between, we find those that benefit from the latter but are at the same time negatively impacted as a consequence of losing space for their manufactures both in their domestic and export markets. South American countries that still retain an important industrial base clearly fit this mould.

The in between economies

Indeed, within South America, we find some commodities' producers that still retain relevant manufacturing capabilities. Brazil and Argentina would stand up in this group. Conversely, there is a second group of countries for which manufactured exports are clearly less significant than commodities' exports. Chile is a good example of the

[133] Juan Paullier, ¿Por qué Venezuela necesita préstamos de China para producir petróleo?, 25 de noviembre 2011, BBC Mundo, <http://www.bbc.co.uk-mundo-noticias-2011-11-111123_venezuela-pdvsa-prestamo-china_2_cch.shtml>.

latter. This country underwent a very purposeful transformation into a commodities' producer while the rest of the region was still involved in import-substitution. Indeed, together with Venezuela and Peru, Chile still relies on commodities for more than three-quarters of their total exports.[134] Uruguay, Colombia, Ecuador, Bolivia or Paraguay would also fall on this side of the fence. So, while this second group of countries mainly benefits from China, the former is in a more nuanced situation. Nations such as Brazil and Argentina have experienced, thanks to China, important growth rates, positive trade balances and strong accumulation of reserves. But, on the other hand, their industrial sectors are shrinking.

Over 90% of Brazilian and Argentinean manufactured exports are under threat due to China's competition. But while manufacturing exports in Mexico represents 72% of its total exports, they just represent 39% in the case of Brazil and 27% in the case of Argentina.[135] Nonetheless, even if the impact of such a threat is substantially lower than in the case of Mexico, and the benefits deriving from the exports of their commodities much higher, it is a very important problem as it implies the potential destruction of a significant part of its manufacturing base.

The high-tech sector is particularly affected in the case of Brazil as 96.7% of the country's high-technology exports, representing 7.2% of all its exports, are being menaced by China. It must be added thus that, unlike Mexico, a fundamental part of Brazilian high tech is endogenously generated. For Argentina and Colombia, around half of all high-technology exports are under threat, but in neither case these do not signify over 2% of total exports.[136]

On top of it, Chinese products also compete inside their domestic markets. "Latin American manufacturing imports from China grew much more between 2000 and 2006 than manufacturing imports from the rest of the world. In fact, while the rate of growth on average for the top 20 Chinese imports was 570%, it was only 89% for

[134] "It's only natural", *The Economist*, *op. cit.*
[135] Kevin P. Gallager and Roberto Porzecanski, *op. cit.*
[136] *ibid.*

the rest of the world for those same 20 products".[137] That immense difference has not only cornered other foreign imports but local producers as well. Displacement of local production by Chinese imports has been high in some of the following sectors: machinery and equipments; textiles, garments and shoes; rubber and plastic products; products derived from metals and chemicals and pharmaceutical.[138]

Brazil and Argentina have not only reacted by imposing tariffs on some Chinese products but are, at the same time, the two Latin American countries with more trade disputes with China:

> The structure of trade with China has brought the subject of deindustrialisation to the discussion table with the displacement of the Brazilian industry from its domestic and regional markets and a return to a primary export economy ... This has resulted in an increasing number of commercial disputes with China, in a wide range of areas, within WTO. Brazil is, together with Argentina, one of the two main regional litigants against China within WTO.[139]

The great majority of anti-dumping investigations initiated in Latin America have originated in the three countries with larger manufacturing capacities: Brazil, Mexico and Argentina. Of those investigations, 49% were initiated by Argentina, 28% by Brazil and 11% by Mexico.[140] The nature of the bilateral trade has aggravated the situation as in 2010, 83.7% of Brazilian exports to China where commodities and 97.5% of imports from China where manufactures, while 95.8% of Argentinean exports to China where commodities and 99.3% of the imports from China where manufactures.[141]

So, while domestic and export markets for manufactures from both Brazil and Argentina are overwhelmed by Chinese goods, China

[137] *ibid.*, p. 55.

[138] CEPAL, *La República popular China y América Latina y el Caribe: Diálogo y Cooperación ante los Nuevos Desafíos de la Economía Mundial.*

[139] Juan Miguel González Peña, *op. cit.*, pp. 13, 14.

[140] CEPAL, *La República popular China y América Latina y el Caribe: Diálogo y Cooperación ante los Nuevos Desafíos de la Economía Mundial.*

[141] Juan Miguel González Peña, *op. cit.*

mainly imports commodities from them. For a high-tech producer such as Brazil, this has been considered to be tantamount to a neo-colonial tainted relation. As a result of pressures from Brazil, though, China agreed to increase the import of Brazilian manufactured products, a good example of which was the acquisition in 2011 of 135 "Embraer 190" airplanes.[142]

As we can see for both Brazil and Argentina, the relation with China is not essentially determined by costs as in the case of Mexico or by benefits as in the case of Chile, but it entails a complex relation of benefits as well as costs. And even if in short-term basis the benefits prevail, in medium- and long-term ones the costs deriving from increased deindustrialisation may be high.

So, there are winners and losers (and in betweens) in Latin America regarding China, but the fact is that even in the best of circumstances, Latin America is just consolidating a primary-export model as the prevailing pattern of its international trade. According to a special report on Latin America published by the World Bank on September 2010, more than 90% of its citizens are located in countries that are exporters of commodities (which includes Mexico as an oil exporter), more than 97% of its GDP comes from such countries, and in 2008 the exports of commodities of the seven largest Latin American countries reached an historical high of almost US$400 billion. Moreover, as observed by HSBC, 74% of South American exports are comprised by commodities and the volumes involved in 2011 (US$462 billion) has transformed this region in the undisputed global chief commodity exporter.[143]

Commodities: Curse or development opportunity?

Nonetheless, one should add that the complexities or the value-add by the commodities business should not be downplayed. There are

---

[142] Georgina Higueras, "El gigante asiático devora las materias primas de la región", *El País*, 8 de noviembre 2011.

[143] "It's only natural", *The Economist*, *op. cit.*; "Reporte del Banco Mundial sobre América Latina", *Observatorio Petrolero Sur*, 20 de septiembre 2010; Andre Loes, *op. cit*

striking instances of the expertise required to establish and develop a globally competitive commodities business. We only have to take a look at some of them. From the marketing ingenuity of Colombian coffee producers to extract a brand premium to its generic coffee, and then successfully diversifying into retailing with its international chain of Juan Valdez coffee shops, to the logistics, technical or marketing requirements to respond to the preferences of grape consumers in different parts of the world by Chileans grape producers. From the logistics required to place and distribute a perishable commodity such as flowers in the American, European and Asian markets by the Ecuadoreans or Colombian producers to the highly successful commercial farming in Peru's fertile coastal strip. From the world class home grown biotech and genetic developments attained by Brazilians in agriculture or cattle raising to Argentina's shown capacity to build the largest vegetable-oil complex in the world. From the Brazilian capability to drill for oil at high deep waters to the Venezuelan control of the downstream and upstream part of the oil business (from exploring and extracting oil to transporting, refining and directly servicing the customers through its own network of refineries and petrol stations in different parts of the world). To be globally competitive in the commodities sector is by no means an easy or elemental task.

Much to the contrary, this has become an increasingly sophisticated sector: "In sum, there is spotty but robust evidence that Latin American countries have been not only moving towards the production of more sophisticated and higher-value-added products within its natural resource-based industries but clustering and production chains are being developed."[144]

It happens, though, that countries overly dependent on natural resources have a tendency to deindustrialise as exports of such resources drives up the value of their currencies making the exports of manufactures less competitive. It is the so-called Dutch disease. That creates a vicious circle where industries are increasingly threatened. And, as the history of the region clearly shows, to become

[144] World Bank, *op. cit.*, p. 37.

dependent on commodities is to be at mercy of economic cycles and high volatility.

Alternatively, it could be argued that dependence on commodities would just reflect a classical international distribution of labour based on comparative advantages. In pure David Ricardo's terms, every country or region has to emphasise those productive sectors where it can become really competitive, letting their own consumers benefit from imports coming from the low-cost producers. If the economy grows, positive trade balances are obtained, strong accumulation of reserves takes place and domestic consumers have access to more affordable goods, then the benefits exceed the costs of contraction of the manufacturing sector. It should not be forgotten that Chile did exactly that, with excellent results, when the rest of Latin America still believed in the import-substituting model.

Not surprisingly, this increased dependence on commodities has generated conflicting points of views by two important multilateral bodies. While the World Bank presents a fairly positive interpretation of such phenomenon, the Economic Commission for Latin America and the Caribbean is mainly pessimistic. For the former, if it had not been for the commodities' export boom, Latin America would not have had the economic strength and resilience to the world economic crisis that it showed. ECLAC, on the other hand, believes that the region is establishing in the 21st century a pattern of relation with China that mirrors the export structure that prevailed during the 19th century.

According to the World Bank, the extreme regional dependence on natural resources should not be seen as a "curse" but, much to the contrary, as a development opportunity. For this institution, there is not much evidence to support the idea that commodities represent an area of slow growth in productivity or that they have a lower potential for generating a positive economic outcome. In the long run, what is important is to administer well this period of bonanza, investing its benefits in human development, infrastructure and innovation so as to guarantee a sustainable growth.[145]

---

[145] *ibid.*; Emily Sinnot, John Nash and Augusto de la Torre, *op. cit.*

For Osvaldo Rosales, Director of International Trade and Integration of ECLAC, the question to be raised is if the nature of the economic association with China would allow for the kind of development that Latin America needs. That is, one based on productive crosslinks, technological innovation and knowledge incorporation. According to him, that cannot be the case when 90% of Latin American exports to China are represented by commodities with a low degree of processing while 88.5% of China's sales to the region are manufactured products. Nonetheless, he acknowledges that China allowed the region to overcome the crisis of 2009, stressing that Latin Americans should take advantage of its high demand of commodities in order to establish long-term contracts containing investments and technological alliances associated to chains of values.[146]

One should remember though that the current state of affairs is based on facts and not on choices. As such the only practical thing to do is to try to improve what exists and not to speculate with what might have been. As Osvaldo Rosales remarks, Latin America should take advantage of the leverage that it enjoys as a privileged producer of commodities in order to extract bigger concessions from China.

In order to redress this inequality, Latin American governments, or to better say South American ones, would need to coordinate their negotiations with China. Up to the present, every South American economy develops its relations with the Asian nation within strict bilateral basis, which creates an obvious imbalance to their detriment. If the region could take advantage of the existing regional or sub-regional institutions in order to define, implement and negotiate joint positions, its leverage would be substantially increased.

Given the fact that most of South American countries would welcome more transfer of technology, more employment creation, more Chinese investments in strategic areas and a greater degree of local processing of their commodities, it would be easy to reach common negotiating grounds. For Brazil and Argentina, that would include as well exporting to China higher percentages of

[146] "Advierte CEPAL desequilibrios en la asociación China Latinoamérica", Notimex, 15 de junio 2011.

manufactured goods. Moreover, within the global chains of value lead by China, services provided from Latin America could play an important role. If emphasis on bilateral relations keeps being the norm only Brazil, given the strength of its GDP and its membership within the BRICS, would be able to exhibit a relative weight in its negotiations with China.

Commodities' producers such as Norway, Canada, Australia and New Zealand have been able to sustain high economic growth rates while creating productive crosslinks of higher value added. That being the case, the only constructive thing for Latin Americans to do is to define a route map that allows obtaining the best possible advantages from the current set of conditions while avoiding risks and minimising vulnerabilities.

Chapter

4

Is There a Future for Latin America?

Between China's torch and technology's Damocles sword

A route map that allows obtaining the best possible advantages from the current set of conditions while avoiding risks and minimising vulnerabilities is fundamental. Such a map should recognise the obvious fact that commodities are at mercy of economic cycles. And, clearly enough the current expansive cycle is highly dependent of China's urbanisation and infrastructural development process, which will reach its ceiling in a not such distant future.

It could be argued, of course, that India with its 1.2 billion people and its current growth rates would take China's place when that moment arrives. Nonetheless, that is far from certain. On the one hand, as mentioned in Chapter 2, India's development model did not follow the classic Asian strategy of labour intensive-export oriented economy, emphasising on the contrary services over industry and high technology over low-skilled manufacturing. As a result, it has been successful in high-end services and capital- and knowledge-intensive manufacturing, but has not been able to create a broad industrial base. Hence, it may never become a magnet for commodities' producers. On the other hand, should India promote a second green revolution with ambitious agribusiness developments, it could not only become self sufficient in food production but also transform itself into a competitor in some Latin American export markets.

Conversely, the Indian government is currently aiming at reaching China's level of investment in infrastructure, which would be 9% of its GDP. A good example of this objective is represented by the project known as the Delhi–Mumbai Industrial corridor. It would be an infrastructural corridor bigger in land size than Japan, stretching from New Delhi down to Mumbai in the West. This US$90 billion plan envisages numerous infrastructural and industrial developments susceptible of tripling the industrial output across the six states through which it runs.[1] The need for infrastructural modernisation is evident as shown at the end of July 2012, when 600 million citizens, in 20 states and Union territories, were affected by a huge electricity blackout that plunged half of India into darkness. If India materialises its ambitions in this field, overcoming the limitations imposed by its boisterous political system, staggering bureaucracy and traditional land battles, it could indeed become a second China.

And, there is of course Indonesia with its 250 million inhabitants with a GDP of around US$1 trillion and an annual GDP growth above 6%. But as a big commodities' producer itself, with a much smaller State dimension, Indonesia could never play the same role or be in the same league of China. So for all practical purposes Latin America cannot assume that when China slows down someone else will take the lead. There would be no doubt about it, many small "Chinas" amid the emerging economies of Asia. Let us just remember that according to Australia's former Foreign Minister Kevin Rudd, in

[1] Matthias Williams and Lyndee Prickitt, "Project will 'change lives' in India", *thestar.com*, 5 November 2011, <http://www.thestar.com/news/world/article/1081409–project-will-change-lives-in-india>.

2017 Asia should represent nearly one-third of the global GDP.[2] Nonetheless, for the Latin American commodities' producers, it may not be enough as many of those emerging economies may be constituted by competitors in such sector. But even if China's role as a big magnet for commodities was to be taken by India or by a combination of smaller emerging economies or by both of them, it is always possible that technology curtails the commodities expansive cycle in dramatic ways.

To begin with, there would be the risk posed by biotechnology, which uses live organisms or processes to make or modify products, improve plants or animals or develop micro-organism for specific ends. This technology began to develop as a consequence of the notable discoveries relating to the genetic code made in the 1950s and became fully useful for commercial purposes since 1980. Its launching platform came that same year when the United States (US) Supreme Court approved the first patent for a genetically created creature, which had been developed with the aim of absorbing oil spills in the sea. In 1987, the US Patents and Trademarks Office, for its part, confirmed the right to patent any creature 'fabricated by mankind', thus recognising for the first time that life as a product might be created.[3]

Since the 90s, some authors began to warn about the potential implications resulting from the association between biotechnology and agriculture. For them, the fundamental problem had to do with the possibility of destroying the ancestral relationship between human beings and soil by creating a world in which foodstuff could be produced in closed laboratories. The essence of the process they referred to was simple. Once you have the genetic code of whatever vegetable, it becomes like any other manufacture that can be produced on large scale through industrial techniques. In that way, producing apples or pears could be the same as manufacturing refrigerators or washing machines.

---

[2] "Tomorrow's Pax Pacifica", *The Straits Times*, 10 February 2012.

[3] Alfredo Toro Hardy, *Tiene Futuro América Latina?* (Bogotá: Villegas Editores, 2004).

According to Paul Kennedy: "It is one thing to have a tomato that is genetically modified to resist disease and which does not quickly rot, and quite another to know that a biotech company can create tomato pulp, orange and apple juice, or tobacco *in vitro* in a laboratory, without needing to plant crops."[4] Moreover, in Jeremy Rifkin words:

> The new advances in science threaten to do away with open-air agriculture by the middle of the next century. Technological shifts in the production of foodstuffs are leading us to a world without farmers, with unforeseeable consequences for the 2.4 billion people who depend on the soil for their survival…Hundreds of millions of farmers thought the world face the prospect of being permanently eliminated from the economic process.[5]

But threats to natural recourses come not only from biotechnology, steam cells technology allows to grow beef for human consumption in laboratories. By generating strips of meat from steam cells, researchers believe they can create a product that is identical to a real burger. Doctor Mark Post, head of physiology at Maastricht University in the Netherlands, announced that his team had successfully replicated the process with cow cells and calf serum. According to his vision, a limited herd of donor animals in the world would be enough to provide the cells for the mass production of meat.[6]

Leap forward advances in biotechnology and steam cells technology hang as a Damocles sword over the head of agricultural and herd producers all over the world. Technological threats for commodities' dependent countries are visible at every step of the way. Clean technology developments could pose risks to oil producers in the same manner in which breakthroughs in tapping untapped hydrocarbons reserves or in mining developments could depress the prices in these sectors. It is not to be certain the same kind of risks that Border's faced

---

[4] *Preparando para o Século XXI* (Rio de Janeiro: Editora Campus, 1993), p. 87.
[5] *O Fim dos Empregos* (Sao Paulo: Makron Books, 1966), p. 134.
[6] *BBC World News*, 21 February 2012.

with the introduction of e-commerce and the digital book or that Kodak did with the digital camera, as commodities inhabit a relatively more peaceful world. Nonetheless such apparent peacefulness makes things all more dramatic when transformational changes appear.

As the world goes, thus, a route map for Latin American commodities' producers has to assume that the current expansive cycle will reach an end sooner or later. China's impressive emergence, and the subsequent bonanza that South American countries enjoy, have to be seen as a window of opportunity to prepare for what may lay ahead. It is the fat cows–lean cows' logic. Moreover, potential seismic shifts in the value of commodities have to be anticipated as otherwise South American economies may simply be razed to the ground. So the big question in the air is: Where do Latin American commodities' producers go from here?

Where does Latin America go from here?

To begin with, there seems to be clarity in at least one thing: Latin Americans cannot look forward to industrialisation as a panacea, as they once did. Indeed, this road seems to be blocked not only at the top but increasingly so at the bottom as well. And that not only includes South American economies but also Mexican-type economies. Latin America's total factor productivity, which is a proxy for technological innovation, higher skills and improved methods of production, has evolved in a negative way during the last 30 years.[7] Latin Americans are clearly not able to compete in the high-tech manufacturing sector. But, at the same time, they are finding extremely difficult to maintain competitiveness in the labour-intensive sector. Not even geographical proximity and free trade agreements have been able to overcome the problems faced in the latter case. In that sense, they are in a typical middle income trap situation, as their economies are unable to compete with advance economies in high-skill innovations and, at the same time, are under continuous competitive pressure in manufacturing exports by Asia's lower income and lower wages

[7] Claudio Loser, "Latin America in the Age of Globalization: A Follower or a Force of its Own?", University of Miami, Center for Hemispheric Policy, 11 June 2012.

economies. As their wages rise and their cost competitiveness decline, possibilities at the bottom side of the equation are becoming increasingly reduced, but on the other hand, they do not have the capabilities to compete at the top with technological innovations.[8]

Only Brazil, Cuba and Argentina have a presence in some endogenous high-technology clusters and niches such as aeronautics, microchips or products associated to deepwater oil drilling in the first case, biotechnology in three of them or tailor-made turbines in the case of Argentina. But clearly, this is the exception not the rule. And, even so, Brazil is not what it used to be in relation to other emerging economies. In 1987, South Korea's technology level was almost exactly the same as Brazil's; Malaysia's level was at 60% and Thailand's at 30% of Brazil's. By 2009, South Korea's technology level was 60% higher than Brazil, Malaysia had almost caught up and Thailand was at over 55%.[9] For the majority of the countries of Latin American, though, endogenous technology is simply a closed door. It should not be forgotten that the market liberalisation imposed by the International Monetary Fund forced the region to abandon its efforts in research and development as shown before when referring to the Mexican case. Today, Mexico exhibits a whole array of high-tech export products but theirs is foreign generated technology. And even though Mexico is yearly graduating an impressive number of engineers, endogenous generated high tech seems to be out of reach.

According to the UNESCO 2005 Science Report and the UNESCO Institute for Statistics, North America's share of gross expenditure in research and development that year was 37%, Asia's 31.5%, Europe's 28.8% and Latin America's 2.6%.[10] For the Iberian–American Network of Science and Technology Indicators, Latin American participation in the total global investments in research and development is even smaller than that, as 42% goes to the US and Canada, 28% to Europe, 27% to Asia and only 1% to Latin America.[11]

---

[8] Asian Development Bank, *Asia 2050: Realizing the Asian Century* (Manila: 2011).
[9] Claudio Loser, *op. cit.*
[10] Dambisa Moyo, *How the West was Lost* (London: Allen Lane, 2011).
[11] Andrés Oppenheimer, "El Desafío tecnológico para América Latina", *La Nación.com*, <http://www.forodeseguridad.com/art/relex/ref_8043.htm>.

As for the intensive-labour products, competition with China has been a true nightmare. And not even if China reduces its participation in this sector will Latin America be safe as other Asian economies such as Vietnam, Indonesia, the Philippines or Bangladesh will be taking its place at the bottom of the wage equation. Asia's supply chain is simply unbeatable. In Robyn Meredith words:

> But during the 1990s, companies began searching for the lowest-cost place to make each component of their products. At the same time, sophisticated technology made reality of what had once been a logistical pipe dream: creating a seamless connection between multiple factories...The last time a manufacturing revolution of this magnitude occurred was in the early 20th century, when Henry Ford revolutionised the business world by popularising the assembly line...In the 21st century, everything has changed...The new system — call it a disassembly line — is the result of companies rushing to break up their products into specialised subassemblies to drive down costs...The manufacturing process is so different from the last century that the term 'assembly line' has been replaced by the phrase 'supply chain'.[12]

And she adds: "The disassembly line has let companies become extremely efficient, by building each piece of a finished good in the country where it is cheapest, then moving the part on to the next factory in line."[13] So, with parts passing from Vietnamese factories to Indonesian ones, to be followed by Bangladeshis', always in the search of the cheapest wage cost for every component, it will be extremely difficult for Latin America to keep pace.

The only spaces where Latin American manufactures can feel protected, Brazil being the only relative exception at the top, are natural resources' processing industries and manufacturing sectors where transport costs from East Asia are relevant. The latter includes, as seen in the case of Mexico, trucks, autos and heavy machinery. In general terms then, the areas where Latin Americans could feel more at ease

[12] *The Elephant and the Dragon* (New York: W.W. Norton & Company, 2007), p. 99.
[13] *ibid.*, p. 101.

include aeronautical industry (endogenous in Brazil and foreign assembly plants in Mexico), the automotive industry, plastics, fertilizers, synthetic fibres, steel, paper, processed feedstuff, spirits, alcoholic beverages, etc. Protecting and adding value whenever possible to those industries constitutes thus a first line of defence.

Within that process, economic integration can play a relevant role. Absence of tariffs or tariff concessions and rules of origin deriving from agreements such as MERCOSUR, Andean Community of Nations or Central American Common Market, are able to provide an additional cushion against lower foreign production costs. Thanks to those mechanism, a growing percentage of manufacturing exports remains within the region. Let us take as examples the case of Argentina that in 1985 directed 31% of its manufacturing exports to other Latin American nations while in 2006 such regional exports reached 69%, or the case of Brazil, that in 2011 exported 22% of its total manufactured goods to a single country: Argentina.[14]

But it is not just the South American countries that have to produce a protective route map against the uncertainties regarding its commodities. The Mexican-type countries have to identify as well economic options against the competition posed by the low wages of China and the East Asian supply chain juggernaut. For different reasons, both groups of countries have to work together on alternative courses of action to their current situation.

Notwithstanding the idea of both groups of countries jointly searching for alternative courses, there are some initiatives specifically tailored for South American commodities' producers. These represent steps to be taken for reducing the uncertainties posed by the volatility of this sector. Diversifying their commodities' offer and adding value to such commodities through branding and clustering are the first common sense steps that have to be taken. In addition to that, but needless even to mention it, emphasis should be given to locally transforming raw materials into basic products with the aim of adding as much value as possible.

---

[14] Kevin P Gallager. and Roberto Porzecanski, *The Dragon in the Room* (Stanford: Stanford University Press, 2010); Andre Loes, "Lat Am trade flows", HSBC Global Research, Economics Latin America, February, 2013.

Commodities exporters' first steps

Not all commodities are equally vulnerable. Let us take as example the case of metals and food. The historical experience of countries, during their industrialization stage, shows that the increase in the price of metals is correlated to that of the per capita income. But that is so until the per capita income reaches a certain plateau, after which the consumption relents. And that plateau is in the order of US$15,000–20,000. On the same token, consumption of higher protein value food increases in direct relation to the increase of the GDP per capita, while that of lower protein value food decreases.[15]

Diversification appears thus as a hedge aiming at compensating the reduction in the consumption of some items through the supply of others that may be more resilient to changes. When China reaches a ceiling in its industrialisation and infrastructural development processes, its demand of iron, copper, steel, or nickel will fall dramatically. But there will still be a gigantic population that needs to be fed. Moreover, as an increasing number of that population becomes more affluent, their intake of higher protein value will increase.

In virtual terms, diversification is tantamount to planting copper, nickel or iron in order to harvest coffee, grapes or cocoa. By the same token, low protein food producers should incursion in animal production or in animal feedstuff. The name of the game is to increase the exportable offer in order to reduce vulnerabilities as not all commodities might be negatively impacted at the same time. A couple of examples can explain the reason for it. In the first half of the 20th century, Paraguay's prime export — cotton — disappeared from the international marketplace after the US began to produce surpluses. During the same period, Brazil's dominant position in the rubber market was destroyed by the sudden appearance of the Malayan production. The impact in both cases was not the same though, as Brazil's much wider offer of commodities allowed the country to overcome such negative situation in an easier way.

---

[15] Bernardo Kosacoff y Sebastián Campanario, *La Revalorizacion de las Materias Primas y sus Efectos en América Latina* (Santiago de Chile: CEPAL, mayo 2007).

Chile is a good example to be followed in this matter. During the mid 80s of the past century, copper represented 80% of its exports. Nowadays, that amount has been reduced to around 38%. In the meantime, more than 2,500 commodities have come to represent their export offer: from salmon to shell food, from timber to grapes, from furniture to paper. The menu of its exportable commodities is indeed a very long one.[16]

But in addition to hedging against changes in the market, diversification protects against the evident fact that many commodities are non-renewable goods. Metals, oil, coal or gas would fall under this category. It may be the case, as it probably happens with Venezuelan oil, that the commercial use of such products may reach an end before reserves are depleted. Moreover, the high prices associated with the scarcity of specific commodities encourage new investments that normally bring with them new discoveries and by consequence additional reserves. Nonetheless, depletion is always a cause for concern in the case of such commodities. Going from copper to timber, as Chile did, means investing the profits of non renewable products in renewable ones.

But in addition to increasing its market offer, commodities' producers should aim at increasing the value add properties of their goods by evolving, whenever feasible, into branded products. While the processing of raw materials generates basic products, both of them are considered to be commodities in as long as they remain bulk unbranded products. Under that assumption, sugar cane is considered a raw material and molasses a basic product. But sugarcane can also be transformed into rum, a typical Caribbean alcoholic beverage. Rums can be highly estimated brand products with some among them competing as high end spirits.

Nonetheless, raw materials and basic products can remain so while obtaining at the same time the equivalent to premium brand recognition through the so-called "Designation of Origin". As a matter of fact, the European Union Law protects the names of special regional foods through its "Protected Geographical Status". The system is

---

[16] Alfredo Toro Hardy, *op. cit.*

similar to "Appellation" systems through the world, such as "*Appellation d'origine controlée*" (AOC) used in France, the "*Denominazione di origine controllata*" (DOC) used in Italy or "*Denominación de origen*" (DO) used in Spain. Such protection is afforded to products that come from a certain area, place or country, whose quality or other characteristic properties are attributable to its geographic origin and whose production or processing takes place within such geographical area. Even if there is no legal protection for these names or products outside their own jurisdiction sphere, bilateral agreements can attain such an aim. Nonetheless, even if proper legal protection is not extended internationally, such products can be associated in the mind of consumers with specific qualities deserving a premium price.

In Latin America, the most obvious and fascinating example of "Designation of Origin" comes from the "*Café de Colombia*" (Colombian Coffee), which extends to all the generic coffee produced in such country. Other cases include Mexican tequila, Venezuelan rum, or Peruvian pisco. Mexico with eight designations of origin tops the list, followed by Peru with five while Venezuela has only three. And so on.

Even though Latin American countries should try to extend the aforementioned list by searching quality products around the region, it is obvious that this is an exclusive club. For those that do not attain membership in the club, branding recognition of processed primary products is the natural alternative to move up in the value chain. Here we can find, by instance, Brazilian chocolates or guaraná (a climbing plant in the maple family produced in the Amazon) soft drinks; Venezuelan corn flours or chocolates; Mexican cement, corn tortillas or wheat bread; Chilean smoked salmon; Argentinean mate leaves tea; etc. These products, amid many others, are identified with well-known regional brands.

Further up in the process we find beer, spirits, or wine. Latin American beers are well-known internationally with some like the Mexican Corona brand enjoying the benefits of global recognition. As for spirits, some of them like the Venezuelan rum or the Peruvian pisco, already enjoy the denominations of origin. Others are just well-known brands. One way or the other, this is an area where the region enjoys an important international reputation. Chile and Argentina and to a much lesser extent Brazil and Uruguay have an important reputation in the wine sector with some of their brands attaining international recognition.

Chilean design furniture, Argentinean and Colombian leather design products or Brazilian fashion clothes, all produced from the top quality of their raw materials, are other examples in the same direction, with well known brands supporting them.

Stepping in and climbing up the brand ladder is the best way to not only add value but to insulate natural processed products from market volatility. This is an area where both the quality of the products and the marketing cleverness matters much. Indeed, a brand is more than a simple tag name attached to a product or groups of products, being the tool through which they can be singularised in the market place. Customisation can become a helpful tool in that process as it allows targeting the preferences of specific groups of consumers adding value to the goods and increasing their degree of protection against the uncertainties of the market.

But besides diversification and branding, clustering is also advisable. Clustering would consist in organizing a set of objects into groups. It was up to Michael Porter to bring this concept into the field of business under the premise that higher degrees of connectivity, spill over of knowledge and synergy emerge when localised agglomeration of similar activities takes place. This allows the creation of value chains.

Silicon Valley is a perfect example of a cluster as the headquarters of 20% of the world's biggest software and electronic companies are located there. Other US-based clusters of information technology include Route 128 on the outskirts of Boston, the Research Triangle Park in North Carolina or Route 270 bordering the city of Washington. Information Technology clusters outside the United States include Bangalore, Taipei, Cambridge, Helsinki and Tel Aviv. But in the high-tech field, we can also find biotechnology or telecommunications clusters in places like Grenoble, Strasbourg, Nice, Toulouse, Barcelona, Ypres and Frankfurt. Creativity and productivity within clusters tend to increase as the conglomeration of know-how and talent has a tremendous multiplier effect.

But needless to say, productive clusters are not limited to high-tech activities as value chains can be generated whenever related and interconnected activities take place within a specific geographic space. In the case in point we refer to commodities' clusters of which numerous examples are available in Latin America. Among them we could mention Antofagasta (mining), Valle del Maule (wine) or Tarapacá (mining-wood-olives) clusters in Chile; Engominas (wood and furniture), Campina Grande (shoes) or Brasilia (textile and apparel) clusters in Brazil; the Asparagus cluster or the Río Blanco and La Granja (mining) clusters in Peru; Costa de Manabí (tuna) cluster in Ecuador; Guayana (mining extraction, mining basic industries and hydroelectric dams), Jose or El Tablazo (petrochemical) in Venezuela; Buenos Aires Province (oil refining and petrochemical), Córdoba (peanut) or Entre Ríos (agro-industrial) clusters in Argentina, etc. Expanding the commodities' clusters, through well defined industrial policies, becomes thus of the utmost importance for the creation of value chains.

But within the road map that all Latin American countries should follow, whether they want to reduce the vulnerabilities of the commodities sector or alternatively face the competition posed by lower Asian prices, a few objectives should be prioritised. Among them we could mention the development of human capital, of international tradable services, of infrastructure and of sovereign wealth funds. Such initiatives can not only improve competitiveness within the region but also widen the scope of available economic options. As such resources and efforts should be primatily allocated to these aims.

The Belindia syndrome

Within the above mentioned road map, human development seems to be the first priority. This brings to the scene the so-called "Belindia syndrome". Indeed, a number of Brazilian economists have given their country the funny name of "Belindia", wanting to signify that the same constitutes a mixture of Belgium and India. While a number of states in Southeast Brazil have the economic dynamism of Belgium, a good part of the nation is plagued by the poverty of India. Needless to say, India itself is the best example of this kind of dichotomy. Part of its economy is at the forefront of the international tradable services and the information technology developments, while the so-called "Bimaru" provinces — Bihar, Madhya, Pradesh, Rajasthan and Uttar Pradesh — impose a great burden of delay and poverty upon the country.

Without reaching the sophistication of Brazil in aeronautics (Brazilian's Embraer is the world's largest producer of short-range jet planes and the third larger aircraft manufacturer after Airbus and Boeing), high-tech engineering services, deep-water oil drilling, biotechnology, or the simple sheer size of its commodity sector, most Latin American countries mirror the same kind of dualism. On the one side, dynamic and competitive niches and clusters which are managed by highly educated elite and, on the other side, third world type of poverty.

Amid the first group, we find the remarkable efficiency of the trade, metals, financial, agro industrial, fishery or wine sectors in Chile; a ensemble of world class companies in Mexico that includes, among others, the telecommunication, entertainment, beer, cement, engineering, oil, tourism, liquor, or bakery sectors; a highly internationalised oil business in Venezuela; a globalised entertainment industry in Columbia; well-known financial and shipping services and a booming construction industry in Panama. And so on.

As for poverty and backwardness, that speaks for itself, with countless citizens around the region excluded from the benefits of economic growth. Under this perspective, the quick footed sectors of society are forced to carry a heavy burden at their shoulders. Speed of movement is not easy under these circumstances. The big question thus is what to do so that the heavy weight of the excluded ones does not end up by pushing societies down? Mexico is a current example of how its drug violence, a perfect by-product of the country' tremendous social gap, threatens with derailing foreign investments and its strong tourism industry.

Well-known Latin American journalist Andrés Oppenheimer wrote a shaking article in 2003, whose numbers may probably have changed but whose premises are still valid. In his words:

> According to the World Health Organization, Latin America is the most violent region on earth with 27.5 murderers for each 100,000 inhabitants, compared with 22 in Africa, 15 in Eastern Europe and 1 in the richest European countries...Kidnapping and other forms of violent crimes are not only putting a brake to foreign investments and tourism, but represent billions of dollars in terms of flight of capitals, hospital expenses, lower labour productivity, high insurance costs and huge protection expenses...Brazilian private sector expends 20 billion dollars a year in health and robbery insurance for its employees, besides 300 million additional dollars in protective measures such as armoured vehicles, electronic alarms and security guards, according to *Gazeta Mercantil*... In 1998, the World Bank estimated that the per capita income in Latin America could be 25% higher if its criminality rates were equal to that of the world average. The Inter-American Bank, on its part, estimated in 1997 that violent crime costs the region 14% of its annual gross national product.[17]

According to Robert B. Zoellick, then President of the World Bank, Central America pays a heavy economic price for its insecurity, which could amount nowadays to 8% of its GDP.[18] But violence is just one of the many consequences resulting from the Belindia syndrome, where the contrast between extreme richness and extreme poverty compounded by lagging levels of education, healthcare and sanitation in the latter, creates havoc in every possible direction. That is why overcoming poverty and inequality becomes fundamental if the region wants to attain development. And even if poverty in Latin America diminished between 2002 and 2009, with several countries showing a substantial improvement, the burden of those left behind is still huge.

[17] "Lo que olvidan los economistas: la violencia", *La Nación*, 9 de diciembre 2003.
[18] "Globalization: Made in the Americas", 30th Anniversary Celebration of the Inter-American Dialogue, Washington D.C., 7 June 2012.

Table 1 Percentage of Population under the Poverty Line

Uruguay	10.7
Argentina	11.3
Chile	11.5
Costa Rica	18.9
Brazil	24.9
Panama	26.4
Venezuela	27.6
Peru	34.8
Mexico	34.8
Ecuador	40.2
Dominican Republic	41.1
Colombia	45.7
El Salvador	47.9
Bolivia	54.0
Guatemala	54.8
Paraguay	56.0
Nicaragua	61.9
Honduras	68.9

Source: Comisión Económica para América Latina y el Caribe.[19]

The percentage of total population under the poverty line in 2009 is shown in Table 1.

Inequality, on its side has been growing stronger in Latin America with the Gini coefficient giving us a good panorama of the situation. The simplicity of Gini makes it easy to use for comparisons across diverse countries, as a coefficient of zero expresses perfect equality while a coefficient of one expresses maximal inequality. The Gini coefficient of several Latin American countries was the following in 2009: Uruguay: 0.433; Peru: 0.469; El Salvador: 0.478; Costa Rica: 0.501; Paraguay: 0.523; Chile: 0.524; Dominican Republic: 0.574; Brazil: 0.576; Colombia: 0.578. In 2008, these

[19] *Panorama Social de América Latina 2010* (Santiago de Chile: Noviembre 2010), p. 50.

two countries had the following coefficient: Venezuela: 0.412 and Mexico: 0.515.[20]

According to *The Economist*: "Income distribution in Latin America remains the most unequal in any continent".[21] As the magazine shows, the region on average slightly surpasses the 0.5 Gini coefficient mark, whereas such coefficient slightly surpasses 0.3 in high income countries, closely approaches 0.4 in South Asia, North Africa and the Middle East and reaches 0.44 in Sub-Saharan Africa.[22]

Indeed, on the one extreme, Latin America is home to 51 billionaires whose combined fortune reaches US$332 billion and which include two of the 10 richest people on the planet: Mexican Carlos Slim as No. 1 worldwide with a fortune of US$69 billion and Brazilian Erike Batista as No. 7 worldwide with US$30 billion.[23] On the other extreme, according to ECLAC, Latin America had 180 million people under the poverty line in 2010, representing 33.1% of the total population of the region. Of that amount, 72 million were destitutes.[24]

In Claudio Loser words: "The recent improvement in Latin America appears to be associated with the emergence of a vigorous middle-class and reductions in poverty, but income continues to be highly concentrated. The actual picture of income distribution may be even more concentrated, since the income statistics fail to capture a significant amount of unrecorded income of the very rich."[25] Under the neoliberal dogma prescribed by the Washington Consensus, there was an easy answer to the problems of poverty and inequality. The economic growth guaranteed by its policies would put in motion a

---

[20] Economic Commission for Latin America and the Caribbean, *Statistical Yearbook for Latin America and the Caribbean*, (Santiago de Chile: 2010), p. 70.

[21] "It's only natural", Special Report: Latin America, 11 September 2010.

[22] *ibid.*

[23] "Los más ricos de América Latina acumulan 332,000 millones de dólares", 9 de marzo 2011, CNNMéxico, <http://mexico.cnn.com/mundo/2011/03/09/los-mas-ricos-de-america-latina-acumulan-332000-millones-de-dolares; http://www.forbes.com/billionaires/gallery>.

[24] Comisión Económica para América Latina y el Caribe, *op. cit.*

[25] *Op. cit.*

trickle-down effect sufficient to end up filling the social pool and hence overcoming the gap. As it happened, though, under the Washington Consensus the region did not have a trickle-down effect, economic growth in itself was highly disappointing, inequality augmented exponentially and poverty thrived.

Conversely, when human development becomes in itself a relevant consideration, a multiplier effect in reverse takes place. Instead of waiting for the social pool to get filled as a result of economic growth, economic growth is boosted by the filling up of the social pool. Education, healthcare, sanitation, civic values, associational patterns, participatory spirit, organisational skills, cooperative development, technical training, support for small businesses. These are but few of the elements with which such pool should be filled up. It is the flourishing from below without which structured societies or sustainable development can never be attained. A single example can illustrate the above. A World Health Organization study suggests that every dollar devoted to improving sanitation and drinking water produces economic benefits ranging from US$3 to US$34, because of healthcare saving, deaths averted and improved productivity and school attendance.[26]

The convergence between the economic growth resulting from the hike in the prices of commodities and the ambitious human development policies put in motion by several Latin American countries, these last few years, have been responsible for reducing poverty in a very impressive way. Argentina, Venezuela and Brazil show the biggest percentages of poverty reduction in the region between 2002 and 2009. Such percentages are shown in Table 2.

Conversely, poverty reduction in Mexico during the same period was scarce, passing from 39.4% in 2002 to 34.8% in 2009. El Salvador, a Mexican-type economy, showed an even meagre reduction passing from 48.9% in 2002 to 47.9% in 2009.[27]

A healthier, educated and productive citizen can become the best turbine for a country's economic take off. Therefore, efforts and

---

[26] Bloomberg, "To improve global health, reinvent the toilet", *Today*, 13 April 2012.
[27] *ibid.*

Table 2 Biggest Percentage of Proverty Reduction

	2002	2009
Argentina	45.4	11.3
Venezuela	48.6	27.6
Brazil	37.5	24.9

Source: Comisión Económica para América Latina y el Caribe.[28]

expenditures directed to these goals should become a key component to confront the "Belindia syndrome" that affects Latin America so much. At the same time, it is the best formula for expanding the aggregate demand within the economic system, creating the foundations for a sustained and balanced economic growth.

Education is a paramount element within this equation, which is why an overview of Latin America's standing in this area, is necessary. To begin with, we must refer to adult literacy percentages in the seven largest economies of the region: Chile 98.6; Argentina 97.7; Venezuela 95.2; Mexico 93.4; Colombia 93.2; Brazil 90.0 and Peru 89.6.[29] According to UNESCO, illiteracy rates have fallen in the region, but at a pace that does not bode well for achieving the objective of education for all by 2015 as nearly 35 million people comprising 15 years of age and older describe themselves as illiterate.[30]

According to a detailed report on this sector by UNESCO and ECLAC, dating back to 2004, regional enrolment rates in primary education between 1990 and 2001 passed from 89% to 94%, which suggested that universal coverage was already within close range. In a subsequent 2008 report by UNESCO, it was stated that primary education completion levels showed that the region had achieved

[28] *op. cit.*, p. 50.

[29] The Economist, *Pocket World in Figures: 2012 Edition* (London: Profile Books Ltd., 2012).

[30] *The State of Education in Latin America and the Caribbean: Guaranteeing Quality Education for All* (Santiago de Chile: Regional Bureau of Education for Latin America and the Caribbean, August 2008).

the goal of universalisation in many of its countries, even though some, basically in Central America, still showed slowness in reaching that aim.[31]

According to the 2004 report during the period 2000–2001 completion of upper secondary education oscillated between 26% and 36% at the lower range (Guatemala and Nicaragua, respectively) and between 70% and 80% in the upper range (Argentina, Chile, Mexico, Uruguay, etc.). Moreover, the economic gap projected itself into this area. While it has been considered that 11 to 12 years of formal education are required to overcome the poverty trap, between 72% and 96% of poor families in the region had then as chief of the household, an adult with less than 9 years of formal education. The average Latin American adult within the richest 10% of the income distribution had 7 years more of formal education than the adult within the poorer 30%. In the 2008 report, on the other hand, it was shown that several countries were in the condition of assuring universal completion of lower secondary and upper secondary education, even though some countries (especially in Central America again) were left behind with completion levels that did not attain 70% for lower secondary education and 50% for upper secondary education.[32]

In 2000, only four Latin American countries dedicated more than 5.5% of their GDP to education, which is the average invested by the Organisation for Economic Cooperation and Development (OECD) member nations. Cuba was at the top of that list with 8.5% of its GDP.[33] By 2007, though, Cuba with 11.9% was the only Latin American country that surpassed the OECD average, followed by Chile with 5.1%.[34]

---

[31] ECLAC/UNESCO, *Financing and Managing Education in Latin America and the Caribbean* (Santiago de Chile: ECLAC, 2004); UNESCO, *The State of Education in Latin America and the Caribbean: Guaranteeing Quality Education for All* (Santiago de Chile: Regional Bureau of Education for Latin America and the Caribbean, August 2008).

[32] *ibid.*

[33] ECLAC/UNESCO, *ibid.*

[34] ECLAC, *Statistical Yearbook for Latin America and the Caribbean* (Santiago de Chile: 2010).

As for third level of education, gross enrolment rate in 2008 had the following percentages in a selected group of countries: Cuba: 121.5; Venezuela: 78.6; Uruguay: 64.9; Chile: 54.8; Panama: 45.1; Ecuador: 42.4; Brazil: 34.4; Mexico: 27.2; El Salvador: 24.6.[35] It is important to mention that Cuba ranks number one in the world in third level education gross enrolment rate, followed by Venezuela in No. 7[36] It could be added that during the period 1999–2007, Venezuela's university population grew from 656,830 to 1,796,507 students, a significant number for a country with a total population of little more than 27 million inhabitants.[37]

The Economist summarises the overall educational situation in the following terms: "Primary schooling is almost universal, except in some of the poorer Central American countries; 70% of the children of the region now start secondary school, up from 60% in 1999 (but 90% do it in rich countries). The number...of tertiary education has risen from a fifth to a third [during the past 20 years]."[38]

Nonetheless, according to the World Bank:

> Over the last two decades, almost all countries in Latin America have greatly expanded the proportions of their emerging labor force with secondary and tertiary education...Notwithstanding these advances, Latin America lags behind other regions in the expansion of education...Since 1990, the rate of expansion by the East Asian Tigers was faster than in Latin America, so by 2010 the gap had widened further, with East Asian Tigers reaching on average 9.5 years (equivalent to completed lower secondary), against 8.4 years for Latin America.[39]

---

[35] *ibid.*

[36] The Economist, *Pocket World in Figures: 2012 Edition* (London: Profile Books Ltd., 2012).

[37] Ministerio del Poder Popular para la Planificación y el Desarrollo, *Logros de la Revolución* (Caracas: Octubre, 2008).

[38] "Societies on the move", *op. cit.*

[39] *Latin America and the Caribbean's Long Term Growth: Made in China?* (Washington D.C.: September 2011), p. 52.

But together with the expansion of the educational system in the region, the quality factor within it is a fundamental consideration. This is easily measured through the Program for International Student Assessment (PISA) exams, which covers math, science and reading comprehension skills of 15-year-olds in 65 countries. Again, according to the World Bank:

> Having achieved very large increases in secondary and tertiary enrolment, the region must now invest in improving the quality of its education systems and the pertinence of education curricula for the labour market (....) The region still reports large achievement gaps compared with the OECD, suggesting the need for a drive to improve quality. The best source of evidence on trends in learning achievements is the OECD's PISA evaluation (....) Most importantly, the gap in PISA scores between most Latin American countries and the OECD remains large — equal to the outcome of about two years of schooling.[40]

According to *The Economist*: "The six Latin American countries that took part in the OECD's PISA study on educational achievement in 2006 all ranked in the bottom third of the 57 countries covered."[41] It must be added, though, that this is a generalised phenomenon in countries with high reliance on commodities. A team from the OECD recently presented a study mapping the correlation between performance in the PISA evaluation and the total earnings on natural resources as a percentage of GDP for each participatory country. In Thomas L. Friedman words: "The results indicated that there was 'a significant negative relationship between the money countries extract from natural resources and the knowledge and skills of their high school population', said Andreas Schleicher, who oversees the PISA exams for the O.E.C.D."[42] In other words, the lack of natural resources incentivises knowledge, which is dependent on education, while its abundance induces to a more laid back attitude in this area.

[40] *ibid.*, pp. 54, 55, 57, 61.

[41] "Societies on the move", Special Report: Latin America, 11 September 2010.

[42] "Pass the books. Hold the oil", *International Herald Tribune,* 12 March 2012.

Countries such as Singapore or Japan are good examples of the former as knowledge and skills become existential tools for viability and success amidst the scarcity of resources provided by nature.

As for tertiary education, the World Bank adds:

> In addition...universities in Latin American countries are perceived of worse quality than their Europeans or Asian counterparts...The latter point is made evident by Thorn and Soo (2006) that show that only 5% of tertiary education teachers in Latin American countries have doctoral degrees (in the UK, this number is above 40%, for example), putting Latin American universities far from the knowledge frontier.[43]

Education is a key element for the attainment of social mobility. Hence, much has to be improved within the Latin American educational system in order to transform it into a turbine of development conducive for the overcoming of the "Belindia" syndrome. At the same time, though, education is a fundamental tool for succeeding in the international tradable services that, as we shall see next, is one of the areas in which Latin America should incursion if it wants to become less dependent on commodities or low wages manufacturing exports.

Services: The new exports frontier

Latin America has proven great strengths and potential in the service sector, which represents the main economic activity of the region, having reached 74.2% of the regional GDP (including the Caribbean) in 2010. Moreover, the service sector generates 80% of the region's urban employment. [44] A good example of that sector is the area of telecommunications, which since the 90s, has received foreign direct investments in the order of US$110 billion.[45] In telecommunications

---

[43] *op. cit.*, pp. 40, 41.

[44] Sistema Económico Latinoamericano, "Informe sobre el proceso de Integración Regional 2011–2012", Caracas (Agosto 2012).

[45] OECD, "Telecomunicaciones en América Latina: Pueden las multinacionales cerrar la brecha?", Percepciones, número 5, Octubre 2007, <http://www.oecd.org/dev/publications/leo>.

as well as in energy, air transport, finance or real state, among other service areas, Latin American transnational companies are growing in importance after a boost to this sector was given.

Services in Latin America have become a fundamental buffer to international economic oscillations as shown in the critical years of 2008 and 2009.[46] Nonetheless, they could become as well a new export frontier. According to Saurabh Mishra, Susanna Lundstrom and Rahul Anand:

> Services have grown as a share of the world's GDP in the last decade accounting for 70% of the global GDP, and service exports in developing countries have almost tripled between 1997 and 2007. Even though manufacturing continues to be a dominant driver of growth, recent developments suggest that we must include the service sector in the debate. Services are no longer exclusively an input for trade in goods but have become a 'final export' for direct consumption.[47]

Within this new export frontier, Latin America has multiple areas where it has shown competitiveness. The first of them is the engineering sector. Several activities can be identified within this area: construction, design, maintenance, consulting, etc. The progressive liberalisation of the engineering sector in developed countries has allowed for an increased participation of foreign personnel and companies in such economies. As a result, a tremendous boost has been given to engineering firms from emerging economies.[48]

Both Brazil and Mexico have engineering companies that successfully operate at the international level. The former is the largest exporter of this kind of services in Latin America with corporations such as Odebrecht and Andrade Gutierrez (positioned at 21 and 106 amidst the global ranking of global contractors: the ENR 2007) and

---

[46] Sistema Económico Latinoamericano y del Caribe, *op. cit.*

[47] *Service Sophistication and Economic Growth.* The World Bank, South Asia Region, Policy Research Working Paper 5606 (March 2011), p. 20.

[48] Andrés López, Daniela Ramos e Iván Torres, *Las Exportaciones de Servicio y su Integración a las Cadenas Globales de Valor* (Santiago de Chile: Comisión Económica para América Latina y el Caribe, CEPAL, marzo 2009).

smaller companies such as Camargo Correa and Queiroz Galvao. In 2006, Brazilian companies billed US$3.682 million for services rendered abroad. Mexico's ICA is also an important provider of this kind of services at a multinational level.[49]

There is an important expertise in Latin America in oil and mining with many local engineering companies operating in these fields. While some of them have been active beyond their national boundaries, others could easily do so as well. Among the first, we can mention the Instituto Mexicano de Petróleo in Mexico, Jantesa in Venezuela, Santos-CMI in Ecuador and Sigdo Koppers in Chile. Engineering service exports is an area with great potential that should be properly promoted.

The software industry has also proven to be very successful in export terms, growing from US$200 million in exports in 1998 to US$1.783 million in 2008. Even though exports have essentially remained within the region, software companies are currently diversifying their markets particularly to the United States and Europe. In order to improve their international competitiveness, software clusters are being created in Argentina, Brazil, Mexico, Uruguay and Venezuela. In 2008, Brazilian exports in this area surpassed US$1 billion, followed by Argentina with almost US$500 million and Uruguay in the third place with around US$200 million.[50]

The entertainment industry is another area where Latin Americans have shown to be creative and highly competitive. Regional multimedia corporations such as Televisa and TV Azteca in Mexico, O Globo in Brazil, Cisneros Group in Venezuela, Caracol and RCN in Colombia or Grupo Clarín in Argentina are internationally relevant by any standards. Latin American soap operas and TV series with Brazilian, Mexican, Colombian or Venezuelan productions are popular around the world and in 2003 generated US$340 million in exports.[51]

---

[49] *ibid.*

[50] CEPAL, "Crece la industria de exportación de software en la región", Santiago de Chile, 11 de noviembre, 2010, <http://www.eclac.org/cgi-bin/getProd.asp?xml=/socinfo/noticias/noticias/0/416220/p41620.xml&base=/>.

[51] *ibid.*

Their musical shows also attract huge audiences within the Spanish and Portuguese speaking countries of the Americas and Europe.

The entertainment industry has a very important value chain effect as a Venezuelan case can attest. Beauty contest is a highly sophisticated sector in that country to the extent that it enjoys of an undisputed world record in the number of Miss Universe, Miss World and Miss International contests. The reason behind this success story is an extraordinarily well-managed entertainment sub-sector One that imbricates with modeling, fashion, fabrics, cosmetics, television, filming and publicity creating a synergy that generates important returns both domestically and internationally.

The cultural sector and the entertainment industry can also become intertwined as another Venezuelan case shows. The hundreds of thousands of classical trained musicians, produced by the Venezuelan Children and Youngster System of Orchestras, have become a formidable pool of available talent for other musical genre. The strength of fusion, jazz, folk or pop music movements in Venezuela, which is proof of the above, has been synergistically integrated with its entertainment industry.

As for the Latin American pop musical talent the list is long: from Buena Vista Social Club and Shakira to Carlos Vives and Ivan Lins; from Juanes and Caetano Veloso to Luis Miguel, Soda Stereo, Oscar de León or Maná. Artists from the region have become international icons which in turn has boosted the international standing of its music and video musical industries. The Latin American film industry has proven as well to have great strength and quality with Mexico, Argentina and Brazil emerging as the main international stars but with other countries following suit. Directors, such as Walter Salles, Alejandro González Iñárritu, Alfonso Cuarón, Guillermo del Toro, Hector Barbenco, Fernando Meirelles, Jaime Osorio Gomez, Adolfo Aristarain and actors and actresses like Benicio del Toro, Gael García Bernal, Ricardo Darín, Diego Luna, Hector Alterio, Norma Aleandro, Rubén Blades, Sonia Braga, Marlon Moreno, Edgard Ramírez or Gastón Pauls, make a very potent combination that has won prizes, praises and revenues from around the world.

The fashion business is another area where Latin America shines with top world designers such as the Venezuelan Carolina Herrera or the Dominican Oscar de la Renta. But besides those two big names, there is a long list of internationally known designers such as Gustavo Cadile or Alan Faena from Argentina; Zuzu Angel, Carlos Miele or Alexandre Herchocovitch from Brazil; Francesca Miranda or Estebán Cotázar from Colombia; Manuel Cuevas or Eduardo Lucero from México and Angel Sánchez from Venezuela. Thanks to them and to many others, six Latin America cities are ranked among the top fashion capitals of the world, according to the renowned fashion publication *Global Language Monitor*. Moreover, according to the above-mentioned publication, within the 2009 global ranking of fashion capitals of the world, Brazil's Sao Paulo was listed as No. 8. It would seem unnecessary to mention the relevance of the fashion industry in the international promotion of Latin American textiles and garments.

Professional sport is another highly productive activity in the region with football and baseball clubs and players projecting themselves internationally and generating huge revenues. Football clubs like Boca Juniors, River Plate, Independiente, Racing, Botafogo, Corinthians, Fluminense, Juventus or Flamengo or baseball clubs such as Aguilas Caribeñas, Tigres del Licey, Diablos Rojos del Mexico, Tigres del Quintana Roo, Leones de Caracas o Navegantes del Magallanes, are widely known outside the region. Latin American football and baseball teams have been consistently producing international stars. Latin football names such as Messi, Ronaldo, Maradona, Pelé, Romario or Ronaldinho are known in the four corners of the world in the same way in which baseball fans around the globe are familiar with names such as Sammy Sosa, Roberto Clemente, Oswaldo Guillén, Edgar Renteria, Omar Vizquel or Andrés Galarraga.

Latin America has also shown to have important competitiveness in the publicity sector. Both Brazil and Argentina are recognised internationally for the quality and the creative talent of their publicity industry. According to the Gunn Report 2007 (based on the awards obtained in the most important publicity festivals around the world),

Argentina and Brazil are ranked respectively in the third and fourth positions. That places them behind the United States and the United Kingdom and before France, Spain, Japan and Germany.[52]

There would be many other examples to be mentioned where Latin American countries have proven to be successful in the area of international tradable services. These, and other similar exportable services, have to be promoted as part of a systematic effort to overcome dependence in commodities or intensive labour manufacturing. Nonetheless, within this sector, there is an area of particular relevance. We refer to the so-called global chains of value.

Global chains of value

Until recently, many services were either tradable in a limited manner or not tradable at all beyond their frontiers, but this situation has changed as a result of the exponential advance in information and telecommunication technologies. Thanks to them, distance has disappeared and many previously domestically encapsulated services have become global. Within the frame of the Information Technology Enabled Services (ITES), an immense variety of services can be provided from distance, giving a tremendous boost to the offshoring of white-collar jobs.

Several reasons can explain this process in motion: (a) the strong diffusion in the technologies of information and telecommunications; (b) the globalisation of competences that has allowed companies to look for the best available talents at the lower possible costs wherever they can be found; (c) the homogenisation of practices of consumption, production and management induced by globalisation; (d) the tendency within corporations to outsource or offshore non core areas.

Within the context of the last of the aforementioned reasons, we have seen the appearance of the so-called "back office", which implies the outsourcing of numerous activities traditionally performed inside the company. Among them the following: accounting, client management, salary payments, data processing, etc. And, of course, whenever

[52] *ibid.*

quality can be maintained and costs can be reduced, outsourcing tends to give place to offshoring, that is, the transference of jobs abroad.

As a matter of fact, we are witnessing the dematerialisation of corporations in the developed economies. Assembly lines and "back office" services are being scattered and offshored around the world in search for the lowest manpower costs. While corporations stick to brands and patents as their core areas, bulk of their activities is outsourced and offshored. According to *Bloomberg/Businessweek*:

> Some observers even believe Big Business is on the cusp of a new burst of productivity growth, ignited in part by offshore outsourcing as a catalyst...As executives shed more operations, they also are spurring new debate about how the future of corporation will look. Some management pundits theorise about the 'totally disaggregated corporation', wherein every function not regarded as crucial is stripped away...The rise of the offshore option is dramatically changing the economics of reengineering. With millions of low-cost engineers, financial analysts, consumer marketers, and architects now readily available via the Web, CEOs can see a quicker payoff. 'It used to be that companies struggled for a few years to show a 5% or 10% increase in productivity from outsourcing', says Pramod Bhasin, CEO of Genpact, the 19,000-employee back-office-processing unit spun off by GE last year. 'But by offshoring work, they can see savings of 30% to 40% in the first year' in labour costs...Professor Mohanbir Sawhney of Northwestern University's Kellogg School of Management, a self-proclaimed 'big believer in total disaggregation', says: 'One of our tasks in business schools is to train people to manage the virtual, globally distributed corporation'.[53]

Chains of value imply the interconnection between manufacturing and services within the context of global processes of production and trade. Moreover, in the future, more products will be sold on the basis of attached services according to experts, which mean that the lines between manufacturing and services are blurring. And more and more the level of services sent abroad increases in terms of knowledge

[53] "The future of outsourcing", 30 January 2006.

based and responsibility services. So far, more than 70% of the offshore white-collar jobs have remained within OECD countries, with India and China strongly emerging from the outside.[54] Nonetheless, that should be seen as the first step in a process that inevitably leads to equilibrium between job quality and the lowest possible job salaries. And, as India and China are showing, emerging economies can become unbeatable in this area.

Up to 2008, 2.3 million service jobs were estimated to have been offshored in the United States and 650,000 in the United Kingdom.[55] Nonetheless, these figures seem laughable when compared to what has been predicted by Alan Blinder, Director of the Princeton University Center for Economic Policy Studies. According to him, impersonal services are in the brink of a gigantic revolution. Such services, which are those that do not require a face-to-face interaction with the customer or patient, will be transferred in their tens of millions to emerging economies, where a gigantic pool of talent converges with much lower costs.[56] In another study that Blinder co-authored together with Alan B. Krueger, their conclusion was that jobs that require a high degree of education and qualification are, if anything, more offshorable than the rest.[57]

According to Saurabh Mishra, Susanna Lundstrom and Rahul Anand:

> The mid 1990s saw two seemingly separate but related developments. First was the revolution in information and communication technology (ICT) and, second, rapid growth in the global forces often referred to as the 3Ts — technology, transportability, and tradability — with the advent of internet age. Both events had a profound impact on the nature, productivity, and tradability of

[54] Andrés López, Daniela Ramos e Iván Torres, *op. cit.*

[55] Robyn Meredith, *The Elephant and the Dragon* (New York: W.W. Norton & Company, 2007).

[56] "Offshoring: The Next Industrial Revolution", *Foreign Affairs,* New York, Vol. 85, (March/April 2006), pp. 113–128.

[57] "Alternative Measures of Offshorability", National Bureau of Economic Research, Working Paper 15287 (August 2009), <http://www.nber.org/papers/w15287>.

> services. This has resulted in rapid growth of what can be called *modern impersonal progressive services*...These services differ significantly from the *traditional personal services*, which demand face-to-face interaction.[58]

We are talking thus of the massive migration of impersonal services jobs to the developing world in the next few decades. From accountants to software engineers, from designers to architects, from doctors to researchers, from financial consultants to lawyers, the areas of service jobs involved can become countless. The legal profession in the United States is currently under the tremendous strain caused by low-end legal work being increasingly handled overseas as corporations demand more cost-efficient fee arrangements. The problem is being considered deep and systemic and is generating a decline in the number of students taking law schools admission tests.[59] That trend is repeated in other professional markets as well. For Latin America, this represents a unique opportunity as well as a gigantic challenge. Both negative and positive elements surround the countries of the region in their possibilities to take advantage of such seismic changes.

The current state of the Latin American educational system stands ahead among the negative ones. And even though Latin American elites enjoy high levels of education, having, in many cases, attended to some of the best universities in the world, averages are still low. Much has to be done in order to improve the general educational levels as otherwise the opportunities derived from these chain of values could simply become a niche for the privileged ones.

Another negative factor is the fact that Latin America is insufficiently integrated to global production chains. According to the World Bank: "There is very little evidence suggesting substantial

---

[58] *op. cit.*, pp. 2, 3.

[59] David Segal, "Law schools see drop in students taking admissions tests", *International Herald Tribune*, 21 March 2012; Ethan Bronner, "Law schools struggle as legal careers falter", *The New York Times International Weekly*, 9 February, 2013.

integration of the region into global production chains. Latin American countries, for instance, do not typically appear in UNCTAD's lists of production centres and their companies are not reported among the large ones involved in global value chains."[60]

Among the positive elements is Latin America's Western heritage and background. As evidenced by the fact that the majority of offshored services jobs have so far remained within OECD countries, it would seem that cultural affinity still plays an important role. If that were to be the case Latin America enjoys of a comparative advantage in the Western world *vis-á-vis* many Asian nations.

Another positive factor derives from Latin America's online culture. According to Basil C. Puglisi, a digital brand marketing consultant formerly with AOL: "Although Latin America makes up only 8.2% of the world's population, they are the second largest consumer of social media. The online behaviour of Latin Americans is evolving right along with the rest of the world, but in many cases, a bit faster."[61] Indeed, Latin America has 118 million Facebook users which mean that 14% of all Facebook users are in the region. Moreover, Argentina and Brazil are currently among the world's leading countries for Google usage while Latin America has 55 million Twitter users and 8.6 million LinkedIn users.[62] According to *The Economist*, Mexico accounts for 26,091,000 Facebook users, Brazil for 20,031,000, Argentina for 15,291,000, Colombia for 14,410,000 and Venezuela for 8,974,000.[63]

Within the positive elements as well is Latin America's special know-how and experience in productive sectors associated with commodities. Such knowledge can be projected internationally through the aforementioned ITES. Among them, we could mention the agro industry in Brazil, Argentina, Chile or Colombia;

[60] *op. cit.*, p. 36.

[61] "Social networking statistics in Latin America", Digital Doughnut, <http://digitaldoughnut.com/social-networking-statistics-in-latin-america>.

[62] *ibid.*

[63] *The Economist Pocket World in Figures*, *op. cit.*

hydrocarbons in Venezuela, Mexico and Brazil; mining in Brazil, Chile and Peru; cattle management in Brazil, Argentina or Uruguay. And so on.

Western time zones also play in favour of Latin America as the region is on equal or close time frame with most of the United States and a few hours behind that of Western Europe. That allows a more direct interaction with foreign operations. Closeness to the United States has also enabled English to become a widely spoken language in the region, which even if not attaining the general use that characterises Indian middle class is nonetheless a familiar second language for many.

Latin America has a tremendous challenge ahead if it wants to become a relevant participant in the projected wave of offshore service jobs. The preparations herein involve three basic directions: education, the creation of an institutional base for supporting efforts in this area and infrastructural development. Education in Latin America requires a complete overhaul, with specific areas demanding special attention. These include massive investments in third and fourth levels of education with ambitious scholarship programs in national and foreign universities; the generalised teaching of English, the universal language of business, and thorough instrumental knowledge of information technology and communication tools.

The creation of an institutional base for promoting Latin American professional services in developed economies which implies, among other initiatives, advising local companies and individuals on how to take advantage of the international chains of value, while helping professionals and companies in linking with the Information Technology Services Qualification Center (for scoring their service performances internationally). The latter is a part of Carnegie Mellon University's School of Computer Science that has attained international recognition in addressing the emerging need for capability models and qualification methods for organisations involved in the Internet economy.

Infrastructural development is another priority field to support the aforementioned effort. Let us just take into consideration a single example in relation to this matter. A joint study by Ericsson, Arthur D. Little and Sweden's Chalmers Technological University on the 33 OECD member countries, concluded that for every 10 percentage points of increase in internet broadband penetration, a country can obtain a 1% increase in its GDP.[64] For a country willing to incursion in global value chains, adequate I.T. and communication technologies' infrastructure becomes essential. Latin American Governments should ambitiously aim at these directions.

Infrastructural development

But infrastructure not only concerns telecommunications and broadband facilities related to the international tradable services. It becomes a necessity for production and exports growth and diversification as well as for human development in general. Electricity, domestic transportation, ports and airports are as important for production and trade purposes as water, sewage and electricity are for human development purposes.

As the case of China and India shows, investment in infrastructure can make a great difference. Even if those two countries are at top of the world in GDP growth, the different levels of infrastructural development have generated a gap between them. Indeed living standards in China, measured through its GDP per capita, surpassed those of India more than 15 years ago. Since that time, China's economy has grown twice as fast as that of India and its GDP is currently more than two times bigger than the Indian one. It is widely accepted that investment in infrastructure has been one of the main ingredients of China's success. The fact of having a better infrastructure is one of the reasons why China was able to attract almost four times more direct foreign investment in 2006 (US$78,000 million) than India (US$19,700 million). In 2005, China spent 9%

[64] "Aseguran que duplicar la velocidad de la banda ancha sube el P.I.B.", TELAM, 8 de octubre 2011, <http://www.telam.com.ar/nota/3605>.

of its GDP in infrastructure compared to 3.6% by India. The Government of India had publicly recognise that its growth has been hampered as a result of its low levels of infrastructural development and it is currently trying to increase it to China's level. According to the Indian Minister of Finance, the inadequate level of infrastructure in his country has reduced its economic growth between 1.5% and 2% a year.[65]

Infrastructural limitations are hampering the possibilities of Latin America for economic growth, competitiveness and poverty reduction. Several studies show that if the infrastructure of the region could reach the level of Korea (which is average within the East Asian tigers), the GDP per capita growth could be increased by close to 4% while inequality could be reduced by between 10% and 20%. Nonetheless, the investment required for such a purpose would be considerable: between 2.4% and 5% of the annual GDP during 20 years. The infrastructural gap between Latin America and the seven East Asian Tigers increased substantially between 1980 and 1997: 48% in fixed telephone lines, 91% in electricity generating capacity and 53% in the longitude of the vial system. This different evolution of its infrastructural developments would explain a 30% gap in the GDP of the two regions between 1980 and 1997.[66]

Of the four classical infrastructural sectors — energy, communications, telecommunications and water — only telecommunications enjoy a good relative position in Latin America. Shortages in the communication sector are evident with particular reference to roads, highways, bridges, airports, ports, etc. Water infrastructure is also insufficient; even though in the hydroelectric subsector some Latin American countries are very well placed with Brazil, Venezuela and Argentina being ranked as No. 2, 3 and 6 world producers, respectively. As for energy developments, different from hydroelectricity,

[65] Laurel Graefe and Galina Alexeenco, "Infrastructure: the Foundation of Prosperity", *Econ South*, Federal Reserve Bank of Atlanta, Vol. 10, No. 2 (Second Quarter, 2008).
[66] Marianne Fay y Mary Morrison, *Infraestructra en America Latina y el Caribe: Acontecimietos Recients y Desafios Principales* (Bogota: Banco Mundial-Mayol Edciones, 2007).

most of the countries of the region are in need of important investments. Brazil, Mexico and Venezuela, though, have world class infrastructural developments in the hydrocarbon subsector with Argentina and Colombia following behind.[67]

According to the World Bank, Latin American governments drastically reduced their investments in infrastructure during the second half of the 80s and the decade of the 90s. This was due to a combination of austerity programs and the transference of responsibilities in this area to the private sector, which resulted from the structural reforms imposed by the IMF. The deterioration of infrastructure in Latin American countries in the 1980s is attributed to a sharp decline in public infrastructure investment owing to large and often abrupt fiscal adjustment. In the 1990s, and in spite of the opening of infrastructure projects to private participation, the private sector did not pick up momentum, thus considerably widening the infrastructure gap between Latin American countries and East Asian Tigers.[68]

Public investments in the six largest economies of the region, which had been of 3.1% of the GDP during the period 1980–1985, plummeted to 0.8% between 1996 and 2001. At the same time, private investment that had been of 0.6% between 1980 and 1985 augmented to 1.4% during 1996 and 2001. In other words, total investments in these countries descended from 3.7% of the GDP during 1980–1985 to 2.2% during 1996–2001.[69]

According to the available data, projected Latin American public investments in infrastructure for the period 2011–2015 amounts to US$450 billion, which would tantamount to 2% of the regional GDP.[70] If that amount was to be complemented by private investment

---

[67] Felipe González, "América Latina: la crisis y el futuro", Cristina Fernández de Kirchner "América Latina como potencia energética" en *Iberoamérica 2020: Retos ante la Crisis*, Felipe González, edit. (Madrid: Fundación Carolina y Siglo XXI, 2009).

[68] *op. cit.*

[69] Marianne Fay y Mary Morrison, *op. cit.*

[70] "América Latina invertirá US$ 450.000 m en infraestructura", *CGLA/Infrastructure*, 20 April 2010, <hhtp://cg-la.con/en/cgla-news?start=650>.

in a percentage similar to that of the period 1996–2001, the total investment would still be below the 4% that many experts believe to be the right percentage of GDP needed. Nonetheless, according to experts, such percentages of private investment are no longer attainable as investors have lost much of the interest that they had in this sector during the 90s and the beginning of the millennium, as returns turned out to be lower than expected.[71]

Brazil is a good example of the problems that infrastructure limitations can pose to a booming economy. According to the BBC News:

> But while Brazil's booming economy has led to an overall feel good factor, investors are concerned about the state of the country's infrastructure, which can add significantly to the costs of getting goods to the market...The challenge is not only moving goods but also people around the country. Air travel has been growing at a rate of 10% a year and an upgrade in the country's main airports is long overdue...The bulk of Brazilian infrastructure, the main roads and ports, as well as the telecommunication network, was built in the 1960s and early 1970's, when the military government embarked on a major program of state investment. The challenge faced by the Lula government and one confronting whoever is elected on 3 October will be to bring this ageing infrastructure back into shape to ensure Brazil's expectations of growth do not falter.[72]

As the above BBC News report mentioned, with a land size of 7,859.269 square kilometres the United States had, in 2008, 4,400.111 kilometres of paved roads whereas Brazil with 8,547,403 square kilometres had, in 2007, only 211,679 kilometres of paved roads. It is obvious that if the region wants to remain competitive in relation to other emerging economies, it will have to do much better than it does in infrastructure, as it is the case as well in education.

---

[71] Marianne Fay y Mary Morrison, *op. cit.*

[72] Paulo Cabral and Liz Throsell, "Clogged roads and ports harm Brazil's development plans", *BBC News*, 29 September 2010, <http://www.bbc.co.uk/news/world-latin-america-11413890>.

Irrespective of whether the issue is human development, services, manufacturing or exports, investments in infrastructure have to increase significantly in relation to what has been projected. That implies the need for higher public investment as a percentage of the GDP in this sector. On the other hand, Latin America (and in this case basically South America), should take advantage of an evolving element that can be of great help: China's increasing investments in the region.

Fortunately, an important group of infrastructural projects with Chinese participation are on the pipeline. In addition to some already referred in relation to Venezuela, we could mention the following: a "dry canal" that involves linking the Atlantic and Pacific coasts by railroad as well as involvement in a host of other projects, including the "Ruta del Sol" and "Autopista de las Americas" highways and the Socomoso and Ituango hydroelectric dams, in Colombia; railway projects including the 1,700 kilometres line from Belgrano to Cargas plus subway lines in the city of Cordoba in Argentina; participation in the construction of the Belo Monte dam (the third largest hydroelectric project in the world) as well as in the construction of the 1,300 kilometres long Gasene pipeline in Brazil; construction of the refinery of the Pacific near Manta plus the Coca Coda Sinclair, the Sopladora and the Toachi-Pilaton hydroelectric facilities, in Ecuador. And so on.[73]

Sovereign wealth funds

Sovereign wealth funds is another area that needs to be covered within Latin America's road map. This is particularly the case for commodities' exporters which have to prepare for the lean cows period while they are amidst a fat cows one. According to Edwin M. Truman:

> Sovereign wealth funds or their near equivalent come in many forms, with a variety of objectives...Consequently, comparisons among them are difficult. Nevertheless, it is possible to outline a core set of

---

[73] Evan Ellis, "The Expanding Chinese Footprint in Latin America", *Asie Visions 49*, Institut Francais de Relations Internationales, Center for Asian Studies (Paris: February 2012).

> common elements that are substantially relevant for all such entities whether the objective is short-term macro-economic stabilisation, wealth transfer across generations, or a combination of objectives, which usually is the case.[74]

Sovereign wealth funds can indeed be divided in two main groups. The first are the stabilisation funds, which are created to reduce the volatility of government revenues and to counter the boom and bust cycles' adverse effects on the national economy. The second are the saving funds, which build up savings for future generations. Such dual objectives can be, of course, combined or enlarged.

Among essentially-oriented stabilisation funds, we could mention the Stabilization Fund of the Russian Federation; the Petroleum Fund of Norway; Chile's Copper Stabilization Fund; Colombia's Oil Stabilization Fund; Mexico's Oil Income Stabilization Fund; Sudan's Oil Revenue Stabilization Account; Venezuela's Macroeconomic Stabilization Fund or the Central Bank of Iran's Oil Stabilization Fund. Conversely, amidst primarily-oriented saving fund, we find the Equatorial Guinea's Fund for Future; Gabon's Fund for Future Generations; Australia's Future Fund; Canada's Alberta Heritage Savings Trust Fund; Norway's Government Pension Fund or Alaska's Permanent Fund.[75]

Sovereign wealth funds may follow other aims as well. They can be used to secure access to strategically needed resources abroad as is the case of the China Investment Corporation or to bolster the country's standing as an international financial centre as is the case of the Government of Singapore Investment Corporation or Singapore's Temasek Holdings.

According to Marc LeBlanc:

> The International Monetary Fund estimates that the total size of sovereign wealth funds investments is roughly US$2 trillion

[74] "A Scoreboard for Sovereign Wealth Funds", Peterson Institute for International Economics, Washington D.C., 19 October 2007, <http://www.iie.com/publications/papers/truman1007swf.pdf>.

[75] "Sovereign Wealth Funds details", *Sovereign Wealth Funds News*, <http://www.sovereignwealthfundsnews.com.phd>.

> to US$3 trillion. The countries with the largest sovereign wealth funds are Saudi Arabia, United Arab Emirates, Norway, Singapore, Kuwait, Russia and China. Some observers see the growth in sovereign wealth funds as an indication of structural shifts within the global financial system and international relations. These shifts are (1) a redistribution in international wealth from developed countries to developing countries that historically have not played a major role in international finance; and (2) a shift in control of funds from the private sector to the public sector.[76]

According to ECLAC, though, sovereign wealth funds represent today US$5 trillion, more than US$4 trillion up since 2002, with Asia, Middle East and Northern Africa accounting for 55% of the total and China alone representing 29%.[77] For Latin American countries, and in particular for those benefiting from the hike of their commodities' exports, preparing for uncertain times should be seen as a rational policy. It must be recognised though that with more pressing development expenditures in their agendas, such as education, healthcare or infrastructure, sovereign wealth funds may not be seen as a priority. With both elements in balance, some kind of trade off should be reached. Indeed, it would seem as irresponsible not to consider the possibility of rainy days in the future as it would be to try to confront such uncertainties at the expense of forgetting urgent current problems such as malnutrition or deficient healthcare. Only common sense can dictate an answer to such dilemma.

South American countries, with those with the largest GDP or GDP per capita leading the way, should invest in sovereign wealth funds, but so should, Mexico. Given the fact that in a few years time the latter may cease being an oil exporter to become an oil importer,

---

[76] "Sovereign Wealth Funds: International and Canadian Policy Responses", Parliamentary Information and Research Service, Library of Parliament, Canada, (February, 2010). <http://www.parl.gc.ca/content/LOP/ResearchPublications/2010-09-e.htm>.

[77] CEPAL, *La República popular China y América Latina y el Caribe: Diálogo y Cooperación ante los Nuevos Desafíos de la Economía Mundial.* (Santiago de Chile: Junio de 2012).

and given the current bust that oil gives to its total exports. Mexico needs an umbrella to anticipate the possibility of rainy days

Up to the present, only five Latin American countries have created sovereign wealth funds: Brazil, Mexico, Venezuela, Colombia and Chile, with Venezuela and Chile counting with two each. Of them, Brazil, Mexico, Venezuela, Colombia and Chile have anti cyclical stabilization funds. Chile also has a saving fund while Venezuela's second fund is clearly directed to domestic development purposes: the National Development Fund.[78] Sufficient allocation of funds for these institutions, and others to be created is thus a priority.

Until here, the overview of a potential route map for Latin America has been provided. And even if the need for such map goes beyond the region's relation with China, it is obvious that a fundamental part of it is determined by the nature of such relations. That becomes quite clear when bearing in mind that Chinese import of Latin American products grew 1,153% between 2000 and 2010 while Chinese exports to Latin America grew 1,800% during the same period.[79] No other economic interlocutor can claim such game changer effect upon the region. Being that the case, the economic association with China should translate into a Latin America White Book defining a strategic vision of the same. Moreover, much of what should be therein contained regards negotiations with China. Both instances — the drafting of a White book and the negotiations — should entail a common Latin American (or at least South American) position.

White Paper and Negotiations

China represents a key trade and economic partner for most of Latin America. As such it should play a relevant role in helping to solve Latin American uncertainties in relation to its economic future. Uncertainties derived in no small measure by China's appearance in the regional scenario. To that aim, Latin American governments should define their relation to the Asian giant on the basis of a tripod

[78] "Sovereign Wealth Funds details", *op. cit.*
[79] Xulio Ríos, *op. cit.*

formed by purpose, credibility and efficacy. A purpose that clarifies the objectives that it wants to attain from such a relation; a credibility based on a realistic assessment of its leverage tools and an efficacy sustained by its ability as a negotiator.

Both purpose and credibility should be formally express in a White Paper that guides Latin American negotiators when dealing with China. Defining a long-term strategy and sustaining the same with a set of identifiable power tools (as would be, by instance, the possession of 15% of the world oil reserves, 25% of the world agricultural lands, 30% the world water or 40% of the world gold and copper reserves), becomes essential when interacting with a cold blooded promoter of its national interest as China. Becoming a passive and reactive member in a partnership with such country, as otherwise would be the case, could indeed be hazardous. Efficacy (which when negotiating with China means basically determination and firm pulse) is undoubtedly helped by certainty in the aims and the means.

Within the context of purpose, credibility and efficacy, acting as a block becomes essential. Alone, Latin American countries are no match for a nation that has been able to overplay the most powerful countries and corporations of the world. The block must express itself both in the definition and execution phases of the above-mentioned process. As for the composition of such group, Latin America could gather together as a whole or as fractions of the whole. Regionally or sub regionally.

The leverage of the whole is obviously bigger but so is the heterogeneity of the interests involved. The choice is thus between embracing more but tightening less, or embracing less but tightening more. Mexican-type countries and Brazil-type countries could each go their own separate ways, with the latter undoubtedly enjoying a better forecast. Or, they could go together. The multiplicity of Latin American integration groups allows for both options and many others.

There is, indeed, an ample menu to choose from when thinking in terms of block power. From MERCOSUR that gathers Brazil, Argentina, Uruguay, Paraguay and Venezuela to UNASUR joined by all South American countries; from the Bolivarian Alternative for the Americas integrated by Venezuela, Ecuador, Bolivia, Cuba, Nicaragua and some English speaking Caribbean countries to the Andean Common Market formed by Colombia, Ecuador, Peru and Bolivia; from the Central American Common Market joined by El Salvador, Honduras, Nicaragua, Guatemala and Costa Rica to the Latin American Integration Association that gathers all Iberian American countries; from the Community of Latin American and Caribbean States formed by all the countries of the hemisphere with the exception of the United States and Canada to smaller free trade agreements.

Obtaining more Chinese infrastructural investments and technological transfers; integrating into value chains led by China; having Chinese firms joint venturing with local companies for the purpose of manufacturing in the region; having China acquiring more manufactured products: these are but a few of the common goals that Latin Americans could attain if they negotiate together within a clear framework of aims.

Curiously enough, it was China that chose the regional body that it wanted to have as a counterpart, which meant taking in their hands a decision that Latin American countries had failed to take. On 26 June 2012, during a Latin American tour that brought him to Brazil, Argentina, Uruguay and Chile, Prime Minister Wen Jiabao implicitly recognised that the representativeness and the scale of the Community of Latin American and Caribbean States (CELAC), made it the best interlocutor and proposed the creation of a China and Latin America and the Caribbean Cooperation Forum that would gather periodically both China and the troika of the CELAC.[80]

Even though it was China and not Latin America who made this decision, the simple fact that the former wanted to discuss and negotiate the big issues of the relation with the latter within an institutionalise framework is very good news. This represents a clear cut difference with the divide and conquers strategy traditionally followed by the United States or the IMF when dealing with the region.

---

[80] Alicia Barcena, "El salto de China en América Latina y el Caribe", *El Universal*, 5 de julio 2012.

On that same occasion, Prime Minister Wen Jiabao set the tone for future relations when aiming at duplicating the amount of trade between China and Latin America and the Caribbean during the next five years so as to reach US$400 billion. Equally important was the statement that China was not looking for a trade surplus with the region and that it was willing to increase the import of Latin American manufactures and higher value added products. By the same token, Premier Wen Jiabao proposed the creation of a cooperation fund between the parties in order to finance joint venture projects in areas such as manufacturing, new technologies and sustainable growth. It announced, at the same time, the opening of a line of credit for the development of regional infrastructures.[81]

Even if China defined the terms of the game, Wen Jiabao's proposals reflected many of the points that should have been included in a Latin American White Book. What was lost in not taking the initiative was won in not having to convince China on the merits of the proposal. If China is willing to "walk the talk", its partnership with Latin America can indeed become very successful for the latter.

---

[81] *idem.*

Conclusion

Acting as a sorcerer apprentice, the West with the United States in front put in motion a market-oriented globalisation process that it was unable to control and that ended up by eroding its competitive capacity and its social stability. Developing economies, which were submitted to ideologically-oriented prescriptions and double standards by the richer countries, ended up by becoming the main beneficiaries of this process. This unintended result was possible thanks to the strength attained by a group of developing economies and very particularly by China.

Greatly benefiting from the race to the bottom of production costs put in place by the West, many developing economies were able to emerge with unsuspected speed. Having China as its main engine, these economies have become increasingly integrated, sustaining in the process a fundamental part of the global trade growth. While this phenomenon was taking shape, market economy excesses generated a seismic crisis that dramatically accelerated the ongoing but up to then slow decline of the West. While the ascendant and descendant curves of developing and developed economies are in the process of crossing each other, a decoupling tendency between the two of them becomes evident.

Relations between China and Latin America, epitomise well the growing integration between emerging economies. Whereas for China the benefits of this economic partnership are clear, they are less so for Latin America. For the latter, this becomes a complex relationship with winners and losers amid its ranks and with opportunities as well as risks surrounding the process. Such situation, nonetheless, emerges from facts beyond Latin America's control and as such there is little to discuss about and much to act upon. Moreover, as no better option than that represented by China is currently on the table for the majority of its countries, Latin America should focus in ameliorating what can be ameliorated within such relation, while defining a route map for the future. Such a map should aim at maximising the opportunities and reducing the risks derived from such economic partnership.

Much is feasible in building a future where natural resources become more protected and valuable but at the same time less relevant and where the current middle income trap that surrounds most of Latin American economies may be overcome. This requires reinventing the nature of that region's economic association with the world, by taking advantage of the window opportunity represented by the high prices of natural resources that benefits so many of them. This is a difficult and demanding endeavour. The same not only requires strategic clarity and perseverance but also substantial efforts in human and infrastructural developments as well as great deal of creativity in taking advantage of the new frontiers in international trade. Saving for the future in also a necessity. In Claudio Loser words, though: "At a time when the world is becoming more integrated and the directions of trade and investment are changing dramatically, there are questions about the sustainability of policies in the region. Although a new spirit of innovation is emerging, a degree of serious complacency remains."[1] Complacency is indeed the biggest threat to the region's future as there is no substitute for success in this process in the same manner in which not moving ahead with change is not an option.

[1] "Latin America in the Age of Globalization: A Follower or a Force of its Own?" (Miami: University of Miami, Center for Hemispheric Policy, 11 June 2012), p. 3.

Bibliography

Akim Cigdem and Kose M. Ayhan. "Changing Nature of North-South Linkages: Stylized Facts and Explanations." International Monetary Fund Working Paper WP/07/280. Washington D.C.: December 2007.

Albert Michel. *Capitalisme contre Capitalisme*. París: Editions du Seuil, 1991.

Alesina Alberto and Spolaore Enrico. *The Size of Nations*. Cambridge: MIT Press, 2003.

Amuzegar Jahangir. "The North-South Dialogue: From Conflict to Compromise." *Foreign Affairs*, Vol. 54, March/April 1976, pp. 56–65.

Arreaza Adriana. "El boom de las materias primas en América Latina: Es suficiente para sostener el crecimiento?" Corporación Andina de Fomento. Caracas: Agosto 2010.

Arroyo Picard Alberto. "El TLCAN 5 años después: Contenidos, Resultados y Propuestas." Comisión de Comercio de la Cámara de Diputados, México: LVII Legislatura, 2000.

Asian Development Bank. *Asia 2050: Realizing the Asian Century*. Manila: Asia Development Bank, 2011.

Attali Jacques. *Survivre aux Crises*. Paris: Fayard, 2009.

Aydon Cyril. *History of Mankind*. London: Running Press, 2007.

Barber Benjamin. *Jihad vs. McWorld*. New York: Ballantine Books, 1966.

Bergsten C. Fred. "The Dollar and the Deficits." *Foreign Affairs*, Vol. 88, November/December 2009, pp. 20–38.

Blinder Alan S. "Offshoring: The Next Industrial Revolution." *Foreign Affairs*, New York, Vol. 85, March/April 2006, pp. 113–128.

Blinder Alan S. and Krueger Alan B. "Alternative Measures of Offshorability." Working Paper 15287, National Bureau of Economic Research, August 2009, <http://www.nber.org/papers/w15287>.

Bremmer Ian. *Every Nation for Itself: Winners and Losers in a G-Zero World*. New York: Portfolio, 2012.

Brown Gordon. *Beyond the Crash*. London: Simon & Schuster UK Ltd., 2010.

Brzezinski Zbigniew. *Second Chance*. New York: Basic Books, 2007.

Cairncross Frances. *The Death of Distance: How the Communications Revolution is Changing Our Lives*. Boston: Harvard Business School Press, 1997.

Chellaney Brahma. *Asian Juggernaut*. New York: Harper, 2010.

China Economic Review. *China by Numbers* 2010. Hong Kong: China Economic Review Publishing, 2010.

Chubb John E. *Interest Groups and the Bureaucracy: The Politics of Energy*. Stanford: Stanford University Press, 1983.

Comisión Económica para América Latina y el Caribe. *Panorama Social de América Latina 2010*. Santiago de Chile: Noviembre 2010.

Comisión Económica para América Latina y el Caribe. *La República popular China y América Latina y el Caribe: Diálogo y Cooperación ante los Nuevos Desafíos de la Economía Mundial*. Santiago de Chile: Junio de 2012.

Cooper Ramo Joshua. *The Beijing Consensus*. The Foreign Policy Centre. London: May 2004.

Cooper Ramo Joshua. *Brand China*. London: The Foreign Policy Centre. London: February 2007.

Das Gurcharan. "The India Model." *Foreign Affairs*, Vol. 85, July/August 2006, pp. 2–16.

Díaz Vásquez Julio A. "China-Latinoamérica: relaciones económicas 2010." *Jiexi Zhonguuo: Análisis y Pensamiento Iberoaméricano sobre China*, Número 2 (Primer Trimestre 2012), pp. 16–22.

Díaz Vásquez Julio A. "Relaciones económicas China-América Latina: Oportunidad o amenaza?" El *Observatorio de la Política China*, 6 de agosto 2011.

Drezner Daniel W. "The New New World Order." *Foreign Affairs*, Vol. 86, March/April 2007, pp. 34–46.

Dussel Peters Enrique. "The Mexico-China Economic Relationship in Electronics: A Case Study of the PC Industry in Jalisco." In *The Impact of China's Global Economic Expansion on Latin America*, edited by Jenkins Rhys. Norwich: University of East Anglia Press, 2008.

Dye Thomas R. and Zeigler Harmon. *The Irony of Democracy*. Monterrey, Cal.: Brooks/Cole Publishing Company, 1987.

Eichengree Barry and Gupta Poonam. "The Service Sector as India's Road to Economic Growth?" Indian Council on International Economic Relations, Working Paper No. 249. New Delhi: April 2010.

ECLAC/UNESCO. *Financing and Managing Education in Latin America and the Caribbean.* Santiago de Chile: Economic Commission for Latin America and the Caribbean, 2004.

Economic Commission for Latin American and the Caribbean. *Foreign Direct Investment in Latin America and the Caribbean 2010.* Santiago de Chile: 2010.

Economic Commission for Latin America and the Caribbean. *Statistical Yearbook for Latin America and the Caribbean.* Santiago de Chile: 2010.

Ellis Evan. "The Expanding Chinese Footprint in Latin America." Asie Visions 49, Institut Francais de Relations Internationales, Center for Asian Studies. Paris: February 2012.

Fay Marianne y Morrison Mary. *Infraestructra en America Latina y el Caribe: Acontecimietos Recients y Desafios Principales.* Bogota: Banco Mundial, Mayol Edciones, 2007.

Ferguson Niall. *Empire: How Britain Made the Modern World.* London: Penguin Books, 2004.

Ferguson Niall. *The Ascent of Money.* New York: Penguin Books, 2008.

Ferguson Niall. *Civilization: The West and the Rest.* London: Allen Lane, 2011.

Forgacs David. *Antonio Gramsci Reader.* London: Lawrence & Wishart, 2001.

Friedberg Aaron L. *A Contest for Supremacy: China, America and the Struggle for Mastery in Asia.* New York: W.W. Norton & Company, 2011.

Friedman Thomas L. *The World is Flat.* London: Penguin Books, 2006.

Fu Zhengyuan. *Autocratic Tradition and Chinese Politics.* Cambridge: Cambridge University Press, 1993.

Gallager Kevin P. and Porzecanski Roberto. *The Dragon in the Room.* Stanford: Stanford University Press, 2010.

Ghesquiere Henri. *Singapore's Success.* Singapore: Thompson, 2007.

Golub Philip S. "Quand la Chine et L'Inde dominaent le monde." *Maniere de Voir*, París: Janvier-March, 2006.

González Peña Juan Miguel. "Una aproximación a las relaciones económico-comerciales entre China y América Latina y el Caribe." *Observatorio de la Política China*, 13 de septiembre 2011.

González Felipe, Edit. *Iberoamérica 2020: Retos ante la Crisis* (Madrid: Fundación Carolina y Siglo XXI, 2009).

Graefe Laurel and Alexeenco Galina. "Infrastructure: the Foundation of Prosperity." *Econ South*, Federal Reserve Bank of Atlanta, Vol. 10, No. 2, Second Quarter, 2008.

Grandin Greg. *Empire's Workshop*. New York: Metropolitan Books, 2006.
Guardiola-Rivera Oscar, *What if Latin America Ruled the World?* London: Bloomsbury, 2011.
Gunder Frank Andre. "The World Economic System in Asia before European Hegemony." *The Historian*, Vol. 56, Issue 2, December, 1994, pp. 259–276.
Gungwu Wang and Wong John, ed. *Interpreting China's Development*. Singapore: World Scientific, 2007.
Gupta Anil K. and Wang Haiyan. *Getting China and India Right*. San Francisco: Jossey-Bass, 2009.
Ha-Joon Chang. *Bad Samaritans*. London: Random House Business Books, 2007.
Halperin Donghi, Tulio. *História Contemporánea de América Latina*. Buenos Aires: Alianza Editorial, 1997.
Haraoka Naoyuki. "The Economic Outlook for Japan in 2012 and Beyond-How can the Japanese Economy help the Global Economy to avoid falling into a Great Depression?" Institute of Southeast Asian Studies Regional Outlook Forum, Singapore, 5 January 2012.
Hernández Rada Silvia. "Venezuela y China: Relaciones económicas en el régimen de Hugo Chávez (1999–2011)." *Observatorio de la Economía y Sociedad China*, Universidad de Málaga, número 15, Junio 2011.
Hout Thomas M. and Pankaj Ghemawat. "China vs. the world." *Harvard Business Review*, December 2010, pp. 95–103.
Huffington Arianna. *Third World America*. New York: Crown Publishers, 2010.
Hungtinton Samuel. *The Clash of Civilizations and the Remaking of the World Order*. New York: Simon & Schuster, 1996.
Hutton Will and Giddens Anthony, edit. *Global Capitalism*. New York: New York Press 2000.
Inter-American Development Bank. *The Emergence of China: Opportunities and Challenges for Latin America and the Caribbean*. Washington D.C., March 2005.
Inter-American Dialogue. "Pobreza y Desigualdad en América Latina." Washington D.C., Noviembre 2009.
International Monetary Fund. *World Economic Outlook Database*. Washington D.C., September 2011.
International Monetary Fund. *World Economic Outlook Database*. Washington D.C., April 2012.
Izquierdo Alejandro and Talvi Ernesto, coord. *One Region, Two Speeds?* Washington D.C.: Inter-American Development Bank, March 2011.

Jacques Martin. *When China Rules the World.* London: Allen Lane, 2009.
Karabell Zachary. *Superfusion.* New York: Simon & Schuster, 2009.
Kennedy Paul. *The Rise and Fall of Great Powers.* London: Fontana Press, 1989.
Kennedy Paul. *Preparando para o Século XXI.* Rio de Janeiro: Editora Campus, 1993.
Kerschener Edward M. and Huq Naeema. "Asian Affluence: The Emerging 21st Century Middle Class." Morgan Stanley Smith Barney, New York, June 2011.
Kissinger Henry. *Diplomacy.* New York: Simon & Schuster, 1994.
Kosacoff Bernardo y Campanario Sebastián. *La Revalorizacion de las Materias Primas y sus Efectos en América Latina.* Santiago de Chile: CEPAL, Mayo 2007.
Krugman Paul. "Dutch Tulips and Emerging Markets." *Foreign Affairs,* Vol. 74, July/August 1995, pp. 28–44.
Krugman Paul. *The Return of Depression Economics and the Crisis of 2008.* London: W.W. Norton & Co., 2009.
Kuttner Robert. *The End of Laissez-Faire.* New York: Alfred A. Knopf, 1991.
Kynge James. *China Shakes the World.* London: Phoenix, 2006.
Lam Willy. "China's 11th five year plan." *China Brief,* 30 April 2006.
LeBlanc Marc. "Sovereign Wealth Funds: International and Canadian Policy Responses." Parliamentary Information and Research Service, Library of Parliament, Ottawa, February 2010.
Lee T.Y. "Crecimiento de las Economías Asiáticas." PECC XII, Papel de trabajo, Santiago de Chile, 30 septiembre–2 octubre 1997.
Leonard Mark. *What does China Think?* New York: Public Affairs, 2008.
Loes Andre. "Lat Am Trade Flows", HSBC Research, Economics Latin America, February, 2013.
Looney Robert. *Routledge Encyclopedia of International Political Economy.* London: Routledge, 1999.
López Andrés, Ramos Daniela y Torres Iván. *Las Exportaciones de Servicio y su Integración a las Cadenas Globales de Valor.* Santiago de Chile: Comisión Económica para América Latina y el Caribe, marzo 2009.
Loser Claudio. "Latin America in the Age of Globalization: A Follower or a Force of its Own?" Miami: University of Miami, Center for Hemispheric Policy, 11 June 2012.
Luce Edward. *Time to Start Thinking: America and the Spectre of Decline.* London: Little, Brown, 2012.

MacFarquhar Roderick, edit. *The Politics of China: The Eras of Mao and Deng*. Cambridge: Cambridge University Press, 1997.

Maddison Angus. *The World Economy: Historical Statistics*. Paris: OECD, 2003.

Mahbubani Kishore. *The New Asian Hemisphere: The Irresistible Shift of Global Power to the East*. New York: Public Affairs, 2008.

Mandelbaum Michael. *The Frugal Superpower*. New York: Public Affairs, 2010.

Mejía Reyes Pablo y Carbajal Suárez Yolanda. "Comportamiento de las exportaciones mexicanas ante la desaceleración estadounidense." *Revista Trimestral de Coyuntura Económica*, México D.F., Julio–Septiembre 2008.

Meier Kenneth J. and Bohte John. *Politics and the Bureaucracy*. Belmont, Cal.: Wadsworth Publishing, 2006.

Meredith Robyn. *The Elephant and the Dragon*. New York: W.W. Norton & Company, 2007.

Ministerio del Poder Popular para la Planificación y el Desarrollo. *Logros de la Revolución*. Caracas: Octubre 2008.

Mishra Saurabh, Lundstrom Susanna and Anand Rahul. "Service Sophistication and Economic Growth." The World Bank, South Asia Region, Policy Research Working Paper 5606, March 2011.

Morris Charles R. *The Two Trillion Dollar Meltdown*. New York: Public Affairs, 2008.

Moyo Dambisa. *How the West was Lost*. London: Allen Lane, 2011.

Naim Moises. "Washington Consensus or Washington Confusion." *Foreign Policy*, Spring 2000, pp. 87–103.

Naisbitt John and Doris. *China's Megatrends*. New York: Harper Business, 2010.

Nat Kamal. *India's Century*. New York: McGraw Hill, 2008.

Ocampo José Antonio and Parra María Angela. "The Terms of Trade for Commodities in the Twentieth Century." CEPAL Review No. 79, April 2003.

Orstrom Moller, Jorgen. *How Asia can Shape the World*. Singapore: Institute of Southeast Asian Studies, 2011.

Paramio Luis. "Perspectivas de la izquierda en América Latina." Documentos del Real Instituto Elcano de Estudios Internacionales y Estratégicos, Madrid, 2003.

Patten Christopher. "Speech of Commissioner Patten at Canning House Gala Dinner." London, Canning House, 4 February 2004.

Prasad Esward and Ye Lei. *The Renminbi's Role in the Global Monetary System*. Washington D.C.: Brookings, February 2012.

Rifkin Jeremy. *O Fim dos Empregos*. Sao Paulo: Makron Books, 1966.

Ríos Xulio. *China: de la A a la Z*. Madrid: Editorial Popular, 2008.

Ríos Xulio. *Mercado y Control Político en China*. Madrid: Los Libros de la Catarata, 2007.

Ríos Xulio. "Crédito y descrédito en América Latina." *Jiexi Zhonguuo: Análisis y Pensamiento Iberoaméricano sobre China*, Número 2, Primer Trimestre 2012, pp. 23–24.

Rohthstein, Robert L. *Global Bargaining: UNCTAD and the Quest for a New International Economic Order*. Princeton: Princeton University Press, 1979.

Sader Emir, Jinkings Ivana *et al.*, coord. *Latinoamérica: Enciclopedia Contemporánea de América Latina y El Caribe*. Madrid: Clacso-Ediciones AKAL, S.A., 2009.

Secretaría Permanente del Sistema Económico Latinoamericano y del Caribe. "Relaciones Económicas de Estados Unidos con los Países de América Latina y el Caribe en Época de Transición." Caracas, Mayo 2012.

Skalair Leslie. *Globalization, Capitalism & its Alternatives*. Oxford: Oxford University Press, 2002.

Simonit Silvia. "Las inversiones chinas en América del Sur." *Jiexi Zhonguuo: Análisis y Pensamiento Iberoaméricano sobre China*, Número 2, Primer Trimestre 2012, pp. 4–15.

Simpfendorfer Ben. *The New Silk Road*. New York: Pelgrave Macmillan, 2011.

Sinnot Emily, Nash John and de la Torre Augusto. *Natural Resources in Latin America and the Caribbean: Beyond Booms and Busts*? Washington D.C.: The World Bank, 2010.

Sistema Económico Latinoamericano y del Caribe. "Informe sobre el proceso de Integración Regional 2011–2012." Caracas, Agosto 2012.

Sistema Económico Latinoamericano y del Caribe. "La crisis en la Zona Euro, su impacto en el proceso de integración europeo y en las relaciones birregionales entre América Latina y el Caribe y la Unión Europea. Líneas de acción desde la perspectiva latinoamericana y caribeña." Caracas, 17 al 19 de octubre 2012.

Sistema Económico Latinoamericano y del Caribe. "Las relaciones entre China y América Latina y el Caribe en la actual coyuntura económica mundial." Caracas, Septiembre 2012.

Solinger Dorothy J. *Chinese Business under Socialism*. Berkeley: University of California Press, 1984.
Spero Joan E. and Hart Jeffrey A. *The Politics of International Economic Relations*. Belmont, Ca.: Thompson/Wadswoth, 2003.
Srinivasan T.N. *Growth, Sustainability, and India's Economic Reforms*. Oxford: Oxford University Press, 2011.
Stiglitz Joseph. *Globalization and its Discontents*. London: W.W. Norton & Company, 2002.
Stiglitz Joseph. *The Roaring Nineties*. London: Allan Lane, 2003.
Stiglitz Joseph. *Making Globalization Work*. London: Allen Lane, 2006.
The Economist. *Pocket World in Figures: 2012 Edition*. London: Profile Books Ltd., 2012.
Toro Hardy Alfredo. *El Desafío Venezolano: Cómo Influir las Decisiones Políticas Estadounidenses?* Caracas: Universidad Simón Bolívar, 1987.
Toro Hardy Alfredo. *El Desorden Global*. Caracas: Editorial Panapo, 1996.
Toro Hardy Alfredo. *The Age of Villages: The Small Village vs. The Global Village*. Bogota: Villegas Editores, 2002.
Toro Hardy Alfredo. *Tiene Futuro América Latina?* Bogotá: Villegas Editores, 2004.
Toro Hardy Alfredo. *Hegemonía e Imperio*. Bogotá: Villegas Editores, 2007.
Truman Edwin M. "A Scoreboard for Sovereign Wealth Funds." Peterson Institute for International Economics, Washington D.C., 19 October 2007.
Turzi Mariano. "Grown in the Cone: South America's Soybean Boom." *Current History*, Vol. 111, No. 742, February 2012, pp. 50–55.
UNESCO. *The State of Education in Latin America and the Caribbean: Guaranteeing Quality Education for All*. Santiago de Chile: Regional Bureau of Education for Latin America and the Caribbean, August 2008.
UNCTAD/UNECE, "The Russian Crisis of 1988", October 1998, <http://www.twnside.org.sg/title/1998-cn.htm>).
Victor David G. and Yueb Linda. "The New Energy Order: Managing Insecurities in the Twenty-first Century." *Foreign Affairs*, Vol. 89, January/February 2010, pp. 61–73.
Villarreal M. Angeles. "The Mexican Economy after the Global Financial Crisis." Congressional Research Service, Washington D.C.: 9 September 2010.
Vogel Ezra F. *Deng Xiaoping and the Transformation of China*. Cambridge: Harvard University Press, 2011.

Wien Byron and Koenen Kriztina. *George Soros.* Rio de Janeiro: Editora Nova Fronteira, 1995.

Woods Ngaire. "Order, Globalization and Inequality." In Held David and McGrew Anthony, *The Global Transformations Reader.* Cambridge: Polity Press, 2000.

World Bank. *Latin America and the Caribbean's Long Term Growth: Made in China?* Washington D.C.: September 2011.

Yeo David and Ng Philip. "China's Twin Paradigm Shift: Beacons in a Sea of Change." *IE Insights*, International Enterprise Singapore, Vol. 1/ July 2012.

Yergin Daniel and Stanislaw Joseph. *The Commanding Heights.* New York: Simon & Schuster, 1998.

Zakaria Fareed. *The Post-American World and the Rise of the Rest.* London: Penguin Books, 2009.

Zea Leopoldo. *El Pensamiento Latinoamericano.* Barcelona: Editorial Ariel, 1976.

Zea Leopoldo. *Latinoamérica, Tercer Mundo.* México: Editorial Extemporáneos, 1977.

Zweig D. David and Jianhai Bi. "China's Global Hunt for Energy." *Foreign Affairs*, Vol. 84, September/October 2005, pp. 25–38.

About the Author

ALFREDO TORO HARDY is a Venezuelan diplomat, scholar and public intellectual. Alfredo Toro Hardy graduated with a Law degree from the Universidad Central de Venezuela, Caracas, in 1973. Between 1973 and 1975 he made postgraduate studies in France under a scholarship of the French government. He acquired a diploma in diplomatic studies from the Institut International d'Administration Publique and a diploma in comparative law from Pantheon-Assas University of Paris, 1975. He received his M.S. from the Universidad Central de Venezuela in 1977 and his Master of Laws from the University of Pennsylvania in 1979. He took a course on international negotiations from Harvard University in 1984.

He is one of Venezuela's most senior diplomats, having served as Ambassador to Washington, London, Madrid, Brasilia, Santiago de Chile, Dublin and, currently, Singapore.

In his role as an eminent scholar, Professor Hardy was Director of the Pedro Gual Diplomatic Academy of the Venezuelan Ministry of Foreign Affairs and Associate Professor at the Simón Bolívar University in Caracas where he was Director of the Centre for North American Studies and Co-ordinator of the Institute for Higher Latin American Studies. He was elected as "Simón Bolívar Chair Professor for Latin American Studies" by the Council of Faculties of the University of Cambridge, but had to decline due to his diplomatic career (previous holders of this Chair include leading Latin American figures such as Literature Nobel laureates Octavio Paz and Mario Vargas Llosa, former President of Brazil Fernando Henrique Cardoso, novelist Carlos Fuentes and economist Celso Furtado). He has been a member of the Advising Committee of the London

Diplomatic Academy (University of Westminster), a Fulbright Scholar and a Rockefeller Foundation Bellagio Center Resident Scholar. A Visiting Professor at Princeton University, he has also taught at the universities of Brasilia and Barcelona and has lectured extensively at universities and think tanks in the Americas, Europe and Asia.

Author of 17 books and co-author of 12 more on international affairs, he received twice the "Latino Book Award" (best book by an author whose original language is in Spanish or Portuguese) at the ExpoBook America fairs celebrated in Chicago and Los Angeles in 2003 and 2008, respectively. Author of numerous papers published in academic magazines, including the *Cambridge Review of International Affairs*, he is a weekly columnist at the Venezuelan newspaper *El Universal* and a frequent contributor in several Latin American and Spanish written media.

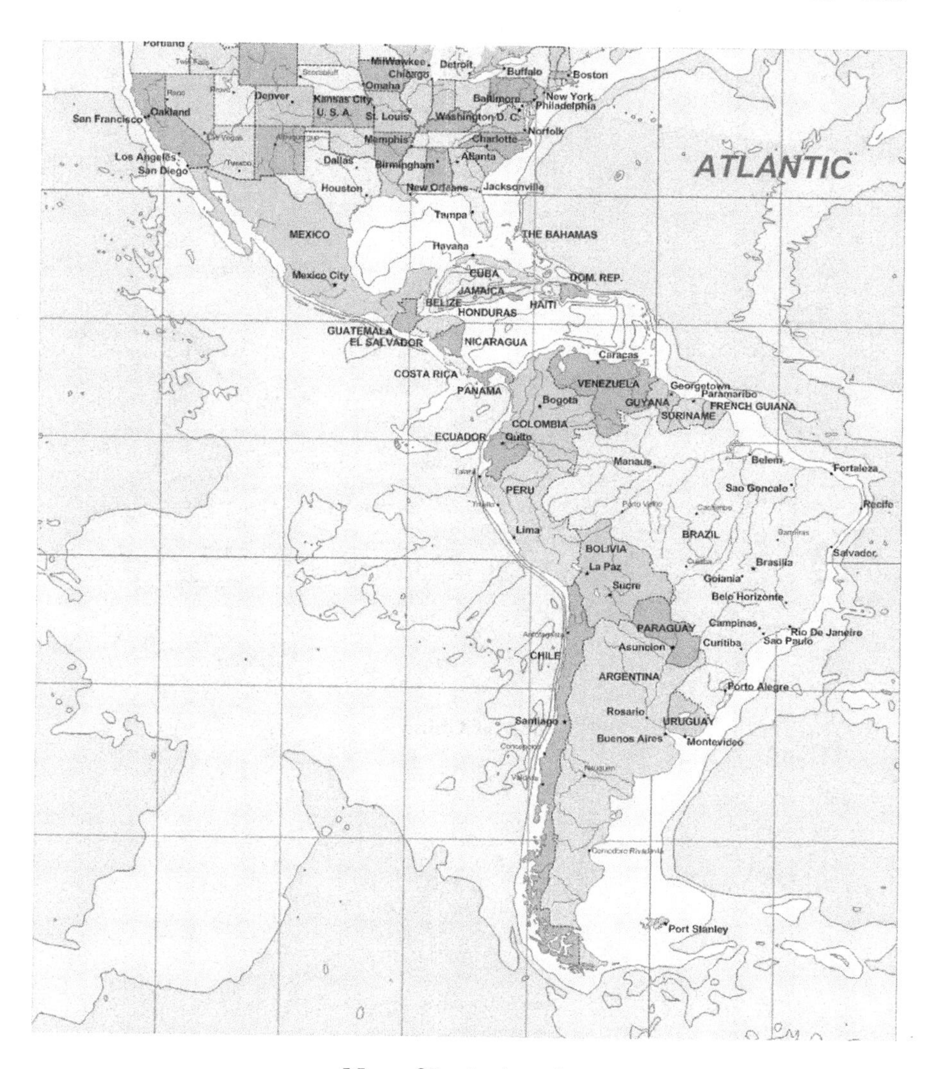

Map of Latin America

Krasnojarsk
Omsk
Novosibirsk
Irkutsk
Qaraghandy
Ulaanbaatar
MONGOLIA
Qiqihar
Harbin
Jixi
Changchun
Jilin
Alma Ata
Urumqi
KYRGYZSTAN
Fuxin
Benxi
Baotou
Beijing
NORTH KOREA
Pyongyang
Dalian
Seoul
SOUTH KOREA
TAJIKISTAN
Yinchuan
Taiyuan
Xining
Qingdao
Lanzhou
Kaifeng
Xian
CHINA
Mianyang
Hefei
Shanghai
Chengdu
New Delhi
Zigong
Yueyang
Huangshi
Ningbo
NEPAL
Jaipur
Agra
Dukou
BHUTAN
Wenzhou
Fuzhou
Allahabad
Guiyang
Xiamen
Taipei
Ahmadabad
Nanning
Shantou
Calcutta
TAIWAN
Surat
Nagpur
MYANMAR
Hong Kong
Ulhasnagar
LAOS
Hanoi
BANGLADESH
Bombay
Pune
Varanasi
THAILAND
VIETNAM

Map of China

Index